Integrating Math and Science in Early Childhood Classrooms Through Big Ideas

A Constructivist Approach

Christine Chaillé
Portland State University

Sara McCormick Davis
University of Arkansas Fort Smith

PEARSON

Boston Columbus Indianapolis New York San Francisco Upper Saddle River
Amsterdam Cape Town Dubai London Madrid Milan Munich Paris Montréal Toronto
Delhi Mexico City São Paulo Sydney Hong Kong Seoul Singapore Taipei Tokyo

Vice President and Editorial Director: Jeffery W. Johnston
Senior Acquisitions Editor: Julie Peters
Editorial Assistant: Andrea Hall
Executive Field Marketing Manager: Krista Clark
Executive Product Marketing Manager: Christopher Barry
Project Manager: Kris Roach
Program Manager: Megan Moffo
Operations Specialist: Carol Melville
Senior Art Director: Diane Y. Ernsberger

Cover Design: Cenveo
Cover Art: Erika Landorf-Kelly
Media Producer: Autumn Benson
Media Project Manager: Allison Longley
Full-Service Project Management: S4Carlisle Publishing Services
Composition: S4Carlisle Publishing Services
Printer/Binder: Courier Westford
Cover Printer: Moore Langen
Text Font: ITC New Baskerville Std, 11/13

Library of Congress Cataloging-in-Publication Data
Library of Congress Cataloging-in-Publication Data is available upon request.

PEARSON

ISBN-13: 978-0-13-714579-9
ISBN-10: 0-13-714579-9

E-text
ISBN-13: 978-0-13-399859-7
ISBN-10: 0-13-399859-2

Dedication from Christine
For my daughter Adrienne Chaille, of Lima, Peru, and son Peter Chaille, of Portland, Oregon, and Coffman Cove, Alaska.

Dedication from Sara
For my late mother, Betty Joan McCormick, and my children Rebecca Noel Davis, of Tahlequah, Oklahoma, and Grant Edward Davis.

Preface

Early childhood teachers today are faced with unprecedented challenges and opportunities. Our classrooms are increasingly diverse, in terms of the cultures, languages, previous experiences, and strengths of the children we teach. We are faced with pressures to provoke the interests and capabilities of children in an increasingly complex world, with higher standards, high-stakes testing, and pressures on children to accomplish more at a younger and younger age.

The Approach of This Book

As a field, we need to do a better job teaching mathematics and science to young children at a time when this is more important than ever. We need to do this without reverting to traditional, non-constructivist practices. And in order to do this, we need to be guided by how children learn—we need to capitalize on the ways children think, explore the world, experiment with materials and ideas, and construct knowledge in contexts that are interesting and meaningful to young children. Standards change and programs come and go, so thinking about who you are in the lives of children needs to guide teaching development.

How to do this? Change how we think about math and science for young children. Instead of separating the disciplines, planning lessons and topics and projects aimed at math *or* science content, let's look at the world the way the child does. Children think in terms of big ideas. And we, as teachers, can capture children's interest and facilitate the construction of both science and math knowledge by seeing this knowledge as interconnected through big ideas.

How This Book Will Help You Understand and Teach Math and Science Concepts

This book offers a way to think about the future classroom and meet the needs of children who come to us with diverse experience, knowledge, and ability. In the first part of the book, we start with the reasons why it is important to think about thinking, and the underlying framework of big ideas as a way to integrate math and science. Assessment is the focus of the second chapter because the teacher must plan for assessment before teaching begins. Then we move into setting up the environment that will support the construction of the big ideas that join math and science.

In the second part of the book, each chapter focuses on a big idea: patterns, transformation, movement, balance and symmetry, and relationships. Each chapter includes two modules to be used for in-depth exploration of different aspects of the big idea of the chapter. The modules can act as stand-alone units or models for lesson planning.

This book is not meant to cover every topic that can come up in math and science; rather, it is meant to be an exploration of learning and thinking, with examples of big ideas that can be used as a framework for integration. The final chapter discusses curriculum planning, and the generation of big ideas beyond those in this book.

Features of This Book

Classroom Scenarios. This book teaches through scenarios to give insight into the teacher's thinking and planning. Rather than a list of activities, we have concentrated on *real-life* experiences that teachers can plan for and take advantage of.

Illustrations. We've provided graphic illustrations to help pre-service educators understand important concepts.

Photos. Authentic photos of children engaged in constructivist activities illustrate how learning should occur.

Modules. In Chapters 4–8, modular explorations are provided so that students can use these to try out, modify, and have first-hand experience with math and science learning activities.

ACKNOWLEDGMENTS

We'd both like to acknowledge the many students and teachers whose ideas and experiences are reflected in this book. We'd also like to thank Erika Landorf-Kelly for her wonderful photos, and Ken Davis for his illustrations. Many of those we work with in teacher education have been seeking a constructivist approach to math and science integration, and we hope that this will inspire and support them in their work. We would like to thank the reviewers for their insightful comments. They are: Kim Cockrell, Wilson Community College; Rosemary Geiken, East Tennessee

State University; Michelle Edwards, Owensboro Community and Technical College; Jana Sanders, Texas A&M University, Corpus Christi; Joan Campbell, Santa Fe College; Lisa Brightman, Edinboro University of Pennsylvania; and April M. Grace, Madisonville Community College.

From Christine Chaillé

I would like to specifically acknowledge the students I have worked with at Portland State University, particularly those from all over the country (and world) in my online Young Child as Scientist course. Particular gratitude goes to the teachers and children of the Helen Gordon Child Development Center, where the school-wide work on big ideas across the school has provoked my own thinking. Ellie Justice, Director of the Helen Gordon Child Development Center, and Will Parnell, faculty colleague and pedagogical director of the center, have been wonderful collaborators in this work. In addition, while writing this book I spent time in Kyoto, Japan, working with St. Mary's School, a private preschool, and in Lima, Peru, where I worked with La Casa Amarilla and the Centro de Formación, two very different cultural experiences that broadened my perspective. My colleagues at Portland State University have provided a constant source of support and caring through this long process, particularly David Bullock and Wendi Laurence. Two of my closest colleagues passed away during the writing of this book—Emily de la Cruz and Frank Mahler—but their support and inspiration is represented in this book. Others to thank include my siblings Raymond and Judith McConnell, and sister-in-law Barbara; the amazing artist and good friend Bob Volke; and my favorite mensch, David Sokoloff.

From Sara McCormick Davis

I want to thank all of my students who are entering the education world excited to bring about change. Their thoughts and questions have provided guidance for this work. Many of the pre-service teachers have now become classroom teachers who have provided feedback and support for my work. I specifically want to thank Margaret Scherrey, Ashley Williamson, Margaret Hall, and Tara Kelton for their willingness to let me hang out in their classrooms. They are all incredible teachers whose passion for teaching and children shines through. My friends and colleagues at the University of Arkansas Fort Smith have been very supportive. I especially want to thank Amy Skypala for providing her unique perspective on science, students, and teaching. Thank you also to Nancy Stockall, whose long-distance support has been incredibly timely. Thank you to my brother Martin and his wife Beverly, and to my dad, retired professor Al McCormick. They are the best family anyone could want. A very special thank-you goes to my husband, artist extraordinaire Kenneth Lee Davis, who has provided the wonderful illustrations for the book and has been my best friend and love of my life.

Brief Contents

PART I
Introduction   1

Chapter 1 Constructivist Curriculum Framework
for the Integration of Math and Science in Early
Childhood Classrooms   2

Chapter 2 Assessment   18

Chapter 3 Creating an Environment for Math
and Science Integration   50

PART II
Integration Through Big Ideas   71

Chapter 4 Patterns   76

Chapter 5 Transformation   100

Chapter 6 Movement   122

Chapter 7 Balance and Symmetry   156

Chapter 8 Relationships   180

Chapter 9 Developing Your Own Curriculum:
Big Ideas and Planning   208

References   228
Glossary   231
Name Index   233
Subject Index   235

Table of Contents

PART I
Introduction   1

Chapter 1 Constructivist Curriculum Framework for the
Integration of Math and Science in Early Childhood Classrooms   2

Children as Theory-Builders 3
   What Is Constructivism? 4
Big Ideas as Tools for Integration 6
   What Is a Big Idea? 6
   Characteristics of Big Ideas 7
Views of Teaching and Learning 7
   The Child at the Center 7
   Celebration of the Diversity of Children 8
   What About Content? 8
   Child-Centered Versus Teacher-Directed Curriculum: A False Dichotomy 10
Background on the Model of Curriculum Integration Used in This Book 11
   Historical Context 11
   Models of Curriculum Integration 12
   The Project Approach 12
   Big Ideas, Projects, Concepts, Topics, and Facts: What Are the Differences? 14
   The Work of Reggio Emilia 15
Review Questions 17
Summary 17
Websites 17

Chapter 2 Assessment   18

Why Begin with Assessment? 19
   Understanding Children's Development 20
Principles of Development 21
   Responding to Children's Needs 22
   Culture and Context 24
Principles of Assessment 26
   Assessment Should Be Valid 27
   Assessment Should Guide Teaching Decisions 27
   Assessment Should Be Part of a System That Is Designed
   to Support the Whole Child 29

Vocabulary Development and Assessment 29
  Teacher Language 31
  Documentation of Children's Learning as Assessment 33
  Documentation Strategies for Integrated Math and Science 34
  Capturing the Documentation 38
  More Formalized Assessment Tools 39
  Science and Math Journals 41
Interviewing for Assessment 43
  Questions That Help with Assessment 44
  Interviewing Activities 45
Standards and Assessment 46
  Standardized Testing 48
  EdTPA 48
Review Questions 48
Summary 49
Websites 49

Chapter 3 Creating an Environment for Math
and Science Integration   50

How Our Beliefs About Children, Teaching, and Learning Shape
  Our Environments 52
  Academic Environment 55
  Physical Environment 57
Classroom Organization 58
  Differentiation Built into the Environment 66
  Animals in the Classroom 67
  Communicating with Families and Others Through the Environment 68
Review Questions 68
Summary 69
Websites 69

PART II
Integration Through Big Ideas   **71**

Chapter 4 Patterns   76

Patterns 77
  What Is Important About Patterns? Why Do We Talk About Patterns
  with Young Children? 77
Elements of the Big Idea of Patterns 78
  Repeating Patterns 78
  Spatial Structure Patterns 79
  Growing Patterns 80

Subitizing 82
    Seriation and Sequencing 83
Patterns Surround Us 84
    Patterns Help Us Predict 84
    Patterns Help Us Make Connections 86
    Patterns Help Us Organize Information 87
Review Questions 88
Summary 88

Chapter 5 Transformation   100

What Is Transformation? 101
    Relationship Building as a Part of Transformation 102
    Equivalence as Part of Transformation 103
Exploration of Transformation 104
    Observation 104
    Estimation 105
    Experimentation 107
    Growth 108
Review Questions 111
Summary 111

Chapter 6 Movement   122

Introduction to the Big Idea of Movement 123
Elements of the Big Idea of Movement 126
    Direction of Movement 126
    Representation of Movement 129
Types of Movement 132
    Movement of the Surface 133
    Sources of Movement 134
    Mysterious Movement 136
    Spinning 138
    The Movement of Time 141
Review Questions 142
Summary 143

Chapter 7 Balance and Symmetry   156

Elements of the Big Idea of Balance 158
    Comparisons 158
    Patterns 159
    The Establishment of Equality 160
Exploration of Balance 162
    The Study of Symmetry 162
    Comparisons and Tools of Measurement 164

The Use of Representations 165
Games That Incorporate Balance: Physical Knowledge 168
Review Questions 170
Summary 170

Chapter 8 Relationships   180

Introduction to the Big Idea of Relationships 181
Elements of the Big Idea of Relationships 183
   Cause and Effect 183
   Part/Whole Relationships 187
   Classification 190
   Perspective-Taking and Interdependence 193
Review Questions 195
Summary 195

Chapter 9 Developing Your Own Curriculum:
Big Ideas and Planning   208

Determining the Big Idea 209
   Coming up with New Big Ideas 209
   Re-thinking an Activity, Project, or Unit 210
   Starting with Children's Interests 210
   Starting with an Event 211
   Starting with Where You Are 212
   Start with an Interest of Yours 212
   Starting with the Standards 213
The Planning Process: Strategies for Thinking About Planning 214
The Planning Process: What Does It Look Like? 215
   Planning for Integration and Inquiry 215
   The Project Approach 216
   Planning with the End in Sight 217
   The Five E Learning Cycle 217
Using Other Areas of the Curriculum to Strengthen Math and Science 220
   Connecting Language Arts, Math, and Science 220
   Connecting Children's Literature, Math, and Science 220
   Cognitively Guided Instruction 221
   Starting with a Standard 223
   Connecting the Arts, Math, and Science 223
   Connecting Social Studies, Math, and Science 224
Review Questions 226
Summary 226
Websites 226

References   **228**
Glossary   **231**
Name Index   **233**
Subject Index   **235**

I

Introduction

In this book, we are intending to provide a framework of "big ideas" for meaningfully integrating mathematics and science in early childhood classrooms, preschool through primary grades. In Part I we will provide the background and context for the big ideas that will follow in Part II of the book.

First, we will discuss the underlying framework of constructivism and big ideas, as well as the different ways of thinking about both curriculum and curriculum integration—both why it is important and the different approaches that influence the one in this book.

We then address the issues of assessment. We see assessment as something that needs to be thought of as an important part of curriculum planning and classroom practice, rather than a disconnected summation of children's learning.

Finally, we discuss the importance of the physical and social environment in which teaching and learning occurs, because classroom environments are an essential part of how we put constructivism and curriculum integration into practice.

1 Constructivist Curriculum Framework for the Integration of Math and Science in Early Childhood Classrooms

Learning Outcomes

After working with the ideas in this chapter, you should be able to:

- Define constructivism and theory-building.
- Describe big ideas and their characteristics.
- Analyze the views of teaching and learning underlying constructivism and big ideas.
- Understand different frameworks for curriculum integration, including the project approach and work inspired by Reggio Emilia.

CHILDREN AS THEORY-BUILDERS

Children do not think in terms of mathematics and science, nor do they separate their activities into disciplinary categories. Children engage in theory-building by experimenting with the world in order to understand it, always applying their theories—what they've constructed to explain what they have experienced—and learning from their experimentation, leading to the construction of more complex theories.

In this process of theory-building, mathematics and science are inextricably linked. Here's an example:

Rebecca has noticed that the carrot that she put into the gerbil's cage in her kindergarten classroom is shriveled up. She takes it out and exclaims, "Look at this! It's weird!" Marsha, her teacher, suggests they talk about this at their morning circle. The children have different thoughts about the carrot, focusing on the ways it is different from a fresh carrot. The children decide to watch what happens to a carrot; they put several fresh carrots on a plate. The children write their predictions of what will happen on a chart—some are focused on the size of the carrot, others on the color or texture of it.

Erika

Integrating math and science through the study of carrots

Based on their predictions, they make documented observations of the carrots. They begin by measuring the carrots, marking their lengths using a string that is put next to each carrot. Rebecca also takes digital photographs of the carrots, posting the pictures on the wall next to the chart. Other children write descriptions of the texture of the carrots— "hard," "wet," "crunchy." In following discussions, Marsha asks questions about what happens to other food that is left out, and brings in resources on decomposition.

In this example, Rebecca's curiosity is capitalized on by the teacher, who facilitates a more extensive exploration of the changes that carrots undergo over time. These changes involve both mathematics and science—measurement and comparison in mathematics, and transformation in science. The questions and interests in this exploration are integrated and linked, and provide a context for the teacher to facilitate the study of both disciplines.

3

What Is Constructivism?

This view of children as theory-builders is grounded in constructivism, a belief that children learn by constructing knowledge. Constructivism comes from Piagetian theory (Piaget, 1977), as well as Vygotskian theory (Berk & Winsler, 1995; Bodrova & Leong, 1996), and is an important way to think about how children learn, with serious implications for our educational practice. What does *constructivism* mean? It means that children have theories or ideas about the world, and that they are constantly applying these theories in an attempt to understand and construct new knowledge. As children apply their theories, they encounter complexity, variation, and differences, and through these encounters their theories build. Take the child who rolls a ball down an incline. She builds a theory that objects roll down inclines. She picks up an object that is not a ball, a cube, and places it at the top of the incline. Her theory is that it will roll, but it does not—it slides. She tries it again; again it slides. Her theory changes—it becomes "round things roll, square things slide"—in response to the variations she experiences in the world. Her theory becomes more complex. This is theory-building, which involves the construction of new knowledge based on applying what is already known.

One interesting and important aspect of theory-building is that it is also grounded in the idea that children are actively seeking to understand the world. There is an inherent motivation to apply the theories that have been constructed. Theory-building does not have to be motivated from the outside, but occurs in the course of all of the child's interactions with the world. This is why children's play is so rich and important for their learning (cf. Frost, Wortham, & Reifel, 2011; Kieff & Casbergue, 2000). This aspect of constructivism constitutes one of the greatest contrasts with the theory of behaviorism, which contends that children's learning is externally motivated—stimuli provoke behavior, and reinforcement is necessary to guide learning. From the constructivist perspective, the child is "wired" to learn. Because of this, the constructivist sees the process of learning as one that is facilitated, not determined, by the outside world, by the environment.

This is not to say that the environment—both social and physical—is not an important element in the learning process. Teachers play an extremely important role in creating the contexts in which theory-building occurs, both in terms of how the physical and social environment is set up and in terms of how teachers provoke theory-building and interact with children to facilitate it, as well as support opportunities for children to theory-build together. Later, we will discuss in more detail the role of the constructivist teacher in creating the context in which theory-building occurs. The physical environment as well provides the opportunities and provocations for the child to engage in theory-building—the physical environment has been called the "third teacher" in the writings of those inspired by the work in Reggio Emilia, Italy, home to an internationally known system of municipal preschools and infant/toddler centers where innovative ideas and practices have stimulated much interest (Edwards, Gandini, & Forman, 1998).

This view of the importance of the environment does not, however, mean that we believe that children's learning is *determined* by the environment. The focus of the constructivist teacher is the child's mind, and learning has to be looked at with the child as the center. And from the child's perspective, there are no distinctions based on discipline; there is no delineation of "mathematics" or "science" or any other disciplinary focus. Curriculum integration comes from taking the child's perspective—as children engage in theory-building, all disciplines blur. So if we as teachers are concerned with ensuring that children learn about different disciplines, we need to understand that we as teachers are imposing the distinctions. In addition, early childhood teachers are challenged by the typical school day that divides the curriculum into distinct periods, which also supports the segmentation instead of integration of the disciplines.

In this book, we are taking the perspective that such differentiation is necessary for us as teachers in order to ensure that we provide opportunities for children to theory-build in the two disciplines of mathematics and science through intentional curriculum. However, we need to be open to the blurring of these lines in actual practice, and to the artificiality of such distinctions from the child's perspective. We need to intentionally provide opportunities for children to engage in activities, projects, and experiences in which mathematics and science are integrated. By doing so, we also open ourselves to the possibility of unplanned curricular integration, where children apply their theories across many different disciplines and domains. This unplanned integration—which comes out of children's ideas, interests, and experiences—should be recognized as a positive development, for it means that children are wrestling with the underlying big ideas, big ideas that transcend disciplines and that could involve many other curriculum domains—social studies, literacy, creative arts, technology. It also means that children are seeking the deeper understanding that goes far beyond disciplines, the big ideas that are the ultimate goal of the educational experience.

●●● **Reflect and Respond**

Cassandra has been in her student teaching placement site for 2 weeks and the cooperating teacher is expecting her to plan a math lesson for the first graders. After looking at the teacher's guide, Cassandra realizes that she could use the math concept of graphing to include real data collection from the children's interest in rocks they have found on the playground. However, the teacher's guide has several pages of data that the children are supposed to transfer to bar-graph worksheets. Cassandra is wondering how she will bring up her idea with her cooperating teacher.

Question to Think About: What would you do or say if you were Cassandra?

BIG IDEAS AS TOOLS FOR INTEGRATION

What Is a Big Idea?

A **big idea** is an overarching idea that engages, inspires, and is relevant to children's interests, an idea that is rich with possibilities. As children play, they interact with their material and social environment, and are naturally actively interested in the big ideas that surround them. Balance, in the broad sense of the word; movement; transformation— these are big ideas. Within each big idea are many concepts that are connected. When children learn concepts under the umbrella of the big idea, deeper understanding is possible. For example, the big idea of balance incorporates concepts such as symmetry, measurement, one-to-one correspondence, and equivalency. Figure 1-1 shows the relationship between big ideas and concepts.

Figure 1-1
Relationship of Big Ideas and Concepts
Source: Sara M Davis

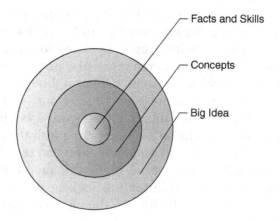

— Facts and Skills

— Concepts

— Big Idea

Characteristics of Big Ideas

Big ideas help children obtain deeper understanding rather than superficial, disconnected content knowledge, or the acquisition of facts. Big ideas allow for connections to be made within and across such ideas and knowledge, through their conceptual links. Big ideas permit children to learn many different things in a larger, more meaningful and engaging context, and allow for the application of knowledge across different content areas. In this way, deeper understanding is constructed.

Returning to the earlier example of Rebecca exploring a carrot, if we were to focus on measurement as the concept to study, our curriculum would be oriented to mathematics, and if we were to focus on biological decomposition, our orientation would be science. But by seeing the big idea underlying both—transformation—integration is at the *heart* of the curriculum. Children then will make connections between the mathematics and the science involved in the context of the big idea. Projects, extensions, and ideas generated from a focus on transformation all have the potential to further this integration.

In this book, we will be using big ideas—such as transformation, balance, relationships—as the underlying framework of the math and science curriculum for the very reason that curriculum integration is natural and meaningful when you do so.

VIEWS OF TEACHING AND LEARNING

The Child at the Center

As noted earlier, it is the child who is the center of this curricular approach, and all of our efforts to develop curriculum start with this premise. This has huge implications for what we do as teachers, because the primary focus is not on the content of what we teach, but rather on the learner, on the learner's efforts to understand the world through inquiry. We are interested in, and learn from, how children are seeing the world, how they experiment and explore it, and what theories they are building. We are concerned about, and learn from, the questions children have, the interests that engage them, and the contexts in which they are motivated to build theories. This is consistent with **inquiry-based learning**, an approach that acknowledges that the source of deep understanding is authentic inquiry that engages children's experimentation and exploration.

Erika

The child at the center.

Celebration of the Diversity of Children

This view of teaching and learning recognizes and capitalizes on the strengths that children bring to the learning experience; it acknowledges their remarkable capabilities. When you focus on children's capabilities you are also acknowledging and cherishing the diversity of the children you teach, diversity of all kinds—diversity of culture, language, socioeconomic class, and ability. For example, if you have a child with limited arm mobility, you look at the ways that she *is* able to engage in a particular activity—for example, drawing with a pencil in her teeth—and develop contexts where this extraordinary capability is both useful and highlighted. Or, if you have a child whose first language is Spanish, you consider incorporating resources and materials that support him in engaging in the activities and learning English, as well as honoring his capabilities in Spanish. From the constructivist perspective, *all* children bring special gifts and needs to the learning experience, and our responsibility is to understand, value, and respond to each child in our classroom.

What About Content?

It is our responsibility as educators to think carefully about what it is that children need to be exposed to and to learn. It is also our responsibility to have educational goals for everything we do. The approach to curriculum that we take in this book is one in which what happens in the classroom is a negotiated dance—one in which the teacher provokes and responds to what children do with goals in mind. But ultimately, the child's engagement is a necessary part of the process, for if the child is not asking his or her own questions, no deep understanding will occur.

And, yes, we are responsible for teaching to content standards, not only in elementary classrooms but also in many preschools, including Head Start centers and some state prekindergarten programs. As teachers we need to be knowledgeable of mathematics and science standards, those of our professional organizations (National Council of Teachers of Mathematics [NCTM], National Science Teachers Association [NSTA]), as well as those of our states (e.g., early learning guidelines) and districts. For example, your state may have adopted the new Common Core Math Standards (National Governors Association Center for Best Practices and the Council of Chief State School Officers, 2010) that you as a teacher need to address. Our responsibility is to ensure that our students come to deep understanding of those standards, not superficial knowledge. Standards can help us to establish our overarching goals, which assist in our planning and assessment. But *how* we meet those standards must be accomplished in a way that is consistent with how children learn using culturally and developmentally appropriate practices, and children need to be given the opportunities to construct knowledge in meaningful contexts in order for this to happen. This is particularly important in early childhood education, where professional organizations acknowledge the differences in how young children learn and how teachers approach content (see, for example, the position statement on early childhood science education from the NSTA, a position statement endorsed by the National Association for the Education of Young Children [NAEYC]).

In this book, we will be discussing the math and science standards that need to be considered as the goals of the integrated curriculum; and we will be discussing the different ways of provoking and assessing how and what children are learning in the context of integrated activities and projects.

Child-Centered Versus Teacher-Directed Curriculum: A False Dichotomy

From the constructivist perspective, there is no dichotomy between child-centered and teacher-directed curriculum—although teacher-provoked (rather than directed) curriculum might be a more accurate term. In some early childhood curriculum approaches, constructivism is misunderstood as implying that children's interests and questions drive the curriculum entirely, with teachers following those interests and questions. In fact, teachers play a significant role in provoking, suggesting, facilitating, and responding to children's explorations and experimentation. Teachers are an important part of the equation—contributing their own vision of what is of value to learn, of what directions to follow and to stimulate. These actions are purposeful and intentional: Teachers are making constant interpretations of children's intentions and understandings, and from those interpretations making decisions about what to focus on, what materials to provide, and what questions to ask. This overarching vision of the teacher is guided by the goals and standards that are worth striving for, the goals and standards that articulate the kinds of things that we want children to learn.

Using standards and goals to guide the planning and implementation of the curriculum has become increasingly valued by educators from different perspectives. Harris, Smith, and Harris (2011) discuss the importance of thinking through carefully and planning around the standards in the context of the project approach to curriculum. And with a focus on assessment, Wiggins and McTighe (2005) are articulating the same approach, discussing it as backward design, an approach being implemented in many schools. This process involves looking deeply at the curriculum that is planned,

Ian Wedgewood/Pearson Education Ltd

Teachers and children collaborate on determining the curriculum.

mapping it to the mathematics and science standards. This enables you to see what may be missing, underemphasized, or overemphasized in your curriculum plan, and to modify your plans as needed to meet your goals.

This puts a greater focus on what the teacher does, and places responsibility on the teacher for carefully monitoring what it is that children are exposed to, what it is that the teacher responds to, and what it is that is provoked and maintained in the classroom as a focus. How much easier to focus on set content and to deliver it in a teacher-directed way! And how much easier to go with the flow of children's interests and spontaneous activities without thought and judgment! The constructivist approach taken in this book puts much more weight on carefully thinking through what the goals are, and carefully observing what it is that children respond to and do, in order that the curriculum is of value. The teacher acts with intention.

BACKGROUND ON THE MODEL OF CURRICULUM INTEGRATION USED IN THIS BOOK

Historical Context

One of the earliest proponents of curriculum integration was John Dewey, who advocated an experiential approach that was grounded in real life: "Relate the school to Life, and all studies are of necessity correlated" (Dewey, 1900, p. 81). Throughout the 1900s, many different approaches to curriculum integration emerged across the grades, approaches summarized by Vars (1996) and Beane (1997). Vars (1996), who examined over 100 integrated curriculum programs that emerged between 1956 and 1995, found that students in interdisciplinary programs do as well as or better than students in conventional programs, regardless of the type of interdisciplinary approach.

With increased emphasis on academic achievement in early childhood classrooms, some question whether integrated curriculum approaches can support student learning. This is addressed explicitly by the Association for Supervision and Curriculum Development (ASCD), which, in its overview of curriculum integration (Drake & Burns, ASCD, 2004), concluded that research supports integrated approaches. The ASCD's overview contends that not only do students in integrated programs do as well or better on standardized tests than those in regular programs, but teaching and learning is a more engaging enterprise as a result.

Putting the current approach to math and science integration that we take in this text into historical context is important—this is not an unprecedented or even unusual approach. However, it is an attempt to make efforts to integrate math and science in the early childhood classroom, both preschool and early elementary, meaningful to and manageable for teachers drawn to a constructivist perspective.

Models of Curriculum Integration

There are several different ways of implementing curriculum integration, and different models that have been used. All of these approaches are interesting and can lead to effective integration, and the approach taken in this text incorporates elements of each but would probably be best characterized as a transdisciplinary approach.

The first is the **multidisciplinary approach**, in which different subject areas are organized around the same theme or topic. One way of doing this is to consider a problem or issue from different disciplines. Problem-based learning is an example of the multidisciplinary approach to curriculum integration.

The second is the **interdisciplinary approach**, in which the focus is cross-disciplinary skills, such as literacy, research, or numeracy. This approach is more commonly applied to middle or high school curriculum.

The third approach is **transdisciplinary**, which is based on the assumption that an issue or problem grounded in the real world incorporates all disciplines. The project approach (Katz & Chard, 2000) as well as the work in Reggio Emilia (Edwards, Gandini, & Forman, 1993) could be classified as transdisciplinary, stemming from children's interests and experiences.

The Project Approach

In the **project approach**, children engage in working in groups on projects that incorporate a variety of disciplines (Katz & Chard, 2000). Curriculum is developed around ideas generated by teachers and children, collaboratively, that result in activities engaged in by children that are connected by a topic or theme. For example, after a visit to a fire station, a group of preschool children might decide to do a project on the fire engine—sketching the fire engine, studying parts of it such as the hoses,

Erika

A project on fire engines

and constructing a fire engine out of cardboard. In the process, mathematics and science can be incorporated into the children's activities—either by spontaneous interest of the children or by the teacher's suggestion and facilitation. One way to do this is that the teacher could make sure that measuring devices are available to the children as they construct the cardboard fire truck, encouraging mathematics applications. And, from a science perspective, children could become interested in the way water from the hose has the power to move objects, and could engage in some experimentation around this on the playground. The science and mathematics here is connected because of the "topic" that is the subject of the project, not necessarily because of the project itself.

Such curriculum integration could be seen as temporal rather than conceptual—the mathematics and science are occurring together in time, but are not necessarily linked by the underlying concepts being investigated. There may be some exceptions to this—children could engage in a project on the movement of objects as a result of their exploration of the fire hose, which takes the project work to the conceptual level rather than the topical level. However, it is more likely that conceptual project work would actually entail a number of projects, and thus would be more similar to the use of big ideas as the underlying curriculum framework.

The distinction between projects and big ideas is an important one, and doesn't just involve using different words. From the teacher's point of view, how you think of the goal of the curriculum and how you plan what to focus on, what to capitalize on, what to extend, and what to provoke is guided by your curriculum framework. If you are thinking of curriculum in terms of projects, you will be guided by the topic under study—a topic that could be purely content driven. Alternatively, you could be guided by the interests of the children, or an event that happens. On the other hand, if you are thinking of curriculum in terms of big ideas, you will be thinking in terms of the conceptual connections that children are making, as well as the broader scope of possibilities within the conceptual framework of the big idea. You would, of course, *also* be responding to the interests and needs of the children, always remembering that children's engagement is a necessary part of constructing knowledge.

One way to think of the difference is to take a project and think about what the underlying (and overarching) big idea(s) might be. Consider a project on buildings, for example, which begins when a construction project is occurring near your school. The children may have noticed the construction and talked about it in class or you may have realized that this is a good opportunity to relate project work to the children's world. The children begin studying buildings, and their work can go in many different directions. The children might show an interest in creating their own buildings, and with support from the teacher, and some planning, the children could engage in wonderful work relating to spaces and enclosures that involves area and perimeter. Or, the children could engage in work relating to transformation— again, depending on their interests and the directions the teacher provokes. For example, 4-year-olds might notice that the bricks going up on the building look like blocks and, with the teacher's help, decide to build walls with their shape blocks. This could lead to a discussion and study of why certain shapes work better than others for different jobs. Similarly, 6-year-olds might notice that the tires on the trucks are much larger than the tires on their family cars. The teacher of the 6-year-olds can set up an opportunity for the children to think about how to measure tires and what tools would be useful for measurement. Different aspects of the project, then, are differentiated according to the standards emphasized, but also according to the children's understanding and interests.

There are many big ideas that could be the focus of a project on buildings—transformation (change) or spaces and enclosures are just two possibilities. If you use big ideas to guide your thinking, planning, and observations, you will think about different ways of extending, supporting, and guiding children's explorations.

Big Ideas, Projects, Concepts, Topics, and Facts: What Are the Differences?

In the following diagram, we have attempted to illustrate the major differences between aspects of the curriculum discussed in the chapter, which have to do primarily with whether the focus is conceptual or topical.

	Description	Example
Lesson plan/ activity plan	A plan for a lesson or activity that includes objectives, materials, introduction to children, predictions of what children will do, and predictions of what they will learn	Building homes: providing children with materials and images for building with blocks
Unit	A set of lesson plans/activities with an overarching objective	A series of activities with different building materials
Topic/theme	"Houses"	Based on discussion of different types of houses, children engage in activities that may not be connected but that share the topic or theme of houses, such as reading books about houses, building different types of houses in the block area, and using small houses as counters in math games
Project	Building a house	Children study different aspects of building a house, including planning, construction, outfitting, and furnishing; might include a field trip to a construction site; culminates in building a house out of cardboard in the dramatic play area
Concept	Stability	Building structures with different materials, testing their stability, comparing the different materials
Big idea	Spaces and enclosures	Exploring different ways of thinking about spaces and enclosures; could include studying different rooms and buildings, building structures, exploring construction; could go in many different directions and could incorporate many disciplines

●●● **Reflect and Respond**

In the past, when Kristin taught a unit about dinosaurs she simply gathered a lot of dinosaur-themed materials and put them around the room. There was not a lot of effort in connecting the idea of "dinosaurs" to the curriculum; it just seemed fun and many of the children loved playing with the dinosaur puppets or painting pictures of dinosaurs. But her principal has told all the teachers that all of their curriculum must be directly related to standards, so Kristin is not sure where to start.

Question to Think About: What can children learn about dinosaurs that would help them understand principles of science? Why do so many teachers use dinosaurs in units and themes? What is the difference between a theme and a project? How does the topic of dinosaurs enable children to learn more about the world they experience on a daily basis?

The Work of Reggio Emilia

By studying the municipal infant, toddler, and preschool centers that are internationally known for the inspiring work that occurs in and around the city of Reggio Emilia, located in northern Italy, we can gain further insights into how curriculum integration occurs in the context of the work of children and teachers who intentionally break down the separation of disciplines. Many resources are available to provide further background on the work of Reggio Emilia (Cadwell, 1997, 2003; Edwards et al., 1993, 1998; Wurm, 2005).

There are numerous ideas coming from Reggio Emilia that underlie the curriculum model of big ideas (Chaille, 2008), and they will not be repeated here. The way that curriculum is developed, however, is particularly relevant for the purposes of this book. In Reggio Emilia, the curriculum is conceived of as dynamic, and yet very intentional. This combination of careful planning and flexibility, based on what children are doing and what teachers interpret through their observations, is captured by the idea of *progettazione*, a form of negotiation. *Progettazione* involves incorporating the voices of teachers and children through dialogue to determine the curriculum. Teachers in Reggio Emilia also have big ideas in mind as they provoke and facilitate what children are doing, and use big ideas to interpret and reflect on what children are doing. For example, all of the schools a few years ago were embarking on the study of writing, with this being very broadly defined and subject to interpretation and variation depending on the particular school, the teachers, and the children. The goal of this large-scale study was to engage in the study of how writing develops. In one school, for example, the very young children and teachers were studying how writing is a form of exchange, of "gifts" from one child to another—an early form of communication. In another school, children and teachers were studying the different ways of making letters, and were inventing alphabets for sounds. The big idea of writing, or communication, is large enough, and conceptual enough, to encompass numerous approaches, interests, and endeavors, all of which are valued and support collaborative study.

●●● Reflect and Respond
Nick has noticed that his second graders are suddenly very interested in an insect someone has brought in from the playground. The next thing on the schedule is math, and Nick feels that there simply isn't time to talk about the insect so he has the child place the insect in a terrarium on a shelf. He goes on with the math lesson, but is struggling to hold the children's attention because the insect has become very active.

Question to Think About: What would you do? How could you capitalize on the children's interest and engagement?

Review Questions

1. What's your definition of constructivism?
2. Can you give an example of theory-building from your work with children or your own learning?
3. What is a "big idea"? Describe one big idea that could be used to integrate the curriculum in a classroom.
4. Discuss the views of teaching and learning underlying constructivism and the focus on big ideas.
5. Describe some of the different frameworks for integrating the curriculum.

Summary

In this chapter, we've presented the theoretical framework and background for the approach we are taking in this book—using big ideas as the approach to integrating science and mathematics for young children in a constructivist classroom. We've looked at constructivism and big ideas, views of teaching and learning, and the different approaches to curriculum integration that have influenced our own. Now that we've set the stage, in the next chapter we'll consider the areas of assessment and creating the environment that will lay the groundwork for this curriculum approach.

Websites

The following websites provide additional information from some of the major professional organizations in math and science, as well as information about Reggio Emilia and the Common Core Standards; they can be found by searching for the keywords below:

National Council of Teachers of Mathematics (NCTM)

National Science Teachers Association (NSTA)

National Association for the Education of Young Children (NAEYC)

NSTA Early Childhood Education Position Statement – endorsed April 2014 by the National Association for the Education of Young Children

Common Core Standards – Mathematics

Reggio Children: This is the official site of the public-private company that manages the educational and cultural exchanges between the municipal early childhood institutions of Reggio Emilia and educators from around the world.

2 Assessment

Learning Outcomes

After working with the ideas in this chapter, you should be able to:

- Define appropriate assessment in a science and math classroom.
- Describe how assessment guides our teaching.
- Analyze the impact of appropriate assessment on children's vocabulary development.
- Create documentation to support assessment.
- Understand the importance of interviewing in assessment.
- Evaluate the use and purpose of standards in assessment.

Margaret had just started teaching first grade. She believed that part of her job was to check children's accumulation of school readiness skills, so she handed out worksheets on the first day of school and asked children to circle certain letters, count groups of objects, draw shapes, and record or respond to other bits and pieces of information. Most of the children struggled to complete the worksheets, and two cried. Margaret was very frustrated by this experience, and disturbed to see that many, if not most, of the children did not seem ready for first grade.

How does this scenario fit into your image of assessment? How do children feel when they are expected to do things that they are not ready to do? If we teach toward children's strengths, how would a checklist help us make decisions? Are the most important ideas we want to assess in math and science readily assessed by tests?

WHY BEGIN WITH ASSESSMENT?

You have probably experienced assessment as grades given at the end of a course, or as a **summative** evaluation of what has been learned, but in this chapter we are concerned with *formative* assessment. **Formative** assessment is what happens every day when the teacher is thinking about the goals of the activities and lessons and how children are meeting those goals and what needs to be done to further children's success. The teacher uses formative assessment on a daily basis by observing children's responses to curriculum, taking notes, working with small groups and individuals, and tracking projects, among many other strategies. Formative assessment is the foundation for teachers' decisions, and guides the design of the curriculum. Formative assessment also can capture experiences that can guide the curriculum in new directions. Formative assessment in early childhood education is done to:

- Plan the curriculum to meet individual children's needs,
- Communicate children's learning to various audiences such as families and the school,
- Support the diagnosis of special needs, and
- Evaluate instructional plans and materials.

Here is one way formative assessment can be structured:

Name	CC.K.CC.4a When counting objects, say the number names in the standard order, pairing each object with one and only one number name and each number name with one and only one object			CC.K.CC4b Understand that the last number name said tells the number of objects counted. The number of objects is the same regardless of their arrangement or the order in which they were counted		
	Sept	January	May	Sept	January	May
Emma	☐	/	☐	☐	☐	/
Sean	/	☐	☐	☐	☐	☐
Gina	☐	☐	☐	☐	/	☐

Formative evaluation form for Common Core State Standards for Math: The teacher would assess each child individually. If the child was able to meet the standard the teacher would check the box; if the child showed partial understanding the teacher would use a slanted line; if the child showed no understanding the teacher would use an X. This information would then be used in planning teaching activities, choosing materials, and communicating with parents and caregivers. At the end of the year the teacher would use an individual activity as a final assessment.

Name Date	Emma June
Met	CC.K.CC.4a When counting objects, say the number names in the standard order, pairing each object with one and only one number name and each number name with one and only one object.
Has not met	CC.K.CC.4a When counting objects, say the number names in the standard order, pairing each object with one and only one number name and each number name with one and only one object.

It *forms* our decisions and *informs* our practice, and our relationships with children and their families. The best formative assessment is woven into the daily life of the classroom and is done *with* children, not *to* them.

In this chapter we will look specifically at the general knowledge needed by early childhood teachers about young children's development in math and science, how formative assessment works in early childhood classrooms where math and science are integrated, and the factors that impact the kind of assessment that may be needed.

Understanding Children's Development

In early childhood education it is essential that the teacher have knowledge about the development of children. It is where we begin when we start planning our educational experiences with and for children.

Normal development in education simply means that the child's physical, intellectual, social, and emotional development falls into a standardized part of the continuum that has been recorded for many children of the same age, but it doesn't mean that all children will have reached the same growth at the same time. Many things can impact a child's development, including family culture, economics, nutrition, place of residence, and genetics. For example, consider the factors affecting the development of each child in the following vignettes:

Aaron's dad was a professional baseball player and his mom received baseballs and bats at her baby shower. Even before Aaron could walk his dad would roll balls to him to hit at with his hand. By the time Aaron began kindergarten he was able to stand at home plate and hit balls tossed to him when most of his 5-year-old friends had to have a stationary ball in order to play. He could count the number of balls he had hit or tried to hit and he could estimate where the ball would go if he hit it.

Seven-year-old Cassandra's mom worked two jobs, so when Cassandra got up in the mornings her mother was still in bed. Her mom put breakfast supplies out for Cassandra the night before, but it was up to Cassandra to eat, get dressed, and arrive at school on time. Cassandra's second-grade teacher noticed that Cassandra could not always use the correct math vocabulary, but she could estimate the amount of liquid needed for a science activity and she could be relied on to prepare the materials correctly for inquiry activities.

One issue in assessment is the expectation that all 4-year-olds or all 7-year-olds are supposed to understand or know the same things simply because of their chronological age. There are theorists in the history of early childhood education (Gesell Institute of Child Development, Ilg & Ames, 1985) who studied children and connected the behaviors they observed to specific and recognizable stages. Unfortunately, this has led some to think that the stages of development are the same for all children of a given age, but they may not be. Stage theories certainly help us understand the development of children in general, but may be less useful when thinking about individual children in today's diverse society.

PRINCIPLES OF DEVELOPMENT

It may be useful to think of development principles rather than stages. The principles of development still apply even when children have physical and mental challenges or when they exceed expectations for a given stage. The principles help us think about what individual children need in order to keep supporting each child's growth.

When thinking about math and science development it is helpful to consider trajectories of development. We can assess a child's understanding of a concept and plan for experiences that will help them construct ideas that move them along the trajectories of development for specific concepts. This does not mean that learning a new concept will follow smoothly from previous learning, but if we know what to look for in concept development we will be ready to support the child's growth.

For example, it has been found that most children have a good conceptual understanding of basic shapes when they enter kindergarten. But teachers have not been building on this knowledge with accurate math education and experiences. Teachers have commonly used one type of triangle to teach the concept of triangle, but children also need to see lots of different types of triangles, and discuss what makes a triangle a triangle. It is important for preschool teachers to understand that children need more than learning the names of shapes (Cross, Woods, & Schweingruber, 2009).

We can spend hours planning our teaching, but if we are not in tune with the learners then we run the risk of nothing being learned. What do we need to understand about young children to maximize the possibility that our plans actually result in the intended learning? Many studies of appropriate pedagogy in early childhood education begin with the development of children (Berk, & Winsler, 1995; Bodrova, & Leong, 1996; Frost, Wortham, & Riefel, 2011).

Some of the principles of developmental assessment in math and science are:

1. The whole child is kept in mind when doing assessments. Many forms of information are used to evaluate the outcome of assessment. Families should be part of the assessment conversation. Special needs are taken into account.

2. Children should be assessed in many different settings. Math and science understanding may look different in a whole group setting as compared to the child's performance one on one.

3. The assessment system should be well planned, consistent, and focused on specific questions. The teacher's background knowledge about what is being assessed should be considered.

4. The information gathered from assessment should produce a picture of learning and movement along the trajectory or path of development. Decisions are not made based on one item.

5. Assessment is used to make decisions about teaching, communicating with parents, and meeting individual children's needs.

Responding to Children's Needs

Teachers knowledgeable about child development understand that their response to one child's needs can support the development of all the children in the classroom. By planning for one child who has specific needs, the teacher can realize how much the other children will be supported by what is planned, as in the following vignettes:

Tim is a third grader with Asperger syndrome. He was easily upset when the schedule was changed, so the teacher knew that planning ways to communicate the daily schedule to the whole class would not only help Tim adjust, but would also help other children who found changes upsetting but didn't act on their anxiety. She also knew that children's understanding of time as a math concept had strong developmental implications. Therefore, planning for Tim helped everyone with multiple math concepts.

Shemeka used a walker in the classroom. The teacher looked at the environment with the perspective of making sure pathways were clear for Shemeka's walker, but this was also helpful to all the children in the class who might not have good large muscle control or were easily distracted and could walk into furniture. It was important to the teacher that all children had access to materials for math and science inquiry.

The teacher also modified her assessments by comparing children's growth over time to her records of where they started.

For example, she knew that Marty, who had impaired vision, should be able to read all the data on charts created by the children as long as the data was large enough; but she also knew that there may be some data that Emily, a child with **Down syndrome**, would struggle with and would take longer to recognize easily. So the teacher modified her goals for Emily. The teacher focused Emily's attention by having her use a cardboard frame that showed one word at a time, so she *made an accommodation for* Emily, but the expectation that Emily would be able to also read the data and use it was the same. So, the *modification* was the amount of time it would take Emily to read and comprehend the data, and the *accommodation* was the added cardboard frame.

All children can learn.

The accommodations for both Marty and Emily supported the rest of the class's ability to participate because they could more easily see the data from a distance and they were free to use the cardboard frames to help them keep track on the list. No distinction was made that the accommodations were there for specific children; all the children accepted the changes as just part of the regular way of doing things.

Culture and Context

For assessment purposes we will define culture as the values, beliefs, and practices that certain social groups share.

Read the following vignettes and discuss what cultural values are being acted on or being referenced. How would the people in these situations feel? What could others do to support their experience? How do our assumptions keep us from learning?

Shelly had just moved to the northwestern United States and begun her new job teaching kindergarten. The weather was not at all what she was used to—she had moved from Arizona, which had a much drier climate. The first time it rained lightly she kept the children inside for recess even though they argued with her. At the end of the school day she was told rather firmly by the principal that in the future she was to send the children outside wearing their rain gear.

Erika

Some areas of the country experience lots of rain. Should children stay inside?

Katsumi, who came from Japan, had been in the United States for two years working on completing his teaching license. He was very excited to begin his teaching career in a school system that could afford to hire science specialists for their elementary schools. The children were seated before class began, and when he walked into the room they not only remained seated, they were all talking to each other and to him. He was very displeased and scolded the children for not standing when he entered the room.

LaVette really enjoyed teaching third grade in a highly diverse school. Her classroom was made up of children from several different nationalities, including children from Vietnam, Honduras, and Russia. She struggled with teaching math because it had never been her strong subject. But she had heard that "math is a universal language," so she thought that surely math would be one of the easier subjects for the children who had moved to her school from their native countries. That's why she couldn't understand why she was having so many problems. The children seemed to not know how to make a "9" or the names for the numerals. She observed them playing games on the playground that involved counting, but then in the classroom they wouldn't respond to her questions about number order.

There is a common misconception that math and science are very objective and do not contain interpretative ideas or cultural concerns. Some think that at least science and math are easy to teach because as curriculum topics they are straightforward. However, science and math are human endeavors. The knowledge we have gained over the years comes from people who are part of their cultures, and is greatly influenced by the cultural context. Number systems, counting language, algorithms, calendars, natural observations, questions about nature, and data collection are all impacted by the cultures in which they developed (Leung, Graf, & Lopez-Real, 2006; Wang, 2009).

A brief search on the Internet makes it very clear that math and science information can change every day. However, traditionally, math and science are often taught as though the answers are static and unchanging. For example, some of us may have learned a mnemonic device to remember the nine planets in the

0	1	2	3	4
5	6	7	8	9
10	11	12	13	14
15	16	17	18	19
20	21	22	23	24
25	26	27	28	29

Ancient Egyptian math system

Dicogm/Shutterstock

Erika

Finding and discussing treasures

solar system, such as "My Very Educated Mother Just Served Us Nine Pizzas." But because scientists have changed Pluto's classification, the sentence no longer fits. If it was the only way you thought of the relationship of planets to each other, then you may have been upset by this change! When math and science are taught as separate, disconnected subjects, with rules and labels to memorize, we are teaching children to think about science and math as things that have already been done with nothing left to discover. If math and science are taught as mainly rules to memorize, we are teaching children to think that math and science only require memorization.

Children are natural mathematicians and scientists. They are constantly wondering, questioning, discovering, and theorizing about what the world is all about. Children can pick up an earthworm from the sidewalk, pluck a flower from the yard, flip a light switch off and on, pour water through a tube, or blow bubbles and see themselves as mathematicians and scientists.

If teachers then hand them a worksheet with words to memorize, lists to number, or even pictures to color, they begin seeing math and science as something that happens at school during a 30-minute time slot in the afternoon, with no connection to their rich lives outside of the classroom. The children in our classrooms come to us with widely differing experiences, understanding, abilities, and interests. When we think about assessment we have to consider each child's individual situation and background. Again, our assumptions about who children are can positively or negatively impact our teaching decisions.

PRINCIPLES OF ASSESSMENT

Assessment has to be sensitive to individuals, but certain general principles in early childhood classroom assessment hold true in most situations. The following assessment principles have been adapted from the

National Association for the Education of Young Children (NAEYC), the National Council for Teaching Mathematics (NCTM), and the National Science Education Standards (NSES). The Common Core State Standards for Math (National Governors Association Center for Best Practices and the Council of Chief State School Officers, 2010) include standards for mathematical practice that can be used as a guide for the integration of assessment into math and science tasks.

Assessment Should Be Valid

Validity means that you are measuring what you intend to measure. Validity means that there is a strong connection between what was taught and what is being tested. The intentional teacher thinks carefully about the connection between what was taught and what will be assessed. For example, if the concept being taught is change over time in the life cycle as a big idea, then the assessments would not necessarily only document children's ability to list the stages of a frog's development, but would also document the child's understanding that the frog goes through big changes over time. Listing the stages would document a child's ability to remember labels in a certain order, but would not indicate that the child understands the idea of change or change over time. Instead we would want to know that the child has begun to understand the connections from one kind of life cycle to another life cycle, whether it is a butterfly, a plant, or a human. Similarly, if we spend all of our time teaching children the rules for adding and subtracting double digits, then we have missed the bigger underlying idea of grouping and regrouping. The children may be able to tell you that when subtracting 25 from 42 you have to mark out the 4 make it a 3 and give a 1 to the 2, but that simply tells you that they can memorize a procedure. It does not tell you that they understand the underlying concept.

Assessment Should Guide Teaching Decisions

Assessment is cyclical. Something is taught, assessment is done and interpreted, and then a decision is made about re-teaching, reinforcing, moving on, or rethinking the goals. Without assessment, teaching would be a series of activities that move forward whether they make sense or not. Good assessment will guide your decisions as a teacher about each child in your class. Formative assessment tells us what to teach next or what project to begin. For example, one math practice from the Common Core is the use of modeling. Teachers can easily use a child's ability to model a math idea as a form of assessment (National Governors Association

Figure 2-1
Rubric for General Knowledge Development

Level	Make sense of problems and persevere in solving them	Reason abstractly and quantitatively	Construct viable arguments and critique the reasoning of others	Model with mathematics	Use appropriate tools strategically	Attend to precision	Look for and make use of structure	Look for and express regularity in repeated reasoning
Planting seeds Looks interested No understanding	I don't know where to start. Loses interest	I do not use math thinking	I don't see any connection between the problem and what others are doing.	I'm not sure what math I am supposed to use. Doesn't have basic number sense/doesn't know numeral names	I did not try to use any math tools.	I did not understand that my response was not accurate.	I looked to the teacher or others for clues where to start.	I see no connections between this problem and others.
Growing Keeps trying Understanding not clear	I started with the part of the problem I knew, but only solved that part.	I have some mathematical thinking.	I listened to others and added to the math conversation.	I used symbols and numbers to express one idea.	I used math tools, but had several errors in use.	I questioned my answer.	I could classify one part of the problem/saw a pattern but had trouble connecting it.	I saw a repeating functions.
Blossoming Follow through Clearly understands	I understood the problem.	I used math to solve the problem correctly.	I could explain my thinking/I could point out issues with other solutions.	I could write/draw 2 different ways to solve the problem.	I chose an appropriate tool and used it correctly.	I knew my first answer was incorrect and changed my reasoning	I saw a pattern during the process and used it to help solve the problem.	I used regularities in math to solve the problems.
Flowering Completes with extended understanding	I understood the problem and used math rules to solve it.	I used the rule to extend my explanation.	I explained other's ideas using correct math terms.	I could write/draw 3 different ways to solve the problem.	I could use more than one tool correctly/and explain why it worked.	I could explain why my solution was correct	I saw more than one pattern/rule during the process.	I could explain how the problem could be extended.

Source: Ken Davis

Center for Best Practices and the Council of Chief State School Officers, 2010). The teacher could create a **rubric** for what parts the model must have to show understanding by the child (see Figure 2-1). Consider the teacher's use of a rubric in the following vignette:

Louise used a rubric to guide her observations of her preschoolers' play with paper-clip chains. She challenged them to find things that were the same length, longer than, and shorter than chains of various lengths. She watched carefully to see if they tried to match the starting points, if they were aware of the size of the units, and if they could match the lengths closely to the objects they found. She noticed that some children had little awareness of these attributes for measuring, but a few actually made chains the exact length of the objects.

You can focus on math or science when doing assessments with rubrics. A general rubric for math might be applied to a science project in order to document children's thinking in specific situations.

Assessment Should Be Part of a System That Is Designed to Support the Whole Child

The intentional teacher chooses assessments that make sense in the context of his classroom, his approach to developing a community of learners and his knowledge of the children, their families, and their needs. If children have been collecting data about their observations of the tree they have adopted, for example, the assessment used would take into account each child's abilities, language, and social development, as well as information needed by diverse audiences—the children, their families, and the administration. The teacher may have to be more focused on certain individual children at times in order to compile a needs assessment request or find out the source of a particular problem in learning. One of the strengths of an integrated math and science approach is the ability of the teacher to work with a child's strengths rather than always focusing on things the child is struggling with.

VOCABULARY DEVELOPMENT AND ASSESSMENT

In today's classrooms, diverse cultures and languages mean that teachers have to be aware of all the ways children communicate and understand ideas. Appropriate and useful assessment is not going to happen without children's communication, and this underscores the importance of language development. Children's vocabulary and ability to talk about their ideas can develop rapidly when they have been genuinely engaged in an interesting topic.

Math and science offer opportunities for engagement that will result in not only the growth of

Children discussing observations of aquarium life.

vocabulary, but also deeper conceptual understanding and communication of ideas through language. In order for this to be supported, the teacher must value children's talk. However, when teachers depend on worksheets and prescribed curriculum, children's talk is kept to a minimum. Those teachers may see teaching as transferring information, which doesn't really leave a lot of room for children's talk, other than simply responding with the answer the teacher is expecting. For some teachers classroom management might mean keeping children quiet and working alone. The idea of the teacher as the center of attention and the controller of all talk is a strong image that is difficult to change.

In order to change this image, it is helpful to consider what constitutes learning. Although you can learn new words by memorizing them, this doesn't help you communicate complex ideas. You have words in your conversational and professional vocabulary that are there because they are useful, meaningful, and interesting. In order to support children's vocabulary development, it is important that classroom teachers provide and support opportunities for language use and language learning that are linked to math and science. Consider the following vignette:

In one first-grade classroom the children were studying physical properties of matter. The teacher had 30 minutes in the schedule each week to focus on concepts in science, and if there was a school assembly or other special event this 30 minutes often got left out. Today she passed out worksheets that had black-and-white drawings of various materials. The children were to circle the pictures that showed matter as a solid, a gas, and a liquid. She walked around the room, keeping the children quiet and helping them find the correct examples. She found herself more and more frustrated by their apparent lack of effort. It seemed so easy to her; she couldn't understand why they were struggling. One child had circled the picture of an ice cube for the example of liquid, and another child circled the picture of a puddle for gas. A few children had completed the worksheet and were now talking to their neighbors, playing with markers in their desks, and disturbing others. It made her think that this 30-minute science period could have been used for more math.

What do you think the teacher might have found out if the children had been encouraged to discuss their choices? What would children be learning from this worksheet? What is assumed by a using a worksheet like this? What could the children be doing instead?

In another first-grade classroom, children were at various stations around the room investigating air. Two children were holding scarves above a homemade wind tunnel and laughing delightedly at the movement of the scarves when they let go of them. Three children were making pinwheels, coloring shapes on

There are many ways to play with the wind.

the wheels that would blur and create new colors. One child was looking at a large illustrated encyclopedia for airplanes, and several more children were fanning objects to make them move. The teacher walked around the room, jotting down things the children were saying, taking photos of some of the products being created, writing down notes about materials she wanted to add to the things available, and listening for ways to support the language being developed. At the end of the project exploration period the teacher had a large chart available so she and the children could record some of the ideas and words they had learned and used. The chart already contained words from an earlier investigation about air, and now the children excitedly added new observations.

How is this scenario different from the first one? How does this scenario support children's learning and our image of teaching? How does this scenario describe children's language development? Why was the teacher in the second scenario not frustrated?

Teacher Language

Research tells us that the language used by teachers is extremely important (Johnston, 2004). In math and science, language becomes a key to communicating ideas clearly and accurately. For example, when teaching children to group and regroup in addition, teachers often say "Carry the 1," but it is not a "1" we are carrying, it is a "10," and we are making a new group, not simply moving a digit. We may think that this is just shorthand for what we mean, but the concept of "1" is very powerful in children's thinking. Similarly, in science we may always refer to insects as being in a classification group separate from people, dogs, birds, and other animals, which is true when talking about classification in one sense, but this ignores the grouping of insects as being part of the Kingdom Animalia.

Jamie Marshall/Dorling Kindersley, Ltd

Insects first belong in the Kingdom Animalia.

Insects are first grouped as animals and then in that grouping are classified further as insects if they have three body parts, three pairs of jointed legs, two antennae, and a hard outer skeleton.

Another aspect of teacher language that we know impacts children's experiences in math and science is the kinds of questions teachers ask. This becomes especially important to think about when doing assessment. If we are constantly looking for the "right" answer we tend to ask questions that have one answer. This does not help us assess children's understanding and thinking. Children do not get opportunities to discuss their theories when teachers create questions that have only one answer. Teachers sometimes say they want the children to participate in discussions, but then they create many rules controlling children's talk.

Suggestions for language that supports assessing science and math ideas include the following:

Instead of	Try This
What is the right answer?	Tell us more about your thinking.
You didn't include _____.	What else do you notice?
What is the name of this shape?	What do you know about _____?
You need to count again.	Can you count another way?
You should raise the ramp to make the car go faster.	What could you do to make the car go faster?
You made a mistake.	Can you show me what you did?

Consider the following vignette:

Asha decided to research children's talk in her third-grade classroom. She took notes and listened carefully to children's discussions when they were in small groups working on projects investigating things they could do to improve their neighborhood's environment. Before she did this, she had thought that the small groups might not be working because the noise level in the room got higher than she was comfortable with; however, after a few sessions of note taking she was pleasantly surprised to find that the children were engaged in very rich discussions about all sorts of environmental concepts. The noise level was just the result of children becoming passionate about their ideas and theories. This helped her realize that the children actually needed a lot more time rather than cutting back on small-group work.

Documentation of Children's Learning as Assessment

When we document children's work we are recording and saving evidence of their thought processes as they write, draw, talk, act out, and communicate, in order to support our understanding and analysis. Documentation of children's work leads to more authentic assessment. Authentic assessment, as opposed to standardized assessment, is a general term referring to the analysis and measurement of meaningful products. Usually authentic assessments are of more use to the classroom teacher because they are sensitive to individual children's abilities, interests, cultural experiences, skills, and construction of knowledge. Sometimes teachers design authentic assessments in connection with children's input. Authentic assessments are generally done often and are collected so they paint a more complete picture of the child's progress and knowledge.

Documentation is also a cornerstone of classrooms inspired by the work in Reggio Emilia (Edwards, Gandini, & Forman, 1998). Educators in the municipal schools in Reggio Emilia believe that documentation is essential. It guides their interpretation of children's learning, provides the basis for ongoing reflection on classroom experiences, and empowers the child, who is involved in the process.

There are many ways teachers can document children's learning, including these:

- Photographing children working and then photographing their final products
- Writing a narrative of the process of a project
- Taking notes about individual children's actions during a project
- Collecting samples of children's work over the course of a project or about specific topics
- Recording comments from others as they view the child's work

- Recording children's comments as they work and as they look at a final product
- Completing checklists of expected behaviors, dating the time and place they occurred, with room for explanatory notes
- Videotaping segments of a project or topic being explored by children
- Creating class-made books that use children's illustrations to tell the story of learning about a topic
- Creating documentation panels that record the steps the class took to learn about a topic

In an integrated math and science classroom all of these might be used, but before this is useful teachers have to understand how to support children's learning and the skills involved in the use of tools. We don't just hand children a sheet of paper and expect them to be able to produce a picture that we can add to their portfolio. Learning to express their ideas and thinking through a variety of forms of representation is an important part of the curriculum. Documentation is integrated into the curriculum, and is an integral part of the curriculum plan.

Documentation Strategies for Integrated Math and Science

There are methods and materials that teachers can use to document children's work in math and science that are particularly powerful, as discussed in the following sections.

Representations

When we talk about drawing or manipulating materials as part of assessment (for example, creating three-dimensional structures) we are not talking about artistic ability, but rather about the representation of thinking. Young children can be supported in representing thinking by looking at their work as a form of communication. In Reggio Emilia classrooms, children's drawings and other representations are a central part of the way teachers interpret what children understand, what they are interested in, what their questions may be, and their planning (Wurm, 2005). It is not necessarily "art"—in fact, there is no time set aside for the arts in Reggio Emilia classrooms, it is woven seamlessly and extensively into the life of the classroom. Creating representations as a form of communication of one's thinking is embodied in the idea that children have "one hundred languages" (Edwards, Gandini, & Forman, 1993). Children are taught the skills for arts-related representations as they are needed and are encouraged to apply them in numerous contexts.

Children need to be taught about, and given access to, many different media and opportunities so they can choose materials that best support the ideas they want to convey. For example, a teacher might plan a lesson where children are focused on moving different parts of their bodies. The children then have that knowledge and can use it to represent their understanding of how a machine works or for acting out the water cycle.

Observational Drawing

Observational drawing requires looking closely. Observational drawing is different from other types of drawing because you pay less attention to the pen or pencil and spend more time looking at the object you are drawing.

Draw what you see!

Erika

Young children are quite capable of observational drawing when given the opportunity as well as experience with the tools needed. To create the best drawings children usually need to use pencils and pens, but the particular tool will vary depending on the child's age. In general, markers are good for coloring in spaces, but not for fine details. Markers are considered more of a painting medium.

We can teach children to be close observers for observational drawing by first having a discussion about the object to be drawn. You can ask the child to look at the lines that make up the object, to find shapes, and to see how the different parts of the object are connected. See Figure 2-2.

The following guidelines support teaching children how to do observational drawing:

- Encourage scribbling. Children's marks indicate an exploration of lines and shape, and provide experiences with materials that can be used with more intention later.

- Avoid labeling what you think a child is drawing, but do describe the shapes and lines that you see: "You have drawn a large circle with lines coming out of it."

- Avoid overt exclamations about how well a child is drawing; this will lead children to believe their pictures are supposed to represent something you think is important. It will also lead them to

Figure 2-2
Close Observation of the Parts of the Plant by a Six-Year-Old Boy

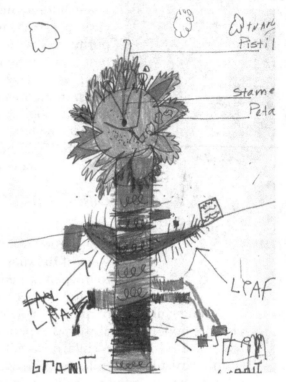

Source: Grant Davis

believe that the drawing is completed, when there may be much more exploration and expression possible.

- Help the children see details and shapes: "Oh look at the sail on the boat; it's shaped like a big triangle."

Consider the observational drawing taking place in the following vignette:

Melissa's second graders were very involved in their project about plants. The children had decided to form small groups that would each study one of the plants found on the school grounds. As part of their research, the children had collected a few samples of their plants and had arranged them in the middle of their group tables. Melissa led the children through close observations of the plants by pointing out parts and labeling them. Each day at least one of the children would carefully observe the plant, sketching the changes that were noticeable. The sketching involved using a good-quality drawing pencil so lines could be erased, lightened, or darkened easily. Another child liked to capture the colors she observed and spent several minutes mixing watercolor paints to get

Erika

Close observation

just the right shades. Still another child liked to use oil pastels to capture the soft colors.

The teacher's role in this situation is to have goals in mind for the learning that may be taking place. Careful observations of the children's work and their conversations holds valuable information. In Melissa's situation she realized that the children needed more support in recognizing the individual parts of the plants, so she found detailed, artistic botanical prints that could be mounted next to the tables so that the children could easily reference the parts of the plants and compare them to the specimens they were drawing. To check for comprehension and see what the children understood about the parts of the plants, Melissa could have them write about plants in general, perhaps encouraging the class to create a book that contained all the information they had gathered.

Three-Dimensional Materials

Teachers often forget that children enjoy expressing ideas with materials that they can use for construction. It is sometimes easier to have paper and pencils stored for children, but there are many ideas they cannot express in two dimensions. Children are much more capable of using three-dimensional materials than we give them credit for.

Clay: Good-quality modeling clay is different from dough. It will hold a shape, whereas most modeling dough is too soft. Children who are trying to create a model of an animal will appreciate the fact that they can make legs that hold the animal up. If you have access to a kiln you can use the kind of clay that requires firing, but self-hardening clay will work also. Just like other materials, young children need a lot of time to explore the qualities and nature of the clay. This has to happen before they can make something that is representational. When you introduce modeling materials to children you can talk about how they are going to be used, how to clean up, and how to store the materials

Waldru/Fotolia

Clay

so they don't dry up. Children are very aware of taking care of materials when they are trusted to use real things.

Once children are familiar with modeling clay, accessories can be added that will help them think of ways to manipulate the clay, such as small sticks, rollers, straightedges, and water. Cookie cutters and other typical dough toys do not support the child's own thought processes and representational abilities and should be avoided, as they limit the possibilities of representation.

Building Materials: There are multiple materials on the market that are designed to support children's three-dimensional work; however, very inexpensive materials can sometimes work as well or even better. Manufacturers create materials that are colorful, but that may be distracting to a child. Some teachers avoid plastic manipulatives and building materials so the children can bring their own imagination to the problem and connect more closely to nature. Sticks used with clay might be a better building material than things made to go together in specific and limiting ways. A collection of cardboard boxes and sheets of cardboard will lend itself easily to representational building.

Capturing the Documentation

Teachers can save two-dimensional representations done by children in portfolios, notebooks, and files. Photos or videos of three-dimensional representations can also be saved. The materials could be organized for each individual child, by teaching objective, by standard, or by topic. The exact material saved and how it is organized is going to depend on the purpose. If the teacher is documenting learning that she wants to share with families at a conference, then she might be focusing on developmental growth and academic goals that would be similar for each child, but would reflect where the child was at the beginning of the assessment period. The materials for that goal would then be saved in an individual child's portfolio. If the teacher is documenting a project that the class has been involved in, then the documentation can be organized temporally, telling the story of the project as it unfolds over time.

More Formalized Assessment Tools

Assessment can be either *formal* or *informal.* Formal assessments are most often tests that are used to evaluate the acquisition of knowledge and are generally not appropriate in early childhood education; they still may be required despite being inappropriate. On the upper end of the early childhood years, tests may be seen more often as part of the school system's accountability framework. Teacher-made tests, which lack standardization, may be more authentic and useful, but still need to be a very small part of the assessment process. Informal assessment is generally done in the context of the classroom.

Rubrics

One type of formal assessment sometimes used for math and science in early childhood classrooms is rubrics. Rubrics are used as scoring guides (Stevens, Levi, & Walvoord, 2012). They generally involve a set of criteria about learning goals, with numerical weights used to separate levels of learning. Rubrics are often written in table form with the criteria listed down one side and the points or values distributed across the top. Each section of the rubric describes the expected qualities for the points or values. Like other more formal forms of assessment, rubrics must be used with caution with young children. Proponents of rubrics maintain that there is a fair appraisal of children's work when everyone agrees on the criteria for quality, but critics of rubrics point out that rubrics limit our imagination. Even though the thought is that rubrics can support authentic learning, the reality is that any assessment tool requires interpretation. There is no formal, standardized assessment tool that should be used by itself. Again, assessment in early childhood education should be a collection of information gathered over time, sensitive to the individual rights of the children and their families. However, there are ways rubrics could be useful in the collection of information about children's learning in a math and science integrated classroom.

There are basically two kinds of rubrics. *Holistic rubrics* have generalized descriptions and can be used with a variety of products. For example, a teacher may have a general rubric that describes what children need to include in their science journals. This would be used by the teacher in assessing what children have done and then could serve as a reference during family conferences or could be added to an educational portfolio.

Analytic rubrics assign partial scores and are more commonly used with procedural projects, such as a documentation panel the child must make to use in a classroom museum.

Sometimes rubrics are used to evaluate a child's individual response when compared to responses from a group. This can give the classroom teacher a place to begin in understanding the child's developmental level of thought. It is important to gather preliminary information about what you expect children to be able to do. This involves having children do a task you can use as a guide for what you will eventually assess. The process is as follows:

- Create an assignment that focuses on what you want to assess.
- Use the children's work to decide what levels of understanding they have. Engage children in a discussion about what the work shows about their understanding. Create a rubric that mirrors these levels of understanding.
- Create a new assignment that focuses on the same concept or topic.
- Use this particular product for your assessment. (Leonhardt, 2005; Lilburn & Ciurak, 2010; Yoshina & Harada, 2007)

Another appropriate way to use rubrics in early childhood classrooms is to have children analyze their own thinking. By giving them faces showing various emotions, for example, children can mark the face that shows how they feel about specific things that have been taught or have happened in the classroom, as can be seen in Figure 2-3.

Figure 2-3
Daily Rubric for Child Input

My Day

Work

Clean-up

Helping

Source: Ken Davis

Science and Math Journals

In a preschool classroom journaling can take the form of a whole-class activity with the teacher acting as scribe. Children can then add ideas through drawing, write their names on a list, make tally marks or checks, and find pictures in magazines to add to the class page. Three interwoven components—drawing, writing, and thinking—are used fairly widely in early childhood classrooms. The intentional teacher knows that he has to plan for the use of these in assessment.

The first component, *drawing*, is so powerful that many children will be motivated to add things in writing too, but beginning with the drawing is important for scaffolding children's thinking. This is not an art opportunity; rather, it is the child's visualization of her thinking process. It is important to allow the child to use pencils or pens that will support the addition of details. There may be a reason for the child to add color, but it is not necessary to have children color all of their drawings.

The second component, *writing*, can be a natural extension. Each day as projects are worked on, children may be more willing to try to write down their observations, new vocabulary, or questions. This could be a description of what they tried, or what someone else did. It could include the child's labels for parts of illustrations. Working in journals is an open-ended activity that will help teachers understand what level of writing children are trying to use.

The third component is the process of *hypothesizing*, or wondering what is going to happen next: What will I try the next time? Why do I think _____ happened?

Having children keep science and math journals or notebooks offers a wonderful way of integrating content with other aspects of curriculum. Teachers often choose to not spend time teaching math and

Science notebook

science because of a concern about time needed for literacy concepts and standards, but journals can give teachers opportunities to assess multiple literacy standards, in contexts that children will find engaging. Science and math journals can become authentic sources for assessing the children's ongoing construction of knowledge. The journals can be reviewed by the teacher during projects for specific concepts, they can be shared among small groups of children for conversations about ideas and what has been learned, they can be shared with parents during conferences, or they can represent part of a larger portfolio of an individual child's progress (Kostos & Shin, 2010).

Notebooks in primary classrooms could be organized with the following structure:

- **Title/Cover.** This can reflect the topic being studied by the whole class or part of the topic as chosen by the child.

- **Table of Contents.** This can be a set list of items chosen by the teacher for the journal or it can incorporate organizational decisions made by the child.

- **Organizational Features.** These may vary according to what the classroom teacher hopes to accomplish but could include page numbers, dates, activity titles, time, and questions being researched.

- **Glossary/Vocabulary.** The children can keep separate areas of the journal for listing and defining the words they need as part of the projects. This part is often shared with the class in the form of a "Word Wall" or topic chart where children can add words as they are explored. Sometimes teachers give the children several words at the beginning of the project and then these words are illustrated as they are needed during the project.

The journals or notebooks then give the teacher ways of assessing children's prior knowledge, procedural understanding, language arts skills, and concept construction. Journals and notebooks can obviously become very elaborate and time consuming, but they can also be a way to support the teacher's ability to collect data and information and give children power over their own learning.

Consider the use of journaling in the following vignette:

In one kindergarten classroom, journals were used as a documentation of children's science wonderings. The journals were five sheets of copy paper folded and stapled with colored covers. This was about the number of pages needed for individual topics being studied or projects that were under way. Each day

15 minutes was set aside for everyone to retrieve their science journals from a centrally located file box. As the children drew and wrote about their project work the teacher was free to circulate around the room, using a stamp date on their pages, taking dictation from those children wanting to write more than they were capable of doing yet, and nudging those who could write more into stretching their efforts. The teacher encouraged some children to add labels to their pictures. As the teacher observed their work, she could tell where each child was in his or her science concept development based on what they chose to draw and write. She was able to take notes about what misconceptions needed to be looked into and what materials would support further exploration. As the journals were completed, the teacher could easily save them for parent conferences and portfolios.

INTERVIEWING FOR ASSESSMENT

There are many ways to interview children in the classroom for information about their knowledge of math and science. The flexible interview was developed by Herbert Ginsburg at Teachers College Columbia (Ginsburg, Jacobs, & Lopez, 1998). This consists of four main parts: presenting the problem, checking comprehension, investigating thought, and interpreting.

> *Presenting the problem:* The teacher gives the child or children a problem that uses materials the child can manipulate. The problem should be very engaging to a young child.
>
> *Checking comprehension:* The teacher makes sure the child understands what she is being asked to do by restating the problem, modifying words, or questioning the child.
>
> *Investigating thought:* The teacher observes the child's response and asks questions to clarify the response, such as, "How did you figure that out?" The teacher does not correct the child's answer.
>
> *Interpretation:* The teacher takes everything he knows about the child to come to an interim conclusion about the child's abilities, thought patterns, skills, and knowledge construction. The teacher needs to know what the child *thinks* about the problem, not whether the child is right or wrong (Ginsburg et al., 1998).

Interviewing for assessment gives the teacher more insight into what is needed to plan for teaching, and to better understand individual children's thinking.

Questions That Help with Assessment

If you need to understand the child's thinking, then most of your questions will be open-ended, but there could still be specific things you may be paying attention to. Questions are designed to probe the child's thinking by having children explain to the interviewer how or why they answered as they did. It is important to set things up so that the children can show the interviewer what they were thinking as they manipulate objects.

There are some basic questions that will help when trying to understand the child's thought process:

- "How did you figure that out?"
- "How do you know?"
- "What do you mean?"
- "Can you show me what you did?"
- "Are you sure?"

The follow-up questions will depend on the child's answer. As the child explains or expands on a thought process, you can ask authentic questions by not taking what the child says as a final statement.

Questions can be part of regular classroom activity; they don't have to be relegated to a conference with the teacher. Consider the following example from preschool:

The preschoolers had been playing with ramps all week. They built them in the block center, they created ramps with books for use with toy cars, and they made tiny ramps with craft sticks stuck in clay. Shelly needed more information for the children's portfolios for parent conferences about their ability to use numeral names. So as part of their play, she helped them make numbered paths out of paper strips the cars would roll onto from the ramps. As they played, she took notes on a clipboard regarding who used number names, who ignored them, and who tried to expand the number paths so the cars would "go to a bigger number." This assessment during play helped her see what the numbers meant to children and who knew the names of the numbers. If she needed more information from a few children who were not as involved in this play, she could casually ask them where the cars had stopped.

Here is an example from third grade:

Kristin was sure that her third graders understood place value; after all, the concept of place value was taught in the first grade and reviewed in the second. But she was also aware that place value was sometimes only understood as the labels for the places in numbers. She had given them a worksheet to assess their ability to recognize place value by labeling the ones, tens, and hundreds in three-digit numerals. They all completed the worksheets successfully. Kristin decided to do a little more assessment by asking individual children to count out 14 buttons and then show her how many buttons were represented by the "4" in "14" and how many represented were represented by the "1" in "14." She was very surprised when she did individual interviews to find that more than half of them could not show her that the "1" in "14" was actually 10 buttons! She realized that the children needed many more opportunities to count groups and record their findings. She found several simple games that the children could play in pairs or by themselves and planned for the whole class to have at least two times a week of math game time.

Interviewing Activities

The following activities, when done for assessment purposes, are not opportunities for teaching as direct instruction. Interviewing for assessment is done solely to *understand* the child's thinking. The image of the teacher as one who gives answers and corrections is very strong, but does not support the constructivist theory of learning.

Preschool

To investigate the concept of one-to-one correspondence with 3- and 4-year-olds, you can have them compare two sets. For example, place a group of five pictures of dog houses on the table and a group of five pictures of dogs. Ask the child to count the pictures and tell you if there are enough dog houses for the dogs. Take note of what the child says. Ask the child to show you what she is referring to. Take notes about whether the child lines up the dog houses with the dogs, and how the child talks about the similarities in the sets. Then present an uneven set of pictures of matching objects and again ask the child if there are enough of each object. Take notes about how confident children are with their answers. If they say that there are enough but the sets are uneven, ask them to show you.

First Through Third Grade

Try this with a child you think should understand place value. Generally children are introduced to place value as a specific math concept sometimes in the first grade, but usually by the second grade they are being asked to add and subtract multiple-digit numbers. Have them count out at least 14 small objects. Then have them write the number "14" on a piece of paper. Ask them to indicate to you by moving the objects how many the "4" stands for. Once they have done that, have them show you how many the "1" stands for. This is not an absolute assessment of their place-value understanding; other forms of counting, grouping, and labeling will be useful too, but it may surprise you to see that their constructed knowledge about this symbol system is not as deeply understood as you thought.

STANDARDS AND ASSESSMENT

Standards and standardized testing are two different things. There has been an ongoing debate in the education world about the role of standards in education.

There are many different content areas of education, each with its own defining ideas about standards. In 2010 national standards for mathematics and English (Common Core Standards) were published by the National Governors Association Center for Best Practices and Council of Chief State School Officers (2010). In 2013, the National Science Teachers Association (NSTA), in partnership with other science groups, released the Next Generation Science Standards (NGSS). These standards are based on *A Framework for K–12 Science Education,* published in 2011 by the National Research Council. States will review the NGSS before adopting them, and national standards for social studies and other curriculum areas may follow.

Standards are designed to give clarity and guidance to the curriculum. The Common Core Standards do not offer advice for meeting individual needs. Classroom teachers trying to implement the Common Core Standards will need a great deal of knowledge and support in implementing the standards. The movement to Common Core Standards is also not without critics, who argue that the implementation of national standards will lead to more standardized testing, less culturally sensitive teaching, and a weaker focus on the learner. This is an extremely important issue to consider, especially in the early childhood years:

> No set of grade-specific standards can fully reflect the great variety in abilities, needs, learning rates, and achievement levels of students in any given classroom. However, the Standards do provide clear signposts along the way to the goal of college and career readiness for all students. (Council of Chief State School Officers and National Governors Association Center for Best Practices, 2010, p. 4)

It has been more conventional for professional organizations to develop standards that are then used by states when developing specific content standards. This is currently true for the National Science Education Standards (Schweingruber, Keller & Quinn, 2012), which are becoming a framework approach to what children need in science education.

It is an important point to emphasize that the Common Core Standards for math and science are not meant to take the place of specific lesson content objectives developed by individual school systems, but are intended to guide those school systems so that there is a greater consistency across the United States for the expectations in math and science education. How those standards are addressed in classrooms is still the responsibility of states and school systems, as well as the individual teachers.

It will be part of your job as a professional educator to become familiar with those standards that your state or school system has created or decided to adopt. However, this does not mean that standards should be used like a checklist and that every child will meet every standard. In early childhood education the focus is on the individual development of each child. The teacher must use the standards as a guide, but with the individual child in mind. Teachers also have to understand that to meet a standard in the third grade, for example, children will need to have experience with the underlying ideas in that standard beginning in preschool. Children will not automatically understand the idea of a fraction in the third grade if they have not had prior experiences with parts and wholes.

Standards can have positive benefits:

- They can define a broad field of curriculum to provide some continuity across many different levels and grades.
- They can create a research base to develop better curriculum.
- They can add a component of professionalism to the field of early childhood education.
- They can provide specific ideas for accountability. (Seefeldt, 2005)

The position we take on this subject is that standards are not a "bad" thing; we need standards to guide our systematic decisions on a large scale. However, when meeting standards becomes the focus of the curriculum, children's understanding runs the risk of becoming a secondary consideration in teaching.

Standardized Testing

Standardized testing means using tests that are designed to be administered and scored the same way for all students. Standardized tests are generally created outside of the immediate context of the classroom and are intended to hold all children to the same measurement criteria. Unfortunately, the use of standardized tests in the earliest grades has grown despite a lack of research to support the reliability and validity of the findings. Research indicates that standardized testing is not appropriate when making decisions about an individual child's educational program (Viruru, 2006). There are many books on the market examining the issues of standardized testing and the problems that develop when standardized testing is used in early childhood to the exclusion of other kinds of authentic, classroom-based assessment (e.g., Harris, Smith, & Harris, 2011; Kohn, 2000).

EdTPA

EdTPA (formerly known as Teacher Performance Assessment) is a national system for assessing beginning teachers during student teaching experiences. It requires video recordings of planned teaching episodes labeled as teaching segments. It is designed to mirror the types of assessments given to other professional occupations for certification. EdTPA requires specific forms of documentation of children's learning. In EdTPA language, documentation is referred to as artifacts and includes the documents used to plan and record the planning involved in teaching. The focus is on the achievement of children resulting from the planned teaching segment.

EdTPA is being adopted by many teacher education programs, but to varying degrees. There is a cost to the student when EdTPA is used by a program to cover the expenses of sending materials out for objective assessment and evaluation.

In sum, assessment is a critical part of curriculum, and it is particularly important in this era of accountability and a focus on standards. Teachers need to be cognizant of the power and limitations of different forms of assessment, and consider formative assessment to be a natural part of their role.

Review Questions

1. What's your definition of appropriate assessment methods for young children regarding their learning and development of science and math concepts?

2. How can assessing young children guide teaching?
3. How can appropriate assessment increase children's vocabulary development? Provide an example.
4. List some types of documentation that can support assessment. Describe what each would include. Finally, create an example and explain how you would share it with a child's parent or guardian.
5. Explain the importance of interviewing when assessing young children's knowledge and capabilities.
6. Name a standard or a couple of sets of standards you will use to assess young children's knowledge and progress in learning about math and science. Explain how you will use the standards to assess and whether they are purposeful or not.

Summary

In this chapter we have looked at the general principles of assessment and also specific strategies and methods for assessing math and science learning in the early grades. Assessment cannot be separated from the curriculum and involves the teacher's knowledge about child development, cultural context, and specific curricular content.

Assessment involves the language we use when teaching, the decisions we make about how and what we teach, the methods we use to document children's learning, and the authenticity of what we expect children to do and learn in our classrooms.

The politics of assessment will impact you in your classroom through the development of common standards and school systems' reliance on standardized tests, but as a professional you will still make decisions that impact a child's experiences in math and science that will form the foundation of their lives.

Websites

EdTPA: The official website for EdTPA shares all the information needed to understand the purpose and goals for beginning teacher assessment.

Teaching Channel: This website provides many videos that show examples of teachers using assessment in their classrooms. Several are specific to early childhood, and many provide overall definitions of assessment concepts.

YouTube: If you search under "assessment in education" you will find videos that show early childhood assessment in action. Dan Huber's YouTube channel provides several of these.

3 Creating an Environment for Math and Science Integration

Learning Outcomes

After working with the ideas in this chapter, you should be able to:

- Analyze personal beliefs about children, teaching, and learning, and their impact on the classroom environment.
- Apply current information about math and science teaching and learning to the organization of the classroom.
- Understand how planning the environment for math and science can meet children's individual needs.

Think about your favorite place to shop. Imagine yourself walking through the doors. What do you look at first? What do you smell? How do you feel being in that environment? What elements do you enjoy and which would you change? How are you treated? Are people who work in this environment friendly and available? Does the environment help you understand where to find the things you need? Are there aspects of the environment that feel chaotic or confusing? Do you enjoy being there by yourself, or would you prefer to have friends with you?

When we talk about environments we are talking about the whole experience of being in a certain space, not just what is on the wall or the shelf. We are talking about how the environment shapes our behaviors and how we can act on and in that environment.

Before children show up for the first day of class, the teacher has thought about how the room will support their learning. The teacher will have thought about how children will manage materials, where they will sit in a group, if everyone will be able to see a centrally located board, and many other group organization concerns. If it is a first-grade classroom the teacher might have looked at folders of information for each child who attended the school the year before. If children are new to the school the teacher will be thinking about how to collect current information and records. However, no matter who the children are, the most important thing in a classroom environment cannot be easily seen. It is the belief the teacher holds about the child's ability to think and problem solve. The image of the child as competent is different than the image of the child as needy.

Can you think of a time someone didn't believe you could do something? How did that person's belief impact your decision to pursue your interest?

This is complicated by our own feelings about our ability to "do" science and math. We may have a feeling that the way it has been taught might not have worked for us, but we don't know other ways of teaching. What we have experienced shapes our teaching. We are most comfortable with things that are familiar. Our own experiences in classrooms have an impact on what we believe about teaching math and science, and what we believe about children's capabilities can become the strongest influence on how we teach math and science.

We may have thought that doing pages of math problems was very boring or we may have been good at math, but the fact is that many of us experienced school as sitting at a desk and following the teacher's directions. This is the image we take with us into the classroom. Science might have been presented as a demonstration carried out by the teacher. Or we might recall having to read a chapter in a science textbook and then answer questions at the end. We might have been in a preschool where there was a "science" table with shells and rocks on it, but with little opportunity to explore and experiment. How can we change those images? What kinds of classrooms support integration of math and science?

HOW OUR BELIEFS ABOUT CHILDREN, TEACHING, AND LEARNING SHAPE OUR ENVIRONMENTS

Let's visit two kindergarten classrooms that are side by side. We will call one of the rooms the Blue Room. The Blue Room is set up with interest centers. There is a book corner, an art area, a math table next to open shelving, and science materials on a table by the window. In the Blue Room everything is neat and clean (Figure 3-1). In fact, there is nothing out of place. An observer may think that children have never entered this room, but it is the middle of the week during the third month of the school year and there are 26 kindergarten children enrolled in this class. A cabinet is sitting in the middle of the room, defining work spaces by separating the math area from the art area. On top of the cabinet sits a lovely green plant, centered exactly in the middle. The cabinet has many shallow shelves and on each shelf is a small stack of duplicated papers ready for the lessons that are already planned for the whole year. There are several low tables arranged around a larger open space. Each table holds pencils, markers, and crayons in similar containers. At the front of the open area is a director's chair with the teacher's name painted brightly on the back. Next to her chair are arranged various large-format books and other teaching supplies. Close

Figure 3-1
Classrooms Can Send Powerful Messages About the Role of the Child

Source: Ken Davis

by is a chart of paper pockets. Each pocket has a child's name on it and is filled with green, yellow, red, and black cards. Next to the chart there is a sign that explains that if children choose to not follow a rule, they must "turn" a card in their pocket on the chart. Another chart has groups of children's names and a schedule of when each group is supposed to visit each center in the room.

On the walls are commercially printed posters reminding children of classroom rules, long and short vowels, the alphabet, groups of objects that are numbered, and so forth. On a low table in front of a window sits a small collection of rocks and a sign, "Science Center." Scissors and construction paper sit on a long table labeled "Art Center." Hanging from the bottom of the art center sign is a craft project that children are obviously supposed to copy. In a corner we find a small cabinet that holds a number of worn books and a small circular rug. The corner has a sign on the wall, "Reading Center," and more rules about being quiet. A cabinet on the wall holds several tubs of small objects such as pattern blocks, Unifix cubes, and Base 10 rods. A table in front of the cabinet has a sign hanging overhead that reads "Math Center."

The classroom next door, which we will call the Green Room, looks very different. It is not extremely neat, but on close inspection we can see that everything seems to have a special spot and many things are labeled. However, the labels are rather messy because the children have created them. On the walls are many graphs and charts, but again, the overall appearance is not terribly neat because the children have made these graphs. This room also has low tables around a larger, open area. There is a chair at the front that is large enough for an adult, but there is another fancier chair next to it with a sign labeled "Royal Reader." An area in front of a window is labeled "Science Center," but we don't really need the sign because it's fairly obvious that many interesting things are going on in this center. We can see a large plastic container that seems to be full of dirt, but on closer inspection we see that the dirt is moving! It is a habitat for earthworms. We then notice that the center next to the science center seems to be the math center because it is full of containers holding all sorts of measuring devices, paper, markers, scissors, tape, and other supplies. The children have made a large chart that holds data from several weeks of observation of the worms. We notice that there is an area that holds many labeled plastic boxes of books, but there are also books all over the room. In the science and math centers there are many books about worms, nature, the Earth, composting, plants, and other topics.

Dainis/Shutterstock

Classrooms can be carefully planned for children to be independent learners.

In this classroom there is no obvious behavior chart, but a short list of rules written in childish handwriting is posted. There is space for the whole class to meet in a circle, and there is a clipboard near the teacher's chair labeled "Issues and Concerns." There is also a pocket chart that seems to be an organizing system for children to keep track of which activity they have planned for the day.

Questions to Consider

1. What qualities of each room support math and science exploration?
2. What elements are children centered and which are teacher centered?
3. What do the behavior expectations have to do with math and science learning?

A brief description of two classrooms cannot really tell us precisely what takes place every day or the relationship between the teacher and the children. But, we can tell from certain signs that the teacher in the Blue Room believes that order and appearance are more important than children's input, and that learning comes from the teacher and is not necessarily something children can generate themselves. The lack of an obvious classroom management system in the second classroom may not, at first glance, seem to have anything to do with how math and science are taught in this classroom; however, the rules written by the children, the system for planning, and the support materials created by the children may tell us that in this classroom children are highly engaged and their input is valued. The teacher in the Blue Room may believe that children are not capable of making good choices without a great deal of control. She may plan around the prescribed curriculum used by her school without considering the role of interest and motivation in the children's *learning* because she is focused on what she is supposed to *teach*.

The teacher in the Green Room recognizes children's innate curiosity, but also believes that it is her job to teach them how to structure their inquiry so they can make good decsions and choices. She thinks that the prescribed curriculum represents the minimal level of learning expected by the school system and that it is her job to make sure the curriculum standards are met and exceeded. She also believes that each child has something to offer and is capable of problem solving and thinking.

Academic Environment

There are many routines, materials, and practices in early childhood classrooms that have become part of the unquestioned curriculum. Many activities commonly done in classrooms actually create routines that don't hold a lot of meaning for children. Routines are very important for classrooms to run smoothly, but they don't necessarily help teach ideas or content.

Looking at One Element in Depth

Let's look at one example of such a routine with a more critical eye. A routine seen often in classrooms for young children is the use of a large wall calendar or other set display used for daily instruction. Quite often the calendar is part of the opening routine of the day. Children are asked to identify the date, find patterns, count the number of days in school, or count the number of days left in the month. But calendars are a way of organizing time, and this should be the focus.

Tara's second graders have no problem identifying dates on the calendar. When asked to point to January 16th they easily find it, and when asked to identify the name of the day that January 12th lands on they can label the day. But a standardized assessment used this problem: "Juan's science fair project was due on February 12th and needed a week of work to complete, but he started it the day before it was due. On what day should he have started?" The children were stumped. Tara walked them through the response by having them put their finger on the 12th and then asking how many days they needed to go backwards to indicate a week. The whole explanation was a struggle and made Tara wonder what children were learning during their daily calendar time.

Questions to Consider_____

1. What do you think the children had learned about calendars?
2. How do *you* use a calendar?
3. What kinds of connections can a teacher help children make with developmental concepts of time?
4. What happens during the school day that helps children understand the organization of time?

Like many of her colleagues, Tara tried to integrate math and science into a very full day. Most of the other second-grade teachers took 15 to 20 minutes a day to go through a routine that used a large calendar, pockets for grouping counting sticks, a weather chart, and other items. But after the problem-solving assessment, Tara began to look for ways to also integrate problems that were real and meaningful to the children. She recognized this issue as an interesting problem for herself and for the children because it was meaningful and could lead to a more educational experience. She began asking the children to help construct problems that they could work together to solve. For instance, Charisse told the class that her birthday was in 3 weeks, but her mom had to order the cake at least 4 days before the party. The class used the calendar to find out exactly on which day Charisse's mom needed to order the cake. A classroom that supports thinking presents children with problems to solve that they are truly interested in solving.

The first week of school could be filled with projects to solve the problem of how calendars are constructed. Children could be presented with wall calendars that have been taken apart and their job could be to notice how the grids work to help us keep track of days and months. Other ways of marking the passage of time could become a mini-project that incorporates not only math and science standards but also social studies.

Preschoolers need much more interaction with thinking about schedules and time in the form of individualized books about themselves showing their personal routines; using calendars is too abstract.

In Tara's classroom the children had become used to doing calendar time every day. It had become an important routine to Tara because she felt that by counting the days of the week, adding days to the number line, and bundling counting sticks into groups of 10 she was providing a learning experience for the children. She thought that through repetition they would "learn" the concepts of counting, one-to-one correspondence, and place value. What was missing, though, was an opportunity for the children to have to think about why adding numbers to the number line was useful or meaningful to their lives. Once Tara started thinking about this problem she immediately thought about how much children look forward to special events and start counting the days. She decided to add events to the number line so that children would be able to connect the counting to the passage of time. This provided **context** to what the children were learning. She realized that the environment could support very meaningful activities—meaningful to both her planned teaching and to children's lives.

Teach to the the why?

Physical Environment

The physical environment of the classroom says a great deal about the image of the child, and the views of teaching and learning, that are held by the school. In the schools of Reggio Emilia, the environment is considered the "third teacher" (Edwards, Gandini, & Forman, 1993). Great thought is put into the physical environment to create a welcoming place that invites children to engage deeply with materials, objects, and each other. Many preschools, and some elementary classrooms, have been inspired to create environments that support children's active engagement. In these classrooms, the teachers think carefully about choices of materials, placement and type of furniture, and issues of accessibility, aesthetics, comfort, and ease of movement.

The physical environment of many American classrooms incorporates practices that are not necessarily a good use of our time and effort. For example, in many elementary school classrooms we use bulletin board trim because everyone does; there are very few schools in the United States where you would not see it used on a bulletin board somewhere in the building. If you were making a list of pros and cons of buying trim, you would need to consider the cost and amount, how much time it will take to cut and fit it to the board, how to attach it, and how it is going to help children focus on the information the board will display. Now, consider using a roll of register tape (this is described in more detail in Chapter 4). You can usually find it in various widths at very low cost. Children can create the pattern for the board, which could be part of the information displayed. Children can measure the board and then the tape, create the designs to be used on it, and talk about how to attach it to the board. The children will appreciate the trim much more when it is their work instead of something bought at the store. These kinds of problem-solving skills are what we want to develop in our classrooms, yet we often give children everything ready to go. By creating an opportunity for the children to make the bulletin board trim, the teacher effectively integrates math (measurement, counting) and science (materials, properties).

CLASSROOM ORGANIZATION

The teacher's approach to classroom organization can also incorporate strategies for supporting math and science learning. The classroom teacher will want to anticipate and think through as many problems as possible before children walk through the door; however, part of what may be thought about are which problems the teacher will deliberately plan for the children to solve.

It is common to hear teachers tell children that the classroom is "theirs" and then to proceed with a list of rules. Materials may be stored out of children's reach and books may have already been selected. It is not surprising, then, that children come to see school as a place where their thinking is not supported.

In a classroom where learning is believed to be constructed through individual problem solving or group discussion, materials and room arrangements will not always be thought of as complete. As projects unfold, children may be asked by their teacher,

"Where shall we store the materials we will need?

What books should we put by the terrarium?

When should we share our work that we have completed on our projects?

How will we decide what to show our parents at open house?"

Teachers understand that the discussions, arguments, sharing of points of view, and language involved in solving these problems should not come only from the teacher, but are an important aspect of a learning environment that supports the construction of knowledge.

There are other elements of the classroom environment that can support knowledge construction in math and science. For example, provide a balance of natural and commercial items. A tub of brightly colored small plastic bears sold as math manipulatives can be found in many early childhood classrooms. The commercially produced counting bears may help the teacher focus on specific attributes such as color. Children may not have counting bears at home, so they may be a novelty. However, a tub of carefully selected rocks could provide the same conceptual activities with the added benefit of connecting children to nature. Here are other ideas for creating a balance of natural and commercial items:

Start with. . . .	and Then Add . . .
Plastic bears	Rocks
Base 10 blocks	Dried pea pods
Attribute blocks	Seashells
Classification objects	Leaves
Rulers	Sticks, string
Pattern blocks	Fabric

Anna/Fotolia

Materials don't have to come from a store.

Anjelagr/Fotolia

Naluwan/Fotolia

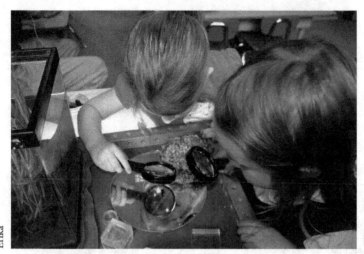

Erika

Tools can help children make close observations.

Many **natural materials**, such as rocks, leaves, and sticks, provide a far deeper experience. Children can use magnifying glasses to sort the rocks according to color, size, hardness, number of points, and texture. They can use the science principles of observation and classification to notice that rocks have different structures. This can lead to questions about how rocks are formed. None of these real connections can come from using brightly colored plastic bears. Materials can support the integration of math and science in natural ways.

The classrooms of Reggio Emilia include many materials that not only come from the natural world, but also have aesthetic qualities that are designed to engage children's experiences with their personal worlds. When people are asked to think about where they spent the best times of their childhood, they often relate details about spending time outdoors in a special area or playing with things found in their environment. Children are attracted to natural materials; their curiosity is piqued by an unusual plant, funny-looking seeds, bird nests, or shiny bugs. Teachers spend hours of precious time and hundreds of dollars purchasing commercially made materials when some of the best materials are the ones found outside their classroom doors. For example, a small part of a flower bed can become a project to study the growth of plants, magnifying glasses taken outdoors during recess can become windows on new worlds, chalk can be used to draw the outline of shadows on the concrete, or water and a brush can be used to exemplify the process of evaporation on a hot sidewalk.

Materials and Tools Should Be Accessible to Children

We cannot always anticipate the problems children may choose to solve. A classroom environment that provides easily accessed tools and materials supports the creative thinking of a child who has a problem to solve. Many classrooms have tubs of used crayons, stacks of assorted construction paper, and dried-up glue sticks and markers. A child who is making a graph to show the growth of a plant or cutting pieces of paper to create a model of his or her observations will tire quickly of digging through the crayons for the right color or looking for a good black marker.

Quite often teachers are dealing with extremely limited budgets, and it seems to be a good idea to buy as many of the cheapest materials as possible so the budget can be stretched, but it is far better to buy fewer materials and make sure they work the way they are intended to. Scissors that hardly cut construction paper let alone string or yarn are not worth having at all.

Accessibility of materials needs to be considered. If materials are stored in closed cabinets and children must ask to use them, then teachers will spend a lot of time directing children to the requested items. If children are asked to think about the best way to store materials, they will feel invested and more responsible for their use.

It may be surprising to know that it takes at least 5 to 6 weeks for classrooms to work well. Teachers know that it is well worth their time and effort to take the time to teach children to be as self-sufficient as possible. The teacher needs to introduce the materials how to access them carefully with the belief that children are quite capable of using real tools and making good decisions.

Technology

When we think of technology in classrooms, we usually think about a Smartboard™ or computer, but digital cameras, real thermometers, and scales that are sensitive to small weights are also examples of technology children can learn to use. When children have used real equipment in the pursuit of information, they can then transfer that understanding to more sophisticated technological models. For example, there is software available for children to manipulate weighted numbers on scales. As a precursor to doing algebra, children are invited to work math problems to find equal equations by moving numbers and "balancing" the results. However, if children have not used a real balance or scale, the physical knowledge of balance may not have been constructed. In a technologically integrated environment, children's exploration of concepts will be supported in many ways.

In the preschool/kindergarten room at an environmentally focused school, children were invited to explore the concept of change over the year. In the spring they began reading books about frogs, which included information about the transformation from tadpole to frog. Many books were collected for the children to use, websites were shared showing the development of frogs, small plastic frogs were placed in the water table, and frog shapes were re-created with textured paint. These are all fairly typical activities that teachers use in a theme approach, but this environmental school went further. Right outside the back door there was a small enclosed garden, pond, and wetland area. The preschool/kindergarten class went outside to capture a few tadpoles from the pond for closer study in their classroom. Data was collected about the development of the tadpoles, information was found about the time involved, pictures were taken, and stories were written with the teacher's assistance. The children used real tools for real research, not simply a coloring sheet showing four stages of a frog's development that children are supposed to color correctly, as can be seen in some more traditional classrooms. Computers around the room were easily accessed for researching any question that came from the authentic thinking, questioning, and investigation children were doing on the topic of frogs. Smartboards were used in this setting to create visual displays of information with much input from small or large groups.

In this example, all of the technology available in the space was a well-integrated part of the life of the classroom.

The Setup of the Room Will Encourage Children to Share Ideas

Talking through our understanding, and listening to others' understanding, is a crucial element of an integrated science and math classroom. Teachers tell children to listen to each other when discussing ideas, but if the children are sitting in a large group facing the teacher, they may think that all of the thinking and sharing of ideas is supposed to come from the teacher. By having space for a large circle of children who are facing each other, the teacher sends the message that making eye contact is important for discussion and that we all have something important to share. The circle indicates to children that each child is equally equipped to add ideas for problem solving

Erika

Light tables can help children notice the properties of materials.

Erika

Children's discussions are very important.

and supports their sense of community.

If desks are lined up in rows that all face the front of the room, a message is being sent to children that their job is to sit, look at the teacher, and listen. Whatever they have to say is secondary. However, if the room space is flexible and children are encouraged to think of ways to work together, the message is sent that their ideas are valid and valued. If there are spaces in the room that allow for small groups, or if desks and chairs are arranged in this way, the environment is suggesting that peer interaction is an important part of classroom activities.

Some teachers use a message system so that children are encouraged to add their ideas to a clipboard for group discussion. This can become an easy way to identify topics and questions for future research and problem solving.

Display Areas Are Used by the Teacher and the Children

Classroom walls covered in commercially produced posters do not convey the belief that children are thinkers and problem solvers. Teachers may believe that a poster showing the steps to adding three-column math problems or a poster with a picture of the parts of a plant are needed to ensure learning. However, the information on the posters is outside the child's experience. Imagine how much better it would be for the children to work in a small group to illustrate how they arrived at a solution to post on the wall, or if they used a variety of materials to create models of plants to display.

Bulletin boards are where children share representations of their work and thinking. The teacher does not have to be responsible for "decorating" a large space. The bulletin board can depict the story of a project. It can document where children were at the beginning of the

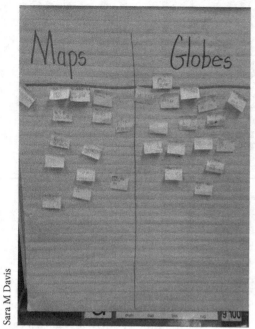

Sara M Davis

Globes and maps can be used for many conversations.

project, what happened next, times and dates that things occurred, comments made by children about the project, and all sorts of examples of what has been learned.

Systems for Planning

Teachers who want to use learning centers or stations in their classrooms have much to consider. They must think about many things, including how much space each work area will require, how materials will be stored in each area, how many children can work in the area comfortably, and what the resources might be. But the most important consideration should be how children will be supported in thinking about what they will do. If the teacher uses a forced rotation system (e.g., groups are timed in each center and at the end of the time they all clean up and move to the next assigned center), new problems arise. How much time will each center require? For example, if forced rotation is used then the activities in each center have to require about the same effort, so having a complex construction activity in one center and a simple counting activity in another center won't work. One group of children will have just gotten started when another group has finished. Having adequate and flexible time schedules can support the idea that children's work determines the time allocated to the project or task.

Questions to Consider

1. Think about a hobby or activity you really enjoy. Would you consider beginning the activity if you only had 10 minutes to work on it?
2. What things do you have to consider before starting a favorite hobby or activity?
3. How does storage impact your work?
4. How do you decide if you have time to work on your project? What constraints do you have to consider?

Sometimes teachers try to avoid this problem by having each group use one center each day during the week, but the opportunities to teach children how to plan and problem solve are lost if we constantly arrange their every move. If the activities at the centers are planned to support ongoing projects, then children will be engaged at

Figure 3-2
One way to organize centers. Children place color-coded sticks indicating which centers they have chosen in a pocket corresponding to the day. The symbols above the columns can be changed every day to send children to specific centers, but as they complete the first center they choose their next center.

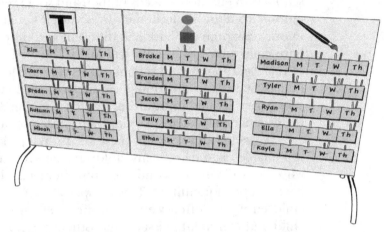

Source: Ken Davis

a much higher level than if the activities are simply planned to keep children busy so the teacher can do other things.

Another issue classroom teachers face with learning centers and schedules is how to be accountable for what children are doing and how to keep track of their choices. Math and science learning centers are not to be ways to occupy the other children's time while the teacher meets with a small reading group. The time in most classrooms is too precious to waste energy on tasks designed to simply keep children "busy."

Swapna used a system in her first-grade classroom during science that supported children's planning. There were several ongoing projects set up around the room in centers. Swapna had cut file folder pockets for each child and the pockets were placed on a board in small groups (Figure 3-2). She placed color coordinated craft sticks in different centers around the room. As children decided what project they wanted to work on, they would retrieve a stick and place it in their pocket. That way, she only had to check their file folder pockets from time to time to see where they had worked. She knew on Friday that Laura had painted a picture of flowers on Monday, planted flower seeds on Tuesday, measured the grass growing in a tub by the window on Wednesday, and estimated where the bean plant would end up on the growth chart on Thursday. She knew then that Laura needed to work on her plant book on Friday because she hadn't done that earlier in the week.

Considering Individual Needs

Most teachers today are teaching groups that include children who may not speak the same language, or who may have physical needs that require special consideration. Some children in our classrooms come to school with emotional needs unmet, and some require more physical attention from the adults in their lives. And it's guaranteed that each child in our classroom will have had different and varied experiences and will have constructed different ideas about the world. As we plan the setup of the classroom before school begins we have to consider all the possibilities. Standard room design elements can help us think about these issues. Space around furniture, access to water, heights of tables and desks, the distance to visual displays, and similar factors all must be considered.

As we talked about in Chapter 2, thinking about one child's needs will enable us to meet many children's needs. There may be one child who has a diagnosed condition, but there may be several others who have not been identified. This is especially true in classrooms of young children. Quite often we are the first person who has worked with a child and can identify issues that others are not aware of. We have to plan for all children in our classroom with the realization that many children may have unrecognized learning or physical concerns.

Differentiation Built into the Environment

Differentiation in the curriculum means planning learning opportunities that support all the different ways children learn and interact. Think about your experiences in traditional science education. Your teacher may have told you to read a chapter in a book and which questions to answer at the end of the chapter. Perhaps a demonstration of the science concept in that particular chapter was shown to the class. What do you remember learning from this? Were there students in your class who seemed to learn a lot from this type of teaching?

In early childhood classrooms the environment must support many different ways of learning. Simply reading text to children followed by a worksheet is not going to help them learn at any meaningful level. At the environmental school mentioned earlier in this chapter, preschoolers were learning in many different ways. Teachers used text, books, trips to the pond, videos, art materials, math materials, charts, graphs, and a specialist to support children's ongoing thinking and questioning. These things were all available to the children; they were not materials and tools that were carefully handed out once a week and used at the teachers' discretion. The study of frogs came late in the year after other projects and studies about chicks, plants, and snakes. Each topic was easily seen through documentation and materials in the classroom.

In a more traditional, teacher-led classroom, children may see a commercially produced poster on the wall showing the life cycle of the frog, listen to a book read by the teacher, and then cut and paste pictures depicting this same cycle. The environment is not seen as the "third teacher" in a classroom like this; only one way of teaching and learning is apparent.

Animals in the Classroom

In any classroom where constructing ideas is important, it is necessary to provide interesting and interactive opportunities for observation, and animals are often included for this reason. Use the following guidelines when considering what animals you will bring into your classroom:

- There are certain animals that are not appropriate for classrooms. You will want an animal that can either be handled or at least cared for easily without any danger to children. There are specific groups of animals that are known to carry bacteria that can make anyone handling them very ill. The following animals are not appropriate for classrooms of children younger than 5, according to the American Association for Laboratory Animal Science web site:

  1. Reptiles
  2. Amphibians
  3. Poultry
  4. Ferrets
  5. Calves, goats, sheep

School-aged children can be expected to better understand the necessity of health and safety precautions, but you will need to carefully consider the maturity or special needs of the group of children you work with.

- Do you have the right conditions to provide a healthy environment for both the animal and the children? Children must wear plastic gloves *and* be able to wash their hands easily when handling animals, their bedding, and their food.

Kitsananan/Shutterstock

Turtles are often brought to school, but children need to wear gloves if they handle the turtles and wash their hands.

- Have you prepared the children before the animal is added to the environment? Do they understand the health routines that must be used? There needs to be a clear structure in place before animals are brought into the classroom.
- What are some of your educational objectives for having the animal in the classroom? What kinds of observation and inquiry will the animal support? You will need to be very purposeful concerning what the animal will add to your curriculum.

Animals are well worth the extra effort to have in your classroom. Caring for and learning about animals is an excellent way to teach environmental connections, support the development of empathy, and provide a variety of ways for children to feel responsible.

Communicating with Families and Others Through the Environment

There are many ways teachers find to communicate with families and others in their schools, such as these:

1. Projects can be documented outside the classroom door and children can be encouraged to explain the parts of the projects.
2. A schedule for the week can be displayed by the door that is made up of photographs of routine activities or children's illustrations of upcoming events.
3. Teachers can provide boxes close to the classroom door with lists of materials needed for projects.
4. A "graffiti" wall can be part of a bulletin board close to the classroom door where messages can be written by families and by children about observations of the weather, for example, or things children are excited to have learned.
5. Families can send authentic artifacts from home to be used in the classroom for a focus on the cultural and social aspects of the larger community.

Each classroom should have a unique environmental connection to communities that speaks to the teacher's belief that children are born scientists and mathematicians.

Review Questions

1. What are *your* beliefs about children?
2. List the responsibilities teachers have in their jobs. Which do you believe are the most important when it comes to creating good environments for science and math?
3. What does it mean to learn something?
4. What is important to learn about math and science?
5. What are the most important ideas about setting up a math and science environment?
6. How does the environment impact individual children's experiences?
7. What do we need to consider about children when we are planning a math and science environment?

Summary

In this chapter we have looked at how classrooms support the integration of math and science. The planned environment supports individual children through thoughtful selection of materials, careful organization, and an awareness of the need to teach children how to make decisions. Teachers consider the kinds of materials available to children, and how those materials are to be used.

Websites

Classroom Architect
Scholastic Tools: Class Setup Tool
These websites provide a drag and drop floorplan to explore different ways of moving furniture in a typical classroom.

Schools Out: Lessons from a Forest Kindergarten
This site has a clip from a movie about a school in the forest.

What is the Reggio Emilia Approach? | An Everyday Story
Resources for incorporating inspirations from Reggio Emilia; the website is designed for homeschooling parents.

Nature Explore
Acorn Naturalists
Two websites that provide science resources focused on the natural world for early childhood classrooms.

II

Integration Through Big Ideas

THE BIG IDEAS TO BE COVERED

In the following chapters, we will be focusing on big ideas that can serve to integrate mathematics and science. Each big idea will be explored first in general, discussing how to think about the big idea as a vehicle for integration, and then with modules that give specific examples of how you would plan activities and lessons related to the big idea. Each module will be specifically linked to mathematics and science standards. The five big ideas are the following:

Patterns

Transformation

Movement

Balance and Symmetry

Relationships

How did we come up with the big ideas that we chose? We carefully chose big ideas that would lend themselves to math and science integration. So, for example, the big idea of **transformation** is an important framework for explorations in science – since change is a theme throughout both physics and chemistry. It is also important in math – because of the importance of observation, estimation, and experimentation in studying transformation. Similarly, the big idea of **balance** is important in science – for example, in terms of symmetry in nature and in optics. It is also important in math – comparisons and measurement as well as algebraic equations are good examples of balance.

We then looked at how best to illustrate each big idea's implementation through modules – examples of activities around one aspect of the big idea. For example, with balance, we provide activities relating to the circus, incorporating tight rope walking, using pictoral equations to represent it. In developing these modules, we mapped each one to math and science standards, and then looked to see if we were capturing the breadth of knowledge desired.

One of the values of the constructivist educator (Brooks and Brooks, 2000; Chaille, 2008) is to support children's learning that is connected, that is not discrete but is linked by important big ideas.

> According to the constructivist, learning takes place when we see the relationships between the many different things that we experience and learn. This focus on connection means that in addition to the importance of living in the moment with children, and appreciating the immediacy of experience, early childhood educators need to think about the broader context of children's experiences, the connections among and between what they do and what they learn. What's particularly important about connection is that it comes naturally for children – they are constantly striving to make sense out of and construct webs among the many different things they experience and learn. By focusing on connection as a basic concept, we are honoring that which children are doing naturally. (Chaille, 2008, pp. 8–9)

Using standards as they relate to big ideas is one way to help teachers make decisions about what to focus on, and why the focus is important.

> . . . The teacher can weave threads across the curriculum, and, through children's experiences in those connected curriculum activities their own world can be woven together. They can start to make implicit, if not explicit, connections across all of the varied interesting things that go on in their lives, and in so doing create more solid and deeper ideas that last and are meaningful. (Chaille, 2008, p. 4)

CONTENT KNOWLEDGE: WHAT DO YOU NEED TO KNOW?

Science and mathematics incorporate a great deal of specific content knowledge that is important, but both disciplines also involve knowledge and skills relating to processes – of inquiry, of problem-solving, of experimentation, of theory-building. One of the reasons mathematics and science education is often shortchanged in preschool and primary classrooms is that the teacher feels inadequately prepared in terms of content knowledge. Because of this, it is important to think about (1) how to draw on our content knowledge, and (2) strategies for gathering content knowledge as needed.

1. Drawing on our experiences and content knowledge.

   Just as we should try to understand what children are bringing to the learning experience – from previous activities, experiences, or readings – we should also try to understand our own knowledge base. Here, think about both everyday occurrences (what happens to food left out) as well as things you've read about or studied. For example, you may recall finding an orange at the bottom of a large bowl of oranges that has partially liquefied. Thinking these things through can give you, as a teacher, some ideas of what questions you might pose to the children about what's happening to the objects being observed.

2. Gathering content knowledge

   As you plan your curriculum, you can identify the areas that might need to be researched for content knowledge, and it is helpful to have some strategies and resources for doing this. For example, there are some important scientific concepts underlying decomposition and these will be described in one of the modules in the chapter on transformation.

   There are many sources for content knowledge that will arise for you, and in science, one of the best resources is the National Science Teachers Association website. Other resources could include science museums (such as the Exploratorium in San Francisco) and children's museums (such as the Boston Children's Museum). A good resource for mathematics is the National Council for the Teaching of Mathematics website. Other resources that support a constructivist view of learning in math can be found on Marilyn Burns' website.

WHAT IS INCLUDED IN EACH "BIG IDEA" CHAPTER?

Each of the chapters in Part 2 will begin by describing the big idea in terms of both mathematics and science, and will provide scenarios of classrooms and children involved in teaching and learning. This will be followed by an explanation of the elements of the big idea that can be explored in an integrated way. How to implement these elements will be the focus of the next part of each chapter, again accompanied by descriptions of classroom practices. We will also include some ideas for exploring your own learning, such as activities you can do and reflections on aspects of the big idea to develop your own thinking. Further reading will include references of content resources as well as broader instructional resources particularly important for the big idea being discussed.

Two modules will follow in each chapter, targeting a concept, topic, or idea that can focus your curriculum. Within each module will be examples describing implementation in preschool through first grade, the other in grades 2 and 3. Each module will begin with the specific mathematics and science standards being addressed, followed by a classroom scenario. Questions will be raised relating to both the scenario and the content of the module. Tools and resources specific to the module (e.g., materials, children's literature, and websites) as well as further explorations of the big idea for teachers and for children, will conclude each module.

4 Patterns

Learning Outcomes

After working with the ideas in this chapter, you should be able to:

- Analyze different kinds of patterns in math and science.
- Define *subitizing* and connect it to foundations of math and science.
- Understand how patterns impact teaching and learning in math and science.
- Create applications for using math and science in the curriculum.

*Common Core State
Standards for Math*

Kindergarten: Counting and Cardinality
Know number names and the count
sequence.
Count to tell the number of objects.
Compare numbers.

Kindergarten: Geometry
Identify and describe shapes.

**Third Grade: Operations
and Algebraic Thinking**
Identify arithmetic patterns and explain
them using properties of operations.

Next Generation Science Standards

K-LS1-1. Use observations to describe
patterns of what plants and animals
(including humans) need to survive.
1-LS1-2. Read texts and use media to
determine patterns in behavior of parents and offspring that help offspring
survive.
1-ESS1-1. Use observations of the sun,
moon, and stars to describe patterns
that can be predicted

PATTERNS

*Ken wanted to focus on patterns with his preschoolers, so he
put out wooden pattern blocks and pattern completion cards,
which were his usual choices of materials for this concept. But
today he also wanted to expand the children's way of thinking about patterns, so he started a list on large chart paper,
"Where Are Patterns?" A few of the children were immediately
interested in what he had written and began finding things
in the room that they thought were patterns. "I see patterns
on the curtains!" said Celia, "They are dots!" "Those aren't
patterns," replied Scott. "They are all the same. They are all
white." Celia frowned and pointed to the lines the dots made,
"But they almost make lines; they are all lined up!"*

What Is Important About Patterns?
Why Do We Talk About Patterns
with Young Children?

Quite often we see patterning being taught as at least
two units that repeat. In many preschool classrooms
teachers have children creating patterns using shape
blocks, and the expectation is that the children will
be able to tell what shape comes next in a series, focusing either on color and shape. But what about this:

Nikolya/Fotolia

Mandalas are an ancient symbol of the universe

How is the idea of pattern used in a mandala? How does it help us understand pattern? If you describe pattern mathematically, you might have to think about it in a different way. More complex patterns do not fit the color/shape pattern traditionally taught to children.

ELEMENTS OF THE BIG IDEA OF PATTERNS

Understanding of patterns includes three different types of patterns: repeating patterns, spatial structure patterns, and growing patterns. Each of these is discussed next.

Repeating Patterns

With **repeating patterns**, there is a unit that recurs over and over. There could be one unit or multiple units that repeat. The units may be easy to see or describe, or may be complex. A unit could be a concrete, visible object or it could be a motion, a behavior, or sound.

Here are examples of patterns that repeat one unit:

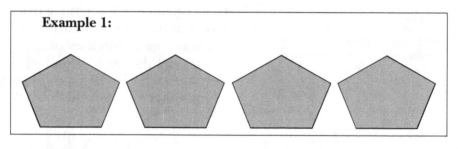

Here are examples of patterns that repeat two units:

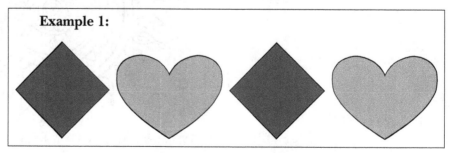

Example 2:

A B A B A B A B

This type of pattern is often seen as one of the only ways patterns are taught in preschool through primary grades. Children are sometimes given pattern blocks that fit an alternating pattern that is commonly referred to as an "AB" pattern, and asked to find the next color or shape in the line. This only requires children to memorize the next color or shape in the line. They don't have to think deeply about the relationship.

It is also important for teachers to refer to one-unit patterns so that children don't think learning about patterning is simply memorizing a rule about alternation. It can be pointed out that the one-unit pattern also repeats.

Spatial Structure Patterns

The **spatial structure pattern** refers to the mental organization of units, objects, and/or groups of objects, as in Figure 4-1.

Being able to organize graphic information into patterns is used in counting and understanding how graphic information is interrelated, such as medical scans and geographical, population, and political mapping. Looking at points on a map requires us to think about how the points might be related; we look for similar or different patterns to see what goes together or has some kind of relationship.

Spatial structure patterns require classification. Classification can be thought of as a patterning process. As children look at a pile of objects, they may be thinking about how to group like items together. They look for patterns of use or other variables.

Deciding what things should go together requires logical-mathematical thinking. Classification is one way science organizes the vast amount of information in our world. When something new is found, scientists look for common attributes or patterns to see what group this new thing might fit into. This is why it is important to think about patterning as a big idea, because the patterns we understand come from our own thinking, our mental organization of what we see and put into relationships. The teacher might set up an activity that requires children to sort and classify a set of materials by color, but what is the purpose? What if the child looks at a red truck, a blue ball, and a green car and thinks, "these are like my favorite toys at home"—is he wrong to classify them like this? The child may be thinking of a pattern of use.

Figure 4-1
Clustered Dots in Six Panels

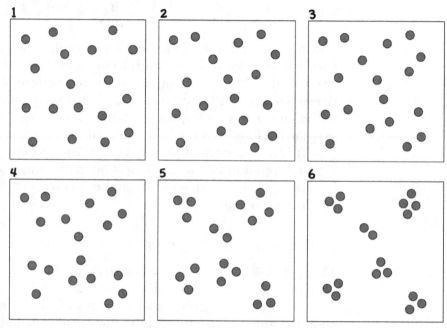

Source: Ken Davis

It is very important for the teacher to be a careful observer and engage the child in a conversation about his thinking. She might ask open-ended questions such as, "How do these things go together?", "I see you chose some different things, what was your rule for choosing these things?" or "Can you think of another way to sort them?" She may provide reasons for sorting such as, "Put all the things together we could use for carrying water to the playground," or "How should we sort and store our art materials?"

Growing Patterns

In a **growing pattern**, the pattern of the unit(s) increases or decreases in a way that is predictable, as in Figure 4-2.

These kinds of patterns are the most challenging for young children, but can be understood by even the youngest. In a study by Papic and Mulligan (2007), 5-year-olds were able to describe growth patterns after having several experiences with them in a task similar to that shown in Figure 4-3.

Children told the researcher that the triangles were getting bigger because there were more dots in each "line," referring to the lines

Figure 4-2
Dots That Form an L

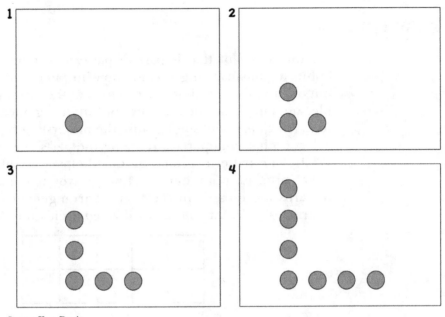

Source: Ken Davis

Figure 4-3
Dots That Form Triangles

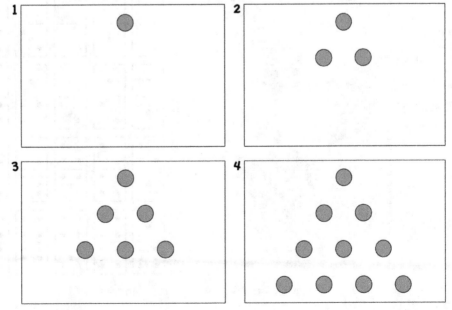

Source: Ken Davis

formed by the dots to create the triangles. They were also able to tell the researcher how many dots the next triangle would be made up of.

SUBITIZING

Another concept that is part of pattern recognition is subitizing. **Subitizing** means being able to know how many are in a group without one-to-one counting. We can look at the pips on dice, for example, and know that there are two or four at a glance. This is referred to as *conceptual subitizing* because the understanding is quick and involves both seeing parts and seeing the parts as a whole (Clements, 1999). The pattern formed on dice helps with subitizing, but having a pattern is not required. However, young children see number patterns more easily in rectangular arrangements such as dice or 10 frames. A 10 frame is a box divided evenly into 5s, such as this:

Children can easily see the combinations for 10 by using the frame.

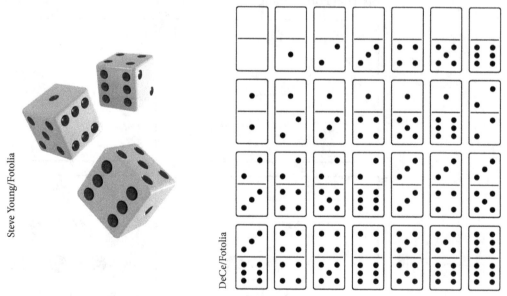

Dominoes and dice are very flexible ways to generate numbers and number patterns.

Pattern recognition in subitizing can happen visually, as in recognizing how many boxes are filled in the 10 frame, or it can be **auditory** recognition of the beats in a rhythm. It can be in understanding that seeing three dots and three dots is going to be six without counting 1, 2, 3, 4, 5, 6. It becomes clear that being able to subitize is foundational to a child's ability to use pattern recognition in his or her construction of number sense.

Seriation and Sequencing

Being able to use seriation and sequencing is the foundation of understanding patterns. When children consider one attribute of an object, they can place multiple objects in a sequence of large to small, little to big, dark to light, and so on. Toddlers will pile things up, and as they become more aware of relationships they will begin using seriation to sequence objects, routines, activities. **Seriation** is thinking about how each attribute relates to the next. **Sequencing** is a supporting concept in that we can think about a time attribute when seriating.

Sequencing can be found in nature

Bogdan Wankowicz/Shutterstock

Gage read "Goldilocks and the Three Bears" to his preschoolers to introduce a focus on seriation and sequencing. He placed three bowls that were similar in color and shape, but were three different sizes, in the drama center. He added three spoons that correlated in size to the bowls. As the children played he observed that they talked about how Goldilocks had eaten from the largest bowl first, the medium bowl second, and the smallest bowl last. Some of the children also pointed out that the largest spoon had to go with the largest bowl, the middle-sized spoon with the medium bowl, and the shortest spoon needed to go with the smallest bowl. Gage was able to use anecdotal notes to record which children were using seriation and sequencing to understand the story.

Patterning, seriating and sequencing are three interrelated concepts that can be planned for and observed, but realistically do not operate as separate ideas in life. Teachers need to understand how using science and math projects can both focus on these ideas and reinforce them.

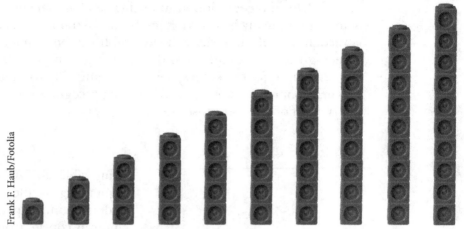

Frank F. Haub/Fotolia

Inter-locking cubes can be used for counting, patterning, seriating and graphing.

PATTERNS SURROUND US

Thinking about patterns goes beyond what we can physically see; it's also what we experience, think about, and use to make predictions. Our routine in the morning helps us get out of bed, get dressed, and get out the door. Because of a pattern of behavior we can predict what we will need over the next few days or change our pattern to fit new needs of the day. As classroom teachers, we use observations of patterns to predict what children will need in the curriculum to meet social, emotional, and physical needs.

Making children aware of all the different ways patterns work in our world helps prepare them for future mathematical thinking. Observing multiple representations of the same pattern helps children to identify the properties of the pattern. When the same pattern is represented in different sounds, movements, colored objects, and letter symbols, children can construct ideas about variables, one of the components for algebra (Casey, Kersh & Young, 2004). Patterns provide a way to understand the world and make sense of it, but in order to use it as a big idea, our thinking about patterns needs to deepen and expand.

Patterns Help Us Predict

We can start with looking at how the word *pattern* is used and talked about in the Common Core State Standards for Math and in the Next

Generation Science Standards (NGSS). In the Common Core math standards, the word *pattern* doesn't appear until third grade. Although we know that this is an expectation for understanding, it doesn't mean that we wait until third grade to suddenly begin introducing thinking about patterns. In the NGSS, the word *pattern* appears in the kindergarten level as a way for children to describe the seasonal changes they see around them. Our expectation is not that children will be able to define the word, but that they are thinking about patterns and how patterns help make sense of the world.

The NGSS use patterns as a major concept because:

> Observed patterns of forms and events guide organization and classification, and they prompt questions about relationships and the factors that influence them. (NGSS, Appendix G—Cross Cutting Concepts, p. 1)

It is a guiding concept because after children begin understanding patterns, they can use them to organize information and ask purposeful questions about why the patterns are there.

Even though the word *pattern* is not used in the Common Core standards for grades K–2, math becomes one way to organize **phenomena** and collect data that help us answer our questions about what we are observing, as in the following vignette:

Kathy had her first graders collect data about their moon observations. She had given each child a large calendar page and they were drawing the moon each evening, if it was observable before their bedtimes. This generated a lot of discussion at school. Kathy set aside time each day for the children to share their observations. Chena said, "I saw the moon when I got out of school yesterday; it was in the sky with the sun!" Several other children said they had seen it too. "It was half a circle," Chena described, "I bet it will be a bigger circle tonight." This prompted other children to predict what they thought they would see. At the end of the month

The moon is also visible during the day

the children brought their calendars back to school and compared the pictures. Kathy suggested that they make a chart showing the shape of the moon for each day. As the children watched her sketch their descriptions, Chena said, "Oh look! I was right, the moon is getting larger and larger, and then we didn't see it at all! What happened?" This led to more predictions about the shape of the moon. Kathy kept the chart up for 2 months, and over time the children's observations became more and more specific. They noticed that the moon followed a pattern, not only of changing shape, but also where it was in the sky.

Questions to Consider _____

1. Why was it important for the children to observe the moon over a period of 2 months?
2. What are some of the other ways the teacher could have collected this information?
3. What should Kathy say or do if the children ask *why* the moon is changing in shape or in its place in the sky? Does Kathy need to understand this? Why or why not?

In this scenario the teacher is using the big idea of patterns to help children make sense of the world. The teacher's objective is not to test children's ability to make accurate observations, but to support their growing understanding about how observations of the world can help them answer their own questions and think of new ones. When children are engaged in answering their own questions they search out new information, so the teacher has to be prepared to go in any direction. In this scenario the teacher can bring in commercially made charts of a year's moon cycle, provide fiction and nonfiction books about the moon, invite a professional astronomer to visit with the class, supply models of the moon, and provide open-ended materials that support children's modeling of what they observe. The moon observations may lead to questions about the sun, light, reflections, color, and seasons, but each topic would also include a focus on how patterns help us understand what is going on.

Patterns Help Us Make Connections

As Cody's third graders studied the life cycle of various organisms, they noticed that insects' body parts were multiples of threes. Brynn pointed this out one day when she was making a chart for her group's animal: ladybugs. "Look Ms. Brown, the ladybugs have two eyes and six legs, but they have three body parts. It's just like when we colored all the multiples of six on the hundreds chart and we noticed it made a pattern." This led to more observations about some of

Anterovium/Fotolia

Common insects like ants are easy to observe

the other group animals: frogs, butter-flies, chickens, and cicadas. Cody knew this was a great connection to the arith-metic patterns they would be studying, so she encouraged the children to use various group findings to create math word problems. Brynn started by writing this problem for her classmates to solve: "If 50 ladybugs flew in the window, how many insect legs would be in the room?"

In this scenario the teacher has the big idea of patterns in mind when teaching about multiplica-tion, but she also knows that she has to intentionally connect the ideas across the curriculum. It is her job to both plan for integration of the curriculum and create opportuni-ties for the integration to happen.

Patterns Help Us Organize Information

The school curriculum guide stated that first graders were supposed to study desert animals. Manny thought that this was a bit of a stretch considering the children lived in the northeastern United States, but he would find a way to help them connect desert life to the wildlife around them as much as possible. He de-cided they would focus on how animals survived in any habitat, and how you could figure out what they did to survive by studying how the parent wildlife took care of their young. He found websites that had recordings of bird calls; the patterns of the songs of the birds were quite obvious. Manny thought the children would enjoy listening to different birds of the desert and that they could then learn the patterns of the bird calls and compare them to those of the local birds.

Questions to Consider

1. How do you think the bird-call patterns could be described?
2. What other sound patterns would most children have had experi-ence with?
3. What else could Manny do to focus on patterns that would help the children connect desert wildlife to their local wildlife?
4. What are some of the ways that music and math are connected?

Review Questions

1. What are patterns in math?
2. What are patterns in science?
3. What is subitizing? Why is it considered basic to a child's math development?
4. How can identifying patterns in math and science help us integrate ideas?
5. Choose one pattern in math and science and create a lesson that would integrate math and science in a real way.

Summary

The big idea of patterns can be described as a way of thinking about relationships. Patterns can be visually observed, recognized auditorily, described behaviorally, and shown graphically. There are three different types of patterns: repeating, spatial structural, and growing. Children need many different experiences with finding patterns in a variety of contexts, using a variety of materials. Teachers need to have conversations with children to support children's construction of pattern relationships.

Modules for Chapter 4: Patterns

MODULE 4-1 FOCUS: PATTERNS IN NATURE

Common Core State Standards for Math

Third Grade: Number and Operations—Fractions
Develop understanding of fractions as numbers.

Next Generation Science Standards

1-PS4-2.
2-LS4 Biological Evolution: Unity and Diversity
3-LS1 From Molecules to Organisms: Structures and Processes

Integrating Math and Science: Leaves

Setting: Third Grade

Jill read Lois Ehlerts's "The Leaf Man" to her third graders. The children were fascinated by the patterns the leaves made to resemble figures, objects, and animals. Jill had a large assortment of leaves she had picked up that morning, and also had asked the children to bring leaves from home. They had looked up ways to preserve leaves, so their collection was quite extensive. They had decided on ways to sort the leaves according to the patterns on each leaf. There was a lot of discussion about what could be seen with their eyes and what required a magnifying glass. Jill told the children, "sketch a picture of something you like; it could be from your favorite sports, characters from books or games, someplace you like to play, anything!" The children were encouraged to make the pictures fill the page. "Now, choose different leaves to create your picture in leaves. When you get it the way you want it you can glue it to the paper." The next day when the pictures were finished, she and the children counted all the leaves they had used. She then had the children make a table that showed the fraction of leaves each picture used. They had to figure out how to describe the leaves, and how to show the fraction of each leaf used. For example, because there were 30 oak leaves, a picture that used 5 of them had used 1/6th of the oak leaves. The pictures were displayed so everyone could see them, and then Jill and the children used them to create Cognitively Guided Instruction (CGI) math problems.

Scenario Questions_____

1. Jill had to plan this project well in advance of carrying it out. What do you think her plans included?
2. The picture book Jill used in this scenario was at a much easier reading level for third graders. What would be some of the advantages of using a book like this for this particular activity?
3. List some of the questions you think Jill used when the children were sorting the leaves.
4. What issues do you think Jill had to plan for?

Content Questions_____

1. How are leaves classified? What attributes do scientists use in grouping leaves?
2. Why would the leaves have to be preserved? What does preservation do?
3. This scenario is one way to incorporate the concept of fractions. What kind of fractions would this represent? What would be a way to use fractions as a part of a whole in leaf exploration?
4. Children quite often ask about leaves turning colors in the fall. Teachers might try to answer their questions with scientific-sounding information, but not really understand the science themselves. What concepts are foundational to understanding what is happening to leaves in the fall?
5. If a teacher lives where seasonal changes do not include leaf color changes, what other local materials might be available to help children understand the cyclical patterns that living organisms go through in their area?

Integrating Math and Science: Day and Night

Setting: Kindergarten

Daylight savings time was going to begin soon and the kindergartners were particularly interested in what that meant. "I don't like to go to bed when it's light outside," said Mariko. "My Mom said that next Monday I'm going to have to go to bed while the sun is still up! My bedtime is supposed to be at night!" Other children in the room agreed: going to bed while the sun was shining was very unfair. This started a big conversation about the sunrise and sunset. Sana asked, "Does daylight savings make the day longer?" Ryan said, "My Dad said that when the sun is shining here, it's nighttime on the other side of the Earth. I don't get it;

how can the sun be shining here and not there?" Their teacher Melinda knew that this was a good opportunity to talk about some science concepts that would help the children think about daylight savings time in a different way. She asked them, "How could we measure the length of the day?"

Using shadows to measure time can be done with any object on the playground

Phspy/Fotolia

Scenario Questions

1. What could Melinda do to help the children see their questions as researchable?
2. Sometimes it is very difficult for young children to listen to others. How do teachers plan for these kinds of conversations?
3. In this scenario the teacher immediately responds to the children's comments, but quite often school-day schedules do not allow that kind of spontaneity. What could the teacher do in this scenario if she didn't have time at that moment to respond to the children's interest?

Content Questions

1. What do you know about the path the sun seems to follow across the sky? Is it always the same? What patterns are involved?
2. How does the sun's gravity affect the Earth?
3. What impact does the sun have on Earth cycles such as weather?

Children's Literature with a Focus on Patterns in Nature

All books listed here have been used with preschool through third-grade children, and may be commonly found in public libraries or school libraries. However, many books can go out of print or be pulled from library shelves. Many teachers find it useful to purchase books they know they will use in their classrooms focused lessons. Almost all books can be found on the Internet and purchased at a very low cost. Two websites that are particularly useful for finding out-of-print books are Powell's City of Books and Alibris.

Campbell, S. C., & Campbell, R. (2010). *Growing patterns.* Honesdale, PA: Boyd Mills Press.

> The Fibonacci numbers are introduced in this book through photographs. The Fibonacci sequence is a series of numbers that are formed by adding the preceding two numbers (1, 1, 2, 3, 5, 8 etc.). The focus on the numbers could be pointed out to older children, whereas younger children would enjoy the patterns revealed in nature.

Driscoll, M., & Hamilton, M. (2004). *A child's introduction to the night sky: The story of the stars, planets and constellations—and how you can find them in the sky.* New York: Black Dog & Leventhal Publishers.

> Astronomy and star-gazing are covered in this informational book. It is a good reference for the classroom.

Ehlert, L. (2005). *Leaf man.* Boston, MA: HMH Books for Young Readers.

> The reader sees an image of a man made up of leaves and acorns. We follow the man as he is blown across the countryside. We see other animals and objects in nature also made up of natural materials as we follow his journey.

Ganeri, A. (2005). *Animal life cycles* (nature's patterns). Chicago, IL: Heinemann.

> This book draws a strong connection between life cycles and patterns.

Sidman, J. (2011). *Swirl by swirl: Spirals in nature.* Boston, MA: Houghton Mifflin Books for Children.

> Very simple, but beautifully written book about all the swirled patterns that can be found in nature.

Swinburne, S. R. (2002). *Lots and lots of zebra stripes: Patterns in nature.* Honesdale, PA: Boyds Mills Press.

> Presents ideas about patterns in nature on several different levels. The wide range of connections helps children think about patterns around them.

Websites

AAAS Science Links for Teachers

This is a searchable website with many rich topics for study. Some of the lessons are British, so the language may be different, but the science is appropriate for young children.

Harvard Graduate School of Education, Center for Astrophysics (CfA)

This website has many links to teaching science through pattern finding, including weather patterns.

Utah Education Network, Science Education Resources

Numerous resources for science education K-12, including some focusing on patterns in nature.

National Geographic Kids

Interesting, child-friendly online resources, including colorful images of patterns.

Further Exploration of the Big Idea for Teachers

1. Observe something in nature over time. Keep track of what you see happening by recording your observations. Pay close attention to things that occur more than once. Can you make predictions based on patterns that may be occurring?

2. Use a live camera feed to observe animal behavior, such as the webcam on penguins on the SeaWorld website. As you watch the animals, keep track of their patterns of behavior by noting what happens in their environment and how they react to it. Try to identify different penguins by the coloring and patterns of their feathers. How does this information help you construct questions about penguins? How does it inform your understanding of penguin behavior?

Further Exploration of the Big Idea for Children

1. Children can also use the live animal cameras to make pattern observations. Sometimes teachers simply project the camera view and leave it up while children are doing other activities in the classroom. The teacher can help them think of ways to document what they are seeing and share patterns of behavior.

2. Create a collage of things collected outside. Encourage children to create categories based on the patterns they see in leaves, rocks, wood, and other natural objects that be brought into the classroom. A water table may provide a good place to create always-changing pictures using the objects.

MODULE 4-2 FOCUS: HOW PATTERNS ORGANIZE INFORMATION

Common Core State Standards for Math

Kindergarten: Counting and Cardinality
Know number names and the count sequence
Count to tell the number of objects
Compare numbers

First Grade: Geometry
Reason with shapes and their attributes

Second Grade: Number and Operations in Base Ten
Understand place values
Use place value understanding and properties of operations to add and subtract

Next Generation Science Standards

2-PS1-3. Make observations to construct an evidence-based account of how an object made of a small set of pieces can be disassembled and made into a new object.
1-PS4 Waves and Their Applications in Technologies for Information Transfer

Head Start Child Development and Early Learning Framework
Math

Number Concepts and Quantities:
Uses one-to-one counting and subitizing (identifying the number of objects without counting) to determine quantity.

Number Relationships and Operations:
Uses a range of strategies, such as counting, subitizing, or matching, to compare quantity in two sets of objects and describes the comparison with terms, such as more, less, greater than, fewer, or equal to.

Patterns:
Recognizes, duplicates, and extends simple patterns.
Sorts, classifies, and serializes (puts in a pattern) objects using attributes, such as color, shape, or size.

Science

Scientific Skills and Method:
Observes and discusses common properties, differences, and comparisons among objects.

Integrating Math and Science: Boomwhackers™

Setting: Preschool

When the preschoolers arrived at school one morning, they found a colorful assortment of plastic pipes in the music center. Sean immediately picked one up and waved it around in the air. His teacher, Liz, noticed Sean's interest and went over to help him. "Look," said Liz, as she picked up another one of the pipes. She tapped it lightly on the edge of a table and then on her hand. "What do you hear?" she asked Sean. Sean's eyes lit up and he replied, "It's music!" Several other children came to play with the Boomwhackers™ too. Soon the children realized that the length of the pipe meant that a certain sound came out. Sean decided to place the Boomwhackers^{TM} from the highest sound (shortest pipes) to the lowest sound (longest pipes).

Scenario Questions

1. What do teachers need to do in order to have sound and/or music in their classrooms? Why is it important?
2. The teacher in this scenario placed new materials in a familiar center. What are the pros and cons of introducing new materials like this?
3. The children in this scenario were encouraged to play freely with the Boomwhackers [R]. How would this same concept be supported with older children?
4. The teacher wanted to support the children's exploration of seriation. What other materials could be used that lend themselves to seriation?

Content Questions

1. What does the shape and size of a musical instrument have to do with how high or low the sound is?
2. Air has to be present in order to hear sound. How would you explain this?
3. Wave technology shows up in many different ways. How are water waves and air waves alike?

Integrating Math and Science: Collections

Setting: First Grade

Today was 100 day in Amy's first-grade class. The children had been given instructions to bring a collection of 100 things to school. Each child

Erika

Hundreds charts can be used in free play.

had been given a small paper sack with the instructions that their 100 things had to fit in the sack. The children were placed in small groups of three. Schyler brought 100 rubber bands of all different colors and sizes, Temperance brought 100 hair clips, and Madison brought 100 pennies. Amy then had the children figure out different ways to sort and organize their collections. She provided small paper cups and other organizing materials if the children wanted to use them. Schyler's group decided to put a penny in the middle of the circles the rubber bands made with a hair clip sitting on top.

Amy then asked the children to show on large graph paper how many things they had all together in their collections. Schyler's group started drawing the circles the rubber bands made but decided that it would take too long to draw all the objects. They ended up making a chart counting by 10s down the edge of the paper for the rubber bands, another list for the hair clips, and another for the pennies. As they added numbers Madison pointed out to her group that there were 30 things across the top of their chart, 30 things in the next row, and so on. "I know that 30 plus 30 is 60. Let's write 60 after the first two rows, and 60 at the next two, and 60 here and here." Schyler said, "We have 3 lists (columns); that means we have 100 here and here and here. That's 300!" Amy had been listening to the children's conversations about the patterns they were finding and made plans to have the children share their charts over the next few days.

Scenario Questions

1. What are some considerations teachers use when creating work groups of children?
2. What kinds of notes do you think Amy was taking while the children worked?
3. How would Amy prepare for the possibility that some children would not bring collections of 100?
4. What are some other ways children could have sorted their collections?

Content Questions_____

1. How do you explain place value?
2. A common way to see place value taught is as follows: "What number is in the 10's place in the number 213?" or, "Label the places in the number 35." Both of these examples are social knowledge. What are some of the problems with teaching place value like this?
3. The words for our number system have no regular pattern until you get to the second decade (20, 21, 22. . . .). In Chinese a regular pattern begins with 11. How does language impact mathematical thinking?
4. How does recognizing patterns help us read large numbers?

Children's Literature Focusing on How Patterns Help Us Organize

Brett, J. (2009). *The mitten.* New York: Putnam Juvenile.
   Jan Brett illustrates a classic story about a little boy who has dropped his mitten in the snowy woods. As animals crawl into the mitten, it stretches and stretches until the smallest creature crawls in.
Buehner, C., & Buehner, M. (2009). *Goldilocks and the three bears.* New York: Puffin Books.
   There are many versions of the story of Goldilocks and the three bears. This version has a skip-rope-jumping, red-cowboy-boot-wearing Goldilocks. The story lends itself to classification and seriation.
Jocelyn, M. (2004). *Hannah's collections.* Toronto: Tundra Books.
   Hannah has *lots* of collections. She can share them for show and tell, but has to solve the problem of how.
Otoshi, K. (2010). *Zero.* San Rafael, CA: KO Kids Books.
   Zero is depressed. She compares herself to other numbers and wants to be "more." This book explores the concept of zero.
Pallotta, J. (2003). *One hundred ways to get to 100.* New York: Scholastic.
   Lots of things to count. Counting by 10s is emphasized.
Wood, A., & Wood, D. (2009). *The napping house.* New York: Harcourt Children's Books.
   Characters stack themselves up on Grandma as she naps, with predictable consequences.

Websites

Bozeman Biology
There are 60 videos explaining the details of the development of the Next Generation Science Standards.
Utah Education Network
Lesson plans focusing on patterns in place value are available here.

Discovery Education
Lesson plans for further science exploration are available here.
Teaching Channel
This lesson shows first graders using patterns of 7 to count by 10s.
Exploring the Science of Light
This website has technical information about how we see colors, shadows,
    optical illusions, and so forth. It is written for much older children or adults.
Math Wire
Math Wire is organized into many topics, with printable games and links to
    online activities.
Illuminations: Resources for Teaching Math
Okta's Rescue. This game reinforces counting and subitizing.

Further Exploration of the Big Idea for Teachers

1. Use several multiplication charts to color in different number facts. How does the pattern that is revealed help you predict the next number?
2. Brainstorm in a small group things you have to organize at home. What rules do people use for organizing? How do they use patterns to help with organization?

Further Exploration of the Big Idea for Children

1. Play beats on an instrument and have the children move to the beats. Add a beat as children learn the patterns.
2. Have the children hold a crayon or marker in each hand. Play various pieces of music and encourage children to "dance" with their arms, marking on large sheets of paper. After the last piece of music, have the children look at each other's papers to see if they can find patterns that match the beats of the music they listened to.
3. Make people patterns. Have the children line up in various patterns of facing forward, boy/girl, arms up/down, and so forth.

Transformation

Learning Outcomes

After working with the ideas in this chapter, you should be able to:

- Define and apply ideas about transformation in math and science.
- Analyze different explorations of transformation.
- Create applications for the integration of transformation in math and science.

Standards Addressed in This Chapter

Common Core State Standards for Math

Kindergarten: Measurement and Data
Describe and compare measurable attributes

First Grade: Measurement and Data
Measure lengths indirectly and by iterating length units

Next Generation Science Standards

K-PS2-1 Plan and conduct an investigation to compare the effects of different strengths or different directions of pushes and pulls on the motion of an object.

K-LS1 Use observations to describe patterns of what plants and animals (including humans) need to survive.

K-2-ETS1-1. Ask questions, make observations, and gather information about a situation people want to change to define a simple problem that can be solved through the development of a new or improved object or tool.

WHAT IS TRANSFORMATION?

Transformation is a powerful big idea that underlies much of what engages children in math, science, and other disciplines. We see children learning about transformation when they transform "the world physically as well as symbolically" (Chaille, 2008, p. 165). Transformation is a conceptual anchor that naturally connects children's experiences across the two disciplines. Children act on their world through manipulating, moving, and exploring objects. Many of these transformations are observable, such as the transformations involving physical movement of objects. Children construct knowledge through playing with objects that can swing, balance, stack, and bounce. These concepts may be thought of as belonging to the science fields, but they are basic for the child's construction of knowledge about math too.

Four-year-old Carson is playing with narrow strips of tag board that have holes punched in each end. The strips are fastened together in different ways using brads to connect them. Four strips are fastened together to create squares, and three strips are fastened together to create triangles (Figure 5-1). The resulting shapes can change as the child

Figure 5-1
Tag-Board Triangle

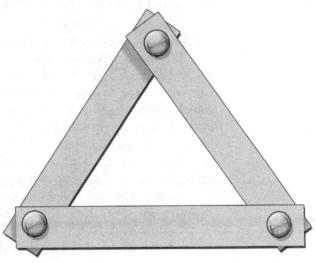

Source: Ken Davis

moves the paper. Carson is exploring the different types of rectangles and triangles he can create with the constructions.

 Later, Carson is looking at two triangles drawn on a piece of paper. He is thinking about differences between the two shapes; one is larger than the other, one is tall and skinny, and the other is fatter. The skinny one is the first one on the page. But Carson is also thinking about how they are the same: They both have three sides, the sides all have points where they come together, and they are both drawn with black lines. He goes over to the shelf and takes out the tag-board triangle, brings it over to the table, and compares it with the different triangles that are drawn on the paper.

Carson's ability to think about the differences and similarities between these two shapes is not unusual. Having opportunities to interact with materials that highlight those differences and similarities helps him make connections and think about the **properties**, or descriptive aspects, of the shapes. His ability to talk about his observations can be supported through conversations with his peers and the caring adults around him. They can help him notice qualities and attributes he may not have been aware of, and make connections that do not occur spontaneously.

Relationship Building as a Part of Transformation

Carson's thought process is an example of logical-mathematical thinking, or relationship-building knowledge. Carson is constructing ideas and making connections that are new to him; he is noticing relationships that are unique to his perspective. If a well-intentioned adult tries to tell him rules for a triangle, Carson may listen respectfully but immediately forget what the adult has told him because it's an idea the adult has constructed and holds little meaning for Carson.

 When we talk about transformations in math and science we are really talking about the mental relationships as something changes from one thing to another. Carson has to construct the ideas involving transformation using his own thinking. We want children to think about how things are different or the same. Thinking about the difference between one object and another object is a mental process that requires thinking about **composition**, what elements things are made up of, and **decomposition**, what pieces would result when taking something apart. This is an idea that seems very straightforward, but is quite complex when thinking about transformations in math and science.

 For example, it is very common for teachers to plan units of study around the life cycle of a butterfly. Many activities can be planned that involve the child in observing the caterpillar making a chrysalis, and then hatching from the chrysalis. But what is happening inside the chrysalis? You can search YouTube for "what happens inside the chrysalis," but even time-lapse photography by itself will not create a deep understanding for young children about the chemical and physical changes happening inside the chrysalis. The child cannot observe the changing structure of the cells that begin the formation of the butterfly. The transformation of the caterpillar into a butterfly remains a mysterious action. However, the time-lapse videos will help children start to understand that transformation involves changes that go beyond a simple cause and effect.

Equivalence as Part of Transformation

To understand transformation, we have to understand equivalence. When we compare two objects, we are thinking about how they are different from each other and how they are the same. We are selecting an attribute or specific descriptive element to focus on. If we notice that the attribute for each object is the same, we are thinking about equivalence.

Mrs. Weber put several addition problems on the board and asked her class of third graders to work the problems and then sort them into groups that were the same kind of addition problem. She used at least three different ways of adding: one known group added to another known group asking for a total; one unknown group added to a known group with a given total; and one known group added to an unknown group with a given total. At first many of the third graders said all the problems were alike because they all required addition, but Mrs. Weber asked them to think about it some more. She said, "Is this problem exactly the same as this one? Is it giving you exactly the same information?" Tina said, "No, some of them tell you how much you start with and some don't." Alfredo commented, "Yeah, they really aren't the same." Mrs. Weber realized that the children needed more experiences thinking about what the word "similar" might mean and what the word "same" means.

Teachers must be able to support children's ability to articulate the transformations they notice. The guiding question becomes, "How are they the same and how are they different?" If Carson's teacher asks him to talk about what he notices is the same and what he notices is different, she is supporting his ability to construct ideas about transformation. Through careful questioning the teacher can understand what attribute the child has focused on and can guide the conversation. Perhaps the child has lined up objects and notices that they go in a stair-step fashion, but they are not aligned on the bottom. The teacher can then ask the child if the objects all share the same starting point.

EXPLORATION OF TRANSFORMATION

In this chapter, we explore transformation in four ways: through observation, estimation, experimentation, and growth.

Observation

Observation refers to the act of noticing details and recording those details in some way. It goes beyond simply looking at something; it means we have a focus, that there is something we are particularly interested in seeing, hearing, and experiencing. Doing mathematical and scientific observations means focusing on seeing and understanding things very clearly and precisely.

When we think about what we want children to learn in math and science, we have to begin by thinking about what ideas the child has constructed. Think about how you would help the child in the following scenario make observations that support thinking about transformation:

Four-year-old Nicki rolled a small piece of clay around until it softened, and then formed a cup-like shape. She placed the cup-like shape in a large clear-sided container of water. She looked at the clay from above the water line, even with the water line, and then got down on the floor and looked up at the shape as it floated on the top of the water. She exclaimed, "It's like a boat! Now I'm going to make it flat." She took the clay out of the water and flattened it and then placed it back in the water and watched with surprise as it sank. Mr. Frank said to Nicki, "What did you see happen?" Nicki replied, "The clay went down!" Mr. Frank suggested she try the boat shape again, this time paying close attention to the water line, and then try it again with the flat shape. Mr. Frank took pictures of Nicki's explorations.

Questions to Consider

1. What does Nicki know about sinking and floating? What does she know about water displacement?
2. How do you know what she knows?
3. What else could Mr. Frank do to encourage Nicki's observations?
4. Why did he suggest that she try both shapes again?
5. What could he do with the photographs to encourage her close observations?

Tools for Observation

Tools for observation refer to the checklists, notes, and forms we may choose to use during an observation to collect information or data. When we decide why we are observing and what we observing we can then make informed decisions about our observation tools.

When planning to address the big idea of transformation, it is important to plan ahead for opportunities to observe by having tools available, such as the following:

- Digital cameras
- Clipboards with plain paper and pencils
- Scales
- Different kinds of measuring sticks
- Magnifying glasses of various kinds, including jewelers' loupes (see Private Eye resource)
- Trays
- Plastic boxes with lids
- Tweezers, spoons, plastic knives, and other tools for separating substances

Having these tools available every day and easily accessible by children is also a key to being able to take advantage of learning opportunities. Early childhood teachers in public school settings are under great pressure to fit many curriculum topics into one day. If they have to stop and find these tools each time, the moment will pass and learning is lost.

Estimation

In math and science, estimation is an idea about an outcome or quantity based on experience and information. It is not a simple "guess." As children have experiences over time, they become better at estimating quantities, making predictions, and asking informed questions. Children need a known quantity in order to make an estimate. Simply putting out a large jar of jelly beans and having children guess how many are in the jar does not fit the defining properties of learning how to estimate. If the jelly beans have been handled, counted, grouped, and measured by the children before being placed in the jar, they can then begin to use their experiences and knowledge to decide, for example, if there are enough jelly beans for everyone to share equally.

When children are using estimation to understand transformation, they need multiple experiences and conversations about what is happening. Learning to estimate a realistic range of possibilities is the goal. When a first-grade teacher asks the children to estimate where a plant will be in its growth pattern in 2 weeks, she has to have first provided other growth experiences. Six-year-olds' sense of time is based on their cognitive development. If they haven't had any experiences with growing plants their estimations will range from no plant growth to "up to the ceiling"!

Mr. Cottrell is making a bubble-blowing solution in a 2-liter soda bottle that will then be shared with his third graders. The recipe calls for water, dish detergent, and glycerin. The children watch carefully as he begins following the recipe, but when the fluid is about 2 inches from the top of the bottle he stops. "How much liquid do you think I can put in the bottle without making it flow over the top?" The children all offer ideas, using the measuring cups to describe their estimations. A few of the children tell him that the dish detergent will sink to the bottom of the bottle and will not cause the liquid to overflow.

Questions to Consider

1. What other ideas are the children revealing in their estimations? What kinds of questions could Mr. Cottrell ask to extend these ideas and learn more about them?
2. What other activities could the children do to increase their ability to estimate volume?
3. How could Mr. Cottrell help the children connect doing this kind of estimation to other things such as number and quantity?

There are many other experiences in science that involve making predictions that rely on being able to estimate amounts. Children testing the absorbency of different brands of paper towels can naturally estimate the amount of water a new towel may hold, providing you give them opportunities to test different brands. Exploring color mixing can involve estimating the number of drops of food coloring needed to change the yellow to orange or make blue a deep purple. Giving children multiple experiences for experimentation, as well as the tools needed to document their estimations, will encourage them to think like scientists and see the value of capturing the numbers that help us understand the outcome.

Estimation can be part of the daily life of children. The teacher does not need to plan a unit on "estimation"; rather, the teacher can plan for ways to provide real problems to solve that involve estimation.

As children use estimation to make sense of their world, they are constructing important ideas about relationships in both math and science.

Estimation is a foundational idea about how numbers relate to each other on a number line. When children look at the following number line they have to think about the magnitude of each number in order to estimate where sequential numbers should be placed. This is also a basic part of rounding numbers.

0——1——2——3——4——5————————————10

If we talk to children about numbers being "closer" to a decade number to round up, then they need to understand the concept of estimating relationships.

As you can see, estimation experiences can lead naturally to other principles of science and math, including opportunities for experimentation.

Experimentation

Understanding transformation means being able to act on objects, trying new ways of manipulating positions, relationships, and perspectives. Experimentation in this sense is simply being able to move things, add things, and take things away, and then being able to observe changing relationships. The child who asks, "How can I make it move?" and then proceeds to carry out his own ideas is using experimentation, which is vital to science being an inquiry, and not simply following the directions in a prescribed "experiment." Many of us have had science and math activities, or can see them in curriculum books, that are much like a recipe from a cookbook. The outcome is known and the student's job is to follow the directions carefully to get to that correct answer. But real science is not a step-by-step production. The nature of science is one of inquiry and questions, and involves exploration and experimentation.

Placing one plant in light over a few days and another in the dark may be a familiar experimentation activity to many adults; however, the question of what might happen to the plant usually comes from the teacher and may not make a lot of sense to young children. Children must be able to construct their own questions—they need to own and care about the experiment—and then be able to follow through with manipulating variables and seeing what happens. The teacher can support the children through preparing an environment that takes advantage of the children's ideas and that gives them the opportunity to see the results of their inquiry.

In addition to creating a supportive environment, the teacher can ask questions that can spark their interest in finding out more about what is being observed. Consider the following example:

Kari has placed brightly colored wooden inch cubes and plastic Unifix cubes in a container on the table, along with a pan balance. As children enter the preschool classroom they gather around Kari as she wonders how many Unifix cubes it will take to balance one wooden cube, which she places in one of the pans. Sean immediately picks up several Unifix cubes and carefully places them on the other pan of the balance. It goes down so he takes them all off. "Can you estimate how many Unifix cubes you will need before you put them on the pan?" Kari asks Sean. This is a challenge for Sean, who then proceeds to experiment more carefully, putting one Unifix cube on the pan at a time. Kari has also placed recording sheets on the table to encourage data collection. Sean decides to try other objects in the room and uses the recording sheet to draw each object as he tries it.

Questions to Consider

1. How can Kari support Sean's thinking about his experiment?
2. What can teachers do to help the whole class think about one child's activity?
3. Kari might sit down and brainstorm other activities that involve comparisons. What other materials might she use?

Activities for Further Explorations of the Big Idea for Teachers

It might seem to some people that Sean is simply "playing." Play in early childhood education has been well researched, and we understand that play at any age can be a way of learning about the world and how it works. Early childhood teachers must learn to advocate for play in the curriculum.

1. Discuss the scenario about Kari with a small group. Write an explanation and rationale for this activity from four different perspectives: children, parents, the principal, and other teachers.
2. Share what your group wrote with other groups in the class. What points are similar for all four perspectives? What points would be specific for parents, the principal, or other teachers?
3. If you were the classroom teacher, what would your response be to someone who voiced a concern about the children merely "playing"?

Growth

Some of the most common experiences children have are related to things changing through growth, and focusing on growth can support children's understanding of the big idea of transformation. Plants can grow and change, and people can grow and change. One of the most interesting ways to examine growth is by looking at patterns of growth. Quite often in early childhood classrooms, teachers focus on patterns as repeating colors, shapes, letters, or numbers; however, scientists and mathematicians know that a pattern of growth can mean other things too. Depositing money in an interest-bearing account is different than putting your money in a box under the bed!

Knowledge of patterns of growth will help children understand, predict, and infer with more accuracy. But they need to have had a variety of experiences with different kinds of growth and a lot of conversation about what they are noticing. <u>Documenting</u> growth over time is one way to focus children's attention on possible patterns. ~~Without documentation—~~ visual or otherwise—young children may miss the small incremental changes that adults take for granted. A craft stick stuck next to a plant in its pot can be marked each day to show how much growth has occurred. Although there may not be much growth on a day-to-day basis, over a period of a week the children will begin to notice change.

Sara M Davis

Documenting plant growth

For example, an activity that can be seen in some early childhood classrooms involves children being shown pictures of things that grow and then being asked to put the pictures in the order that would show what happened first, second, and so on. An activity like this does little to teach children about growth. However, if photographs are taken of actual plants each day and children are given the opportunity to manipulate the pictures and compare the pictures to the actual plants, the teacher will be able to assess the children's understanding of the sequential aspects of growth by listening to their questions and comments.

Understanding growth as part of the big idea of transformation requires many different and varied experiences. The conceptual idea of growth goes beyond a plant growing. And, in terms of mathematical understanding, it is important to see that the foundational thought process for algebra begins in early childhood with thinking about patterns of growth in number. Consider the following vignette:

Mrs. Stockall's second graders are planning on selling donated heart-shaped lollipops to other children in school to raise money for a field trip to the local science museum. They know that it will cost each child $2.00 to get into the museum, and there are 25 children in the class.

She helps them figure out that they will need a total of $50.00 for the class to enter the museum. This is a large amount of money and the children are a little overwhelmed. They are concerned that they may not have enough lollipops to get everyone in. Mrs. Stockall suggests that they create a chart to understand how many lollipops they will have to sell to get everyone into the museum. They can sell the lollipops for 20 cents each. She draws a table on chart paper and labels the top row "number of lollipops" and the bottom row "cost of lollipops." She works with the children as they add the information for the chart. Mrs. Stockall uses this opportunity to encourage pattern finding by the children.

Number of Lollipops	1	2	3	4	5	6
Cost of Lollipops	20 cents	40 cents	60 cents	80 cents	100 cents (1 dollar)	120 cents

Mrs. Stockall puts this information into the chart and then asks the children to work with a partner to figure out how many lollipops they will have to sell. After they have worked in groups, Mrs. Stockall brings them back together as a class to discuss their findings. After much discussion with differences of opinion, the children decide that they will have to sell at least 10 lollipops per child. This seems like a reasonable number and the children are visibly relieved that they will be able to accomplish this important task.

Questions to Consider

1. Why didn't Mrs. Stockall just tell the children at the beginning how many lollipops they would need to sell?
2. What does Mrs. Stockall believe about the capabilities of the children?
3. How does a problem like this compare with worksheets or problems from a textbook?

The Common Core State Standards have included algebraic thinking by emphasizing the concepts needed for understanding big ideas

Figure 5-2
Possible Trajectory for Developing Understanding of Estimation

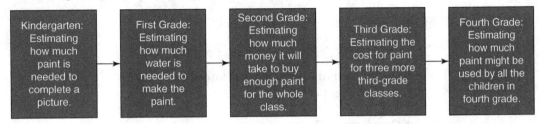

Source: Ken Davis

about transformation: "Identify arithmetic patterns (including patterns in the addition table or multiplication table), and explain them using properties of operations. For example, observe that 4 times a number is always even, and explain why 4 times a number can be decomposed into two equal addends" (Common Core State Standards, Grade 3; National Governors Association Center for Best Practices and the Council of Chief State School Officers, 2010, p. 23). Kindergartners who have transformed amounts and constructed ideas about growth will be third graders who can understand this algebraic principle. Figure 5-2 shows a possible trajectory for the development of children's understanding of estimation.

Review Questions

1. What does transformation mean? Give an example of transformation in math and an example of transformation in science.
2. Choose one example of transformation in math or one in science. Show how the transformation can be used to help children think about the progression of change.
3. Create a lesson that uses transformation in math and science.

Summary

Children think about transformation through close observation, estimation, experimentation, and the study of growth. In the following two modules, we will highlight one of the four ways transformation can be explored. As you read each module, think about how each activity could be done differently to focus on any of the four ways transformation could be explored.

Modules for Chapter 5: Transformation

MODULE 5-1 FOCUS: CLOSE OBSERVATION

Common Core State Standards for Math

Kindergarten: Measurement and Data
Describe and compare measurable attributes.

Next Generation Science Standards

K-LS1-1 Use observations to describe patterns of what plants and animals (including humans) need to survive.

Integrating of Math and Science: Rotting Pumpkin

Setting: Kindergarten

Mrs. Albert's kindergarteners had enjoyed their pumpkin unit; they had learned about seeds, food growth, weighing, and measuring. In her hurry to leave for Fall Break, Mrs. Albert forgot to remove the pumpkin from the science center. As she came into the kindergarten room after Fall Break, she immediately noticed a sharp odor and saw to her dismay that the pumpkin had become a soft, sodden mass. But instead of scooping it up and throwing it away she left it on the table. As the children entered the room they exclaimed over the changes in their pumpkin. Jasmine was the first to notice, "Hey, our Jack-o-lantern on our front porch looks just like this! "What happened to our pumpkin, Mrs. Albert?" said Stevie. "I think it got rotted," added Tymber. Mrs. Albert had the children notice all the changes the pumpkin was

now displaying. They noticed the liquid underneath the shell, the way the shell could be pushed and prodded, and the sharp odor. Markus looked at the chart next to the pumpkin that listed the weight of the pumpkin from earlier in the unit, "I bet our pumpkin is heavier now," Markus declared, "look how it's leaning over in the middle. Mrs. Albert asked the children if they could think of a way to find out if the pumpkin had become heavier as it rotted.

A rotting pumpkin can be very interesting.

Scenario Questions

1. Some children might be upset about the pumpkin's condition. Why? What would you do as the classroom teacher to help them?
2. How might Mrs. Albert set this up the next year to ensure that the children would have more data?
3. If you were the teacher, what would you do in this scenario if you wanted the children to focus on estimation or experimentation?
4. How would the rotting pumpkin be addressed in a third-grade classroom? What kinds of data collection could be introduced to third graders? What math standards could be addressed?

Content Questions

1. How would you help children understand decomposition? Why is it an important concept to understand?
2. What else decomposes? What are the possible causes of decomposition?
3. Why do we call regrouping a number "decomposition"?
4. What other materials could children weigh that could be weighed in two common forms? What ideas might children construct from several activities involving before and after weight?

Common Core State Standards for Math

3. MD
   Represent and interpret data.

Next Generation Science Standards

2-ESS1-1. Use information from several sources to provide evidence that Earth events can occur quickly or slowly.
3-LS4-1. Analyze and interpret data from fossils to provide evidence of the organisms and the environments in which they lived long ago.

Integrating Math and Science: Rocks

Setting: Third Grade

Mr. South knew that his third graders had to study the Earth's formation because his school system had given him a list of topics to be covered in third grade. The textbook had a chapter about different kinds of rocks and an activity that used information from the book. However, Mr. South also wanted to improve his students' overall ability to observe and understand transformation, so their homework over the weekend included bringing a

Sometimes the best manipulatives are right under our feet!

collection of small rocks to school. As the children arrived, he had them place their rocks on their desks with blank sheets of paper and magnifying glasses he had already provided. For the first 5 to 10 minutes of class the children looked carefully at the rocks, noting appearance, details, weight, hardness, and size by writing and drawing. Mr. South then picked the papers up and had the children put their rocks into a basket. The next day the children were given someone else's observation sheet and worked in groups to find the rocks that were described on the sheets. "I think this rock is this one on the sheet; see, it has the same dark spots," offered Tim. "Yeah, but it says that the rock was really flaky and I can't get anything to flake off of this one," added Anna. Juan reached over and plucked a small rock from the pile, "I bet it's this one; see, it has the dark spots and it's got little flaky pieces coming off." Mr. South divided the children into small groups to create charts of data. Each chart compared one property of the rocks; so there was a chart comparing weight, one comparing hardness, and one comparing size. Over the next few days each group then shared its findings with the rest of the class.

Scenario Questions

1. Why did Mr. South decide that the textbook did not have all of the information he wanted the children to learn?
2. How would you collect the data the children generated? What questions do you think the children might have if they revisit the information about their rocks?
3. What could Mr. South do to modify this activity for a child who has vision problems?
4. There is a lot of conversation and discussion going on in the classroom. How could Mr. South make sure all of the conversation is about rocks? How could he document the children's comments?
5. How could Mr. South keep this study going in his classroom without planning whole-group instruction?

Content Questions

1. How do scientists judge the hardness of rocks? What kinds of tests are done on rocks to judge their hardness? How could this information be adapted for young children?

Alexlukin/Shutterstock

2. Children are told that fossils are the calcified remnants of ancient plants and animals. What do they need to understand about the rock cycle in order to understand fossils?
3. Where do rocks come from? What is the connection between soil and rocks?
4. What are some of the functions of soil?
5. Mass and weight are two different things. Describe the differences.

Children's Literature with a Focus on Observation

These titles emphasize descriptive language, observing details, and classification. They are also supportive of real experiences children can have in their own communities.

dePaola, T. (1985). *The cloud book.* New York: Holiday House.
   Includes common cloud types and weather associated with them.
Hart, L. (1997). *How many stars in the sky.* New York: HarperCollins.
   A little boy and his father spend the evening observing a sky full of stars.
Jocelyn, M. (2004). *Hannah's collections.* Toronto: Tundra Books.
   A little girl wants to take her many collections to school, but there are too many. She decides to solve her problem by classifying some items from each group.
Rosinsky, N. M. (2006). *Rocks: Hard, soft, smooth, and rough.* Mankato, MN: Picture Window Books.
   Highly descriptive text about rocks and their properties.
Yolen, J. (1999). *Bird watch.* New York: Puffin Books.
   Poetic descriptions of birds and their environments. Scientific information is included about the birds.

Websites

Science IDEAS
Science IDEAS supports teaching science through an integrated model that includes reading comprehension and writing.
First Hand Learning
This website supports children's learning through direct experience with the world.
The Private Eye
This website supports using close observation to integrate the arts with science.
National Geographic
This website is a great resource for all of the science content you may not be sure about. There is a link on the home page just for teachers where you can find resources and lesson ideas. The link on the website for children provides games, videos, information, and activities to engage children's imaginations and increase their science skills and content knowledge.

Andy Goldsworthy
British artist Andy Goldsworthy manipulates nature to create beautiful art
that transforms over time.
Science With Me
A commercial website that includes free resources for children and
teachers.
National Geographic
National Geographic's website for children provides games, videos, informa-
tion, and activities to engage children's imaginations and increase their
science skills and content knowledge.
Science with Me
Games, activities, and information are designed to be used by children.

Further Explorations of the Big Idea for Teachers

1. Choose a plant outside that you can observe every day for a set
   amount of time. Sketch the plant and label the parts of the plant,
   research information about the plant, take pictures as often as
   possible, and write notes about the weather at the time of your
   observation. At the end of your observation period, decide how
   you can organize and represent your information so others can
   see what you've observed.
2. Create a polygon out of tag board or other heavy paper that is at
   least 4 inches across. Place the shape on a large piece of paper
   using one point of the polygon as the center of your design. Trace
   the polygon and then turn it a few inches and trace the shape
   again. As the design reveals itself, notice how the shape seems to
   change and transform into other patterns. How can you color the
   shapes in your design to show new patterns?
3. Research how observation is taught in the criminal sciences or
   medicine. What elements of observation are the same or different
   for various careers?

Further Explorations of the Big Idea for Children

1. Have the children use observational drawing to illustrate vocabulary labels in the classroom. For example, a drawing of the clock,
   labeled, "clock" could be part of the chart for the class schedule.
2. Memory games like Lotto, Concentration, and What Is Missing
   lend themselves to using close observation.

MODULE 5-2 FOCUS: ESTIMATION

Common Core State Standards for Math

First Grade: Measurement and Data
Measure lengths indirectly and by iterating length units.

Third Grade: Measurement and Data
Solve problems involving measurement and estimation of
intervals of time, liquid volumes, and masses of objects.

Next Generation Science Standards

K-PS3-1. Make observations to determine the effect of sunlight
on Earth's surface.

Head Start Child Development and Early Learning Framework
Science

Observes and discusses common properties, differences, and
comparisons among objects.

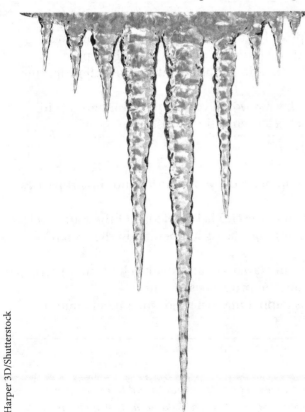

Harper 3D/Shutterstock

Icicles can be studied using extra caution.

Integrating Math and Science: Ice
Setting: Preschool

*A cold snap had hit the area and
Miss Reed's preschool class of 3- and
4-year-olds had become very interested
in the icicles hanging from bushes
and trees. Of course the children
were hoping for snow and snowman
building. Miss Reed decided that,
based on the children's interest, this
was a good time to consider some
physical properties of water, so she
started by asking the children to
share what they had seen.*

*Tommy: I saw some ice hangin'
down on my house!*

Sasha: I seen some too!

*Miss Reed nodded and wrote on her
chart, "Tommy saw some icicles" and
"Sasha saw some too." She then read to
the children what she had written.*

*Lauren: I saw some too, but they
were drippy.*

117

Miss Reed: They had water dripping off of them?

Lauren: Yeah!

Miss Reed added to the chart, "Lauren saw some water dripping from an icicle." She thought aloud, "I wonder why there was water dripping from the icicle?"

Tommy: I betcha it was melting!

Lauren: Yeah! The sun was shining on it and it got hot!

Miss Reed wondered aloud, "Will the big icicles take longer to melt?"

> *Each child had a different idea about how long it would take for the icicles to melt.*
> *The children decided to make a table at the bottom of their chart to record everyone's guesses of when the biggest icicle would be completely melted. Miss Reed noticed that some children's guesses were that it would take months and some children guessed that it would take minutes.*

Scenario Questions

1. What does Miss Reed now know about children's concepts of time? How can she provoke thinking about concepts of time? Could this be done through the children's record keeping?
2. What other kinds of estimation could children do with properties of water and time?
3. If you were Miss Reed, what would you do next to help the children gather data to check their estimations?

Content Questions

1. What is the relationship between temperature and the properties of water?
2. What happens in the water cycle? Is knowledge of the water cycle important to understanding what is happening in the scenario? Why or why not?
3. What might a teacher in Hawaii do to provoke children's interests and observations about the properties of water?
4. What is heat? What is happening to a solid when it generates heat?

Integrating Math and Science: Classroom Pet

Setting: Second Grade

Mr. Hugo's second graders were very excited about the addition of mice as class pets. Different jobs were assigned to each child on a rotating basis so everyone would have responsibility during the month to care for the mice. Jose was the second, after Alana, to be in charge of feeding the mice.

Jeff Foott/Nature Picture Library/Alamy

Mice are good for classroom observations.

Jose noted, "Mr. Hugo, I gave the mice their food this morning and they have already eaten all of it. I looked in the box and I don't think there is enough left to last the rest of this week.

Mr. Hugo peered into the box. "You might be right, Jose. How much food do you think the mice will need?"

Alana joined the conversation, "I used the smallest measuring cup last week and I counted that I used six by Friday."

When the children came to school the next day their problem of the day was on the board. Mr. Hugo had written, "The mice are eating 6 to 8 quarter cups of food a week. The box of food holds 2 cups of food. I am going to the store today and I need to buy enough food for our mice for the rest of the month. How many boxes of food should I buy?"

The children began writing the numbers down that they thought were important and a few began drawing pictures of boxes of food labeled "2 Cups." One child thought about using a calendar to see exactly how many weeks were left in the month.

Rose: Mr. Hugo, I think we'll need about three more boxes.

Mr. Hugo: How did you arrive at that number, Rose?

Rose: I counted the number of quarter cups Alana used and I figured out that it was almost 2 cups, so then I estimated for the rest of the month.

Marquis: Uh, I disagree. I think we'll need two more boxes. I used the cups to count the food in the box and I scraped it off the top with my pencil.

Mr. Hugo asked several children to share their estimations, and the class agreed that two boxes was a good prediction. Mr. Hugo suggested they see at the end of the month if the prediction was correct.

Scenario Questions

1. What can Mr. Hugo tell about the children's ability to use estimation? What can he do to strengthen their ability to estimate mass?
2. Measurement relies on comparing quantities and understanding units. What other activities can Mr. Hugo plan that will help children understand that the results of measurement depend on the size of units?
3. How do you think Mr. Hugo had his classroom set up in order for children to manipulate materials as they needed or wanted to?

Content Questions

1. What are some of the issues in understanding the difference between volume and mass?
2. We don't commonly refer to an object's mass in everyday conversation. How does that impact our ability to estimate it?
3. What other concepts would be connected to understanding volume, weight, and mass? For example, if you were standing on the moon, how would your weight change?
4. What activities do preschoolers need to participate in that would help them understand weight and measurement concepts in third grade?

Children's Literature with a Focus on Estimation

Clements, A., & Reed, M. (2006). *A million dots.* New York: Simon and Schuster Children's Publishing.

Interesting facts are connected to the illustration of a million dots.

Fromental, J., & Jolivet, J. (2006). *365 penguins.* New York: Abrams Publishing.

Many penguins mysteriously arrive over time at a little boy's house. No one knows who is shipping the penguins to the boy and his family, but as they arrive one at a time over the course of the year, they present many problems. They have to be counted, sorted, arranged, and cared for.

Goldstone, B. (2006). *Great estimations.* New York: Square Fish.

Great Estimations helps the viewer train the eye to use different techniques for estimating quantity through counting strategies.

Goldstone, B. (2008). *Greater estimations.* New York: Henry Holt and Company.

Themes for counting from *Great Estimations* are continued in this book with the addition of estimating length, weight, area, and volume.

Murphy, S. J., & Bjorkman, S. (2003). *Coyotes all around: Mathstart 2.* New York: HarperCollins.

Clever Coyote adds in her head as she hunts for lunch. Estimation in rounding is introduced as a way to add numbers.

Myller, R. (1991) *How big is a foot?* New York: Yearling.

This classic explores the problem of building a bed without using standardized units of measurement.

Websites

Mathwire

Provides links to activities, lesson plans, worksheets, and other resources for planning and teaching.

U.S. Geological Survey

How much do you know about the properties of water? This website provides rich background information for the teacher.

National Library of Virtual Manipulatives
This website has many interactive activities that guide children through
thinking about patterns, properties, operations, estimation, and other
math concepts.

Further Exploration of the Big Idea for Teachers

1. Make a list of all the times you use estimation. Compare your list
with others. What do your lists have in common? What do you
think is important to understand about estimation?
2. Think about a time that you used estimation. Write about it as
though it were a story. Analyze your story for what you had to
think about in order to get close in your estimation.
3. Search for estimation strategies on the Internet. Find at least
three different strategies. Choose one strategy and apply it to
both a science and a math context. Compare your ideas with
those of others in a small group. Survey your group members
about which strategy they like best and why. Decide with your
group how the strategy could be used in direct instruction and
still make sense to as many children as possible. Think about how
strategies can be similar across different contexts.
4. Create an estimation activity. Share your activity with a small
group. Pay attention to how people interact with the planned activity. Edit your activity in response to your group's comments. Use
the activity with a child or small group of children. Write down the
children's responses and edit your activity based on their thinking.

Further Exploration of the Big Idea for Children

1. Create a classroom store. Children could use play money to "buy"
things.
2. Have the children plan the next classroom party. Ask them to
estimate how many cookies, napkins, punch glasses, and plates
will be needed.
3. Plan for things that require measuring. For example, children
could build a house for an imaginary creature using specific size
criteria.
4. Use child-friendly recipes for classroom snacks.
5. Let the children plan activities for the day, estimating start times
and end times.

6

Movement

Learning Outcomes

After working with the ideas in this chapter, you should be able to:

- Define and describe key elements of the big idea of movement.
- Analyze and create activities for at least two of the different types of movement, including movement of the surface, sources of movement, mysterious movement, spinning, and the movement of time.
- Create applications for the integration of math and science using the big idea of movement.

Standards Addressed in This Chapter:

Common Core State Standards for Math

First Grade: Measurement and Data
Measure lengths indirectly and by iterating length units

Second Grade: Measurement and Data
Measure and estimate lengths in standard units. Relate addition and subtraction to length.

Third Grade: Measurement and Data
Solve problems involving measurement and estimation of intervals of time, liquid volumes, and masses of objects

Next Generation Science Standards

K-PS2-2 Analyze data to determine if a design solution works as intended to change the speed or direction of an object with a push or a pull.
3-PS2.1. Plan and conduct an investigation to provide evidence of the effects of balanced and unbalanced forces on the motion of an object.
3-PS2-2. Make observations and/or measurements of an object's motion to provide evidence that a pattern can be used to predict future motion.
3-PS2-3. Ask questions to determine cause and effect relationships of electric or magnetic interactions between two objects not in contact with each other.

Head Start Child Development and Early Learning Framework

Geometry and Spatial Sense
Understands directionality, order, and position of objects, such as up, down, in front, behind
Recognizes and names common shapes, their parts, and attributes.
Combines and separates shapes to make other shapes.

INTRODUCTION TO THE BIG IDEA OF MOVEMENT

Many of the activities of children are centered around movement, and much of the **physical knowledge** that is constructed by young children relates to the movement of objects. Think about some of the most common interests children have—balls rolling, vehicles, slides, water—many activities children engage in with delight are related to their interest in, and inquiry about, the movement of objects. Movement as a big idea is so pervasive in young children's lives, and we will try to zoom in on some particularly important elements of it, elements that lend themselves well to the design of curriculum that integrates math and science.

In Jason's kindergarten classroom, there is a reading loft where children can spend time surrounded by pillows and read books. Donna, Jason's teacher, has restricted the children's access to the loft because of behavior problems— some of the children, Jason included, have become interested in dropping things from the loft, creating a safety hazard. But Donna wants to encourage the use of the reading loft, and so poses the problem to the group at meeting time, asking the children to help her solve this problem. Jason speaks up. "We could make an elevator for the books! Then they wouldn't fall on our heads." The children seem interested in this idea, so Donna has them work to design an "elevator" for the books. The problem the children are dealing with is: How can we safely move the books up and down to the loft without carrying them?

Many ideas are generated, some of them quite imaginative. Donna decides to bring in some books, pictures, and materials to suggest some practical ways they might answer the question. After looking at some of the books and pictures with the children, Donna notices that the children seem intrigued by pulleys, based on looking at the book Lights Out *by Arthur Geisert. She brings into the class a simple pulley, and demonstrates to them how it works. She also brings in an incline that is long enough to reach from the loft to the ground.*

123

In this classroom, the teacher has set the stage for the children to engage in experimentation with movement, and has created a context where the children's questions and interests are the basis for learning about both mathematics and science. She is articulating the problem that has come up—how to safely move the books up and down from the loft—and supported them in engaging in the problem-solving process.

Three of the children create an incline using the plastic gutter that the teacher has brought in. They first create a long incline that stretches across the room. Susan puts a book on the incline, and it doesn't move. "It's too long! It needs to be steeper!" The children work to shorten the incline and make it a steeper drop, and the book drops instead of sliding down the incline. Susan and Jason decide to try the incline at different lengths. Donna, the teacher, provides them with chart paper and meter sticks to keep track of how each incline works (see Figure 6-1).

The science in this scenario is seen in the application of the **scientific method**—systematic experimentation that involves varying the length of the incline and recording the results—as well as in

Figure 6-1
The Children's Chart of Their Incline Experiments

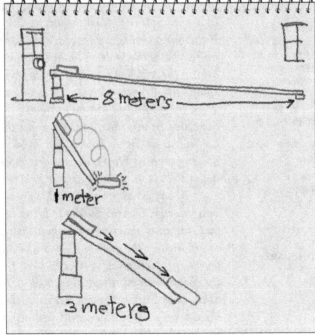

Source: Ken Davis

learning about the relationship between the steepness of the incline and the speed of the object down the incline. The mathematics is seen in the measurement of the length of the incline, and the relationship between the angle of the incline and the results. This experimentation effectively combines math and science, and takes on a life of its own, in the service of an authentic problem that interested the children, and with the support of the teacher in both articulating the problem and providing opportunities for the children to generate possible solutions and try them out.

An important part of the scientific method involves determining the relationship between **variables**, such as the angle of the incline and the speed of the object sliding down it. The effort the child uses is another variable in this specific example—how hard the child pushes the object down the incline—but this is a difficult variable to control. Children's ability to control the variables, and to see the results of their variations, is an essential part of facilitating their construction of knowledge.

And this construction of relationships underlies the development of **logico-mathematical knowledge**, another type of knowledge discussed by Piaget (1977) that is the focus of Constance Kamii's (1985) important work on early childhood mathematics learning. Unlike physical knowledge, which is empirical and exists in the physical world, logico-mathematical knowledge exists in children's minds—because it is the relationship between variables that the child is imposing on the world. For example, the incline is "steep" only in relationship to another incline that is less steep. In order for children to construct logico-mathematical knowledge they must interact with the world through theory-building, just as they do to construct physical knowledge. In fact, the two are intertwined in experience, as you can see—one of the other underlying reasons that mathematics and science are integrated, naturally, in the child's world.

Questions to Consider

1. What do you think children learned from the experience described in the scenario?
2. Think about the choice that Donna made in responding to this situation. What were the other choices that she had in terms of her approach to the problem of the loft?
3. What would the children have learned if Donna had provided cameras? What are some other directions in which she could have taken this project?

ELEMENTS OF THE BIG IDEA OF MOVEMENT

We will be discussing here two elements of the big idea of movement that are particularly helpful in focusing on the integration of math and science: (1) direction of movement and (2) representation of movement.

Direction of Movement

The simple act of throwing a ball creates movement. But it is in the direction of movement that the nature of the movement is made visible. For example, if a child is throwing beanbags to knock over targets made of Styrofoam blocks, she has to think about the direction of the movement of the beanbag, as well as the **force** of the throw. When she misses the target, then she has to think about how to change her aim or the power of her throw in order to be successful.

Liza, who is 4 years old, is at the water table, putting different materials in the water. She places a flat piece of aluminum foil in the water, and as she splashes the water, the foil moves on the surface. She delightedly says, "I made a boat!" Other children at the table begin to take pieces of foil and make them in different shapes, and one of the children discovers that he can make his foil boat move by blowing on it through a straw. The children decide to have a boat race, and some of the children start to put marbles on their boats.

Think about the different variables that the children are considering in this scenario: the shape and structure of the foil boat, the positioning of the straw in relation to the boat, the weight added by the marbles, and the distance and speed that the boat moves across the water. Many possibilities emerge that can be supported and extended by the teacher to support both math and science in just this one simple episode.

Christine Chaille

Experimenting with foil boats

Questions to Consider _____

1. What are some ways Liza's teacher could have responded to focus the children on particular variables involved in moving the boats across the water?

2. What is the role of the particular materials made available to the children in an activity? How can the teacher consider the choices of materials, limiting them as needed to focus children's attention?

Another way to focus on movement is through the study of mazes. In a maze, a ball or marble is directed through a path toward a goal. Sometimes mazes incorporate lanes in which the marble rolls; other times there are other obstacles to either target or avoid.

Alex's first-grade class has some small maze puzzles that are available to play with in the game center. They have also been engaging in math games of various kinds to support their math skills—mostly card and dice games. With the support and encouragement of Samuel, their teacher, they have also been creating their own games. Alex has the idea of making a maze math game. Samuel provides cardboard boxes and other materials, and the children create targets on the maze with numbers on the targets. The children roll the marble by moving the box, and, using addition, see how many points they can accumulate in a period of time. There is much excitement about the game, and Samuel capitalizes on this excitement by introducing challenges to the game—using negative numbers and multipliers on the maze. This becomes one of the children's favorite games.

Samuel sees the value of games as a way to support the children's understanding of, and practice with, arithmetic, and incorporates games into the curriculum. As a result, the children become quite capable and fluent with their addition and multiplication, and can quickly figure out their scores, either using paper and pencil, or, in the case of many of the students and depending on the problem to be solved, in their heads.

In addition to supporting the children's mathematical understanding, they are also experimenting with the direction of movement, and the effects of their actions—inclining the cardboard box, in this case—on the movement of the marble.

Questions to Consider

1. Why are games a good way to support children's developing arithmetic understanding?
2. How could Samuel communicate to parents the value of games?
3. How could you, as a teacher, support the use of mathematical games at home?

Mazes can also be used with younger children without incorporating numbers as Samuel's first-grade class did, as in the following scenario:

The 3- and 4-year-old children in Lory's class are introduced to a simple cardboard box maze, on which she has made targets on the box sides. The children aim for the targets as they incline the boxes. She then introduces a box with marble-size holes cut in it. As the children play with it, some of them try to get the marble to drop through the hole; others try to avoid the holes.

Micki gets some small strips of colored paper, and tapes the ends onto the box to create hoops through which to direct the marbles. The children start creating their own box mazes, using holes, hoops, and targets to make them increasingly complex.

Lory's use of mazes is particularly interesting because of how the children can pose their own goal for the use of the maze, avoiding the hole or aiming for the hole, for example. She also is encouraging the children to create new variations on the maze activity.

Lory has been interested in getting the children to work together, instead of always creating their own individual mazes (see Figure 6-2). She brings in

Figure 6-2
Small, Individual Maze

Source: Ken Davis

Figure 6-3
Large Maze Requiring Cooperation

Source: Ken Davis

large cardboard box tops, large enough that one child cannot manipulate the maze by him- or herself (see Figure 6-3).

Micki begins working on the large cooperative maze with another child. As they work, they have to make decisions about what kind of maze to make, and then together have to use the maze. As they do, they find they have to communicate with each other to coordinate how they are tilting the box—"I'll put this side up while you put your side down."

Much problem solving and resolution of conflicts is necessary during this process, which was one of Lory's goals.

Representation of Movement

When children experiment with movement, varying how, where, or how fast something moves, it is sometimes difficult for the different effects of those variables to be visible. And, in order to effectively experiment, children need to be able to track those differences. One of the ways to support this tracking is to create ways that movement is represented. This allows comparisons across actions that are otherwise problematic.

Figure 6-4
Cardboard Incline with "Tunnel"

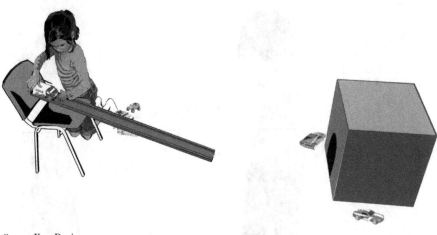

Source: Ken Davis

Think about a child rolling a ball toward a target. If the target is missed, it is difficult to gauge the aim of the first trial without some record of it, some trail. If, on the other hand, the ball leaves a mark as it rolls, then it is easier to change the aim to be successful. Here is an example of representation of movement, using a car whose wheels are dipped in paint to represent the car track as it rolls:

Five-year old Adrienne is rolling a car down a gently sloped cardboard incline to try to get it through the tunnel that is drawn on a large box (Figure 6-4).

She aims and releases the car several times, and eventually is able to get the car to go into the tunnel. Peter, who is watching Adrienne, says, "I know— let's dip the wheels in paint the way we did when we rolled marbles on paper!" The teacher hears this, and helps them get the paint they need to add to this activity. The two children then carefully aim their cars toward the tunnel, and because they can see the track the car makes, are able to make the adjustments needed to be successful. They then can reproduce their success over and over. "See, we made a path!" says Adrienne, excited.

When movement is represented, it is easier for children to make direct comparisons of each trial. Older children could look more carefully at a variable such as the angle of the path, and could measure it using a compass.

Questions to Consider

1. What are some other ways that children could represent the movement of the car?

2. How could the teacher encourage the documentation of the children's experimentation? What forms of technology could be introduced and incorporated into the activities to support this?

One of the difficulties in experimenting with movement is that often it happens too fast to explore in depth. Think about a child throwing a ball—he can see it at point A, when he releases it, and at point B, when it hits a target. But the path the ball takes is happening too fast to even see clearly. Technology can help with this, as in the following scenario:

Laura has set up a game of target ball for the children in her second-grade class, and after the children have played it for a while, they have a discussion about how the ball hits the target. She asks the children to draw the trajectory of the ball, and they compare drawings, which are not consistent. One of the children suggests that they videotape the ball, and then slow down the picture. They ask Laura to do filming, and then upload it to the computer. Samantha and Dennis work on the digital video, creating sloweddown versions of the scene and stopping it frame by frame. They print out the different frames, and put them on the wall where the drawings are also displayed. The children make comparisons of their drawings and the frame-by-frame pictures.

Dennis notices that the computer program also can put the time on the frame, so they start to compare the speed as the ball moves through the air. After sharing this with the class, some of the children decide to time each throw, comparing point A to point B. They begin to experiment with the force of their throws, as well as the differences depending on the arc of the throw.

Laura encourages these experimentations by providing suggestions for documenting their efforts, and posting charts in which they can record the different efforts. She documents the different experiments with a timeline, and the children refer to the timeline as they begin each new exploration.

The class is as excited about the idea of the frame-by-frame pictures as they are about the ball throwing, and Laura suggests that they brainstorm different

Incorporating technology in the early childhood classroom

things they could study using this technology. The class collects other video clips of actions to study, including clips of a soccer game on the playground. As they study the soccer game, they notice the different ways that children are running, and begin to focus on this.

Laura supports these extensions because they are engaging, and because they are good ways to incorporate measurement and technology use into the study of movement. They are also introducing different ideas about velocity, and in the case of the study of running, the functioning of the human body. She envisions the latter extending to the study of other animals and how they run, and the relationship between body structures and movement.

Teachers who are concerned about children's engagement in activities, and the degree of their interest, have to make decisions about what direction the curriculum is going. This requires teachers to have the big picture in mind—what are the science and math standards that are being addressed? What directions should be supported and encouraged, and which should not? Laura's decisions are based on her observations of the children's explorations, as well as her knowledge of the curriculum content for her second-grade classroom.

Questions to Consider

Laura may find that what she has planned for the children is not what they end up doing. There is a balance in a constructivist classroom between planning and flexibility.

1. Think about how you would feel if you planned what you thought would be an engaging activity, and the children take it in another direction. Would you be willing to let go of your plans and expectations, and alter the activity to respond to the children's ideas?
2. Can you think of a direction the children might have taken this activity that you would *not* support or encourage? If so, why not? How would you handle redirecting the children?
3. What are the benefits of planning? Of flexibility?

TYPES OF MOVEMENT

Here we consider various categories of movement that are helpful in generating ideas, including movement of the surface, sources of movement, mysterious movement, spinning, and the movement of times.

Movement of the Surface

Another way to move objects is to move the surface on which the objects lie—rotating the surface, or moving it back and forth.

At Jean-Paul's preschool, the children have been interested and concerned about news reports of a large earthquake in Japan. Many have seen news reports of the damage, including videos of buildings, both inside and outside, during the earthquake.

Linda, the teacher, decides to address the children's questions by studying what happens when the earth moves under buildings, thinking that this could lead to healthy discussions about the children's concerns. She consults a friend who teaches high school science, and he loans her a wooden base that moves back and forth, commonly known as an "earthquake board." At morning meeting time, Linda introduces the earthquake board to the children, and suggests that they might want to build houses on the base. Initially she puts out small unit cubes for the children to use.

Jean-Paul and two of his friends build two structures, one a tall, narrow building and the other a wider, two-cube-high building. When Linda releases the lock, they gently move the base back and forth. The tall building falls over immediately, and the shorter building doesn't. Jean-Paul suggests that they see how high they can make a building before it falls down. After building a three-cube-high building and moving the surface, one of the children says that it fell down because he shook it harder. After much discussion and argument, Jean-Paul suggests that they build all the buildings on the base and shake them at the same time.

Linda is impressed with the children's reasoning, as it reflects the idea of keeping variables constant in order to see the effect. She also notices that the children are very engaged and do not seem anxious about experimenting with "earthquakes," and so she decides to support continued experimentation.

Linda finds some videos that show a brick building and a wooden building in an earthquake, and the comparison is striking. She shows the children the videos, and asks them why they think this happens. After putting forth many different ideas, she suggests that they try some different materials in their constructions. The children create Lincoln Log structures, Lego structures, and toothpick structures, and compare the different strengths of their constructions.

Linda could have put out different materials, and posed questions to the children about their predictions relating to the different constructions. Instead, she decided to provoke the children's *own* questions by showing a video.

Questions to Consider

1. Why would it be different if Linda had posed the question directly about structures made out of different materials instead of showing a video?
2. How do you think children feel when they engage in activities that come out of their own questions?
3. How do *you* feel when you are working on a project of your choice versus being assigned a topic?

Another way to study the movement of surfaces is to look at what happens to objects on a rotating surface, as in this scenario:

Grant, a 3-year-old, is playing with a large plastic lazy Susan that has been put on the table. He first spins it, laughing, and then Peggy comes over and

places a small toy dog on the lazy Susan. Grant spins it again, and the toy dog flies off. Peggy and Grant do this over and over, laughing each time.

Their teacher is watching them and quietly places a small basket of different sizes of small animals on the table. Grant and Peggy start trying the different animals, and Peggy exclaims, "Look, the lion flies more slowly!"

Rebecca, reluctant to interfere with the repetitious experimentation that Grant and Peggy are engaged in, instead "suggests" variations using other materials simply by making them readily available. She realizes that they may ignore her suggestions, and understands that the simple repetition may be sufficient experimentation for them, but is interested to see how they explore the different objects.

Sources of Movement

Think about the many different ways that objects are made to move.

Exploring a moving surface

Erika

They can be propelled by air or water or thrown by a child, for example, or they can be self-propelled. One consideration in developing activities is to consider whether and how the child can either vary the movement of the object in a systematic way, or can examine the effects on the movement of the object (how the object varies).

Recall the example of the foil boats being moved in the water. The children can change *how* they cause the boats to move—instead of blowing on the boats through straws, they could use a battery-operated fan, which more effectively delivers a constant speed. In this case, children can vary the position of the fan and how they aim it toward the boat. Then, you need to think about how the children can observe the effect on the boat's movement—how do they measure the effect? Do they look at the time it takes for the boat to get across the water? Or do they look at which boat gets to a particular point first?

A simple way to look at different sources of movement is to pose the question to children: "How can we make this move?" This question can be embedded in a context, such as trying to move a boat across the water, or it can be raised more generally. And depending on the objects used, say a car versus a paper ball, the children may be more likely to focus on the movement of an object across a surface or through the air.

Rachel brings a basket to the morning meeting of her kindergarten classroom. The basket contains lightweight scarves, paper balls, cotton balls, and flat pieces of paper. She asks the children, "How can we make these things move through the air without touching them?" The children call out, "Blow on them!" "Hit them with a stick!" "Drop them from the loft!" The children decide to begin with dropping them, and when they do this they notice the different ways the objects move through the air.

Questions to Consider

1. If you were Rachel, teaching a kindergarten classroom, what are some other arrays of objects you could bring to the meeting and ask "How can we make them move?"
2. What would your predictions be about the kinds of experimentation they might engage in using those objects?
3. What would you do differently for 3- and 4-year-old children? For second-grade children?

Some sources of movement are direct, and others are indirect. An interesting indirect source of movement, which could also be seen as movement of the surface, is vibration.

Frank's 3-year-olds have been exploring sound, and a parent has brought in a large drum, 2 feet across, that sits on the floor. The children, fascinated with this instrument, have been playing with it when Elisa places a plastic dog on the drum. As Joshua bangs the drum with a mallet, the dog bounces, moving across the surface of the drum until it falls over, and continues to bounce off the side. Elisa says, "Uh-oh!" and picks up the dog up, setting it upright on the drum again as Joshua continues to hit the drum. The dog falls over again, and Elisa picks it up once more. Joshua hits the drum more lightly, trying to keep the dog upright, but it falls over again. He then hits the drum harder, and the dog jumps around on the drum's surface. The children laugh, repeating this over and over. Jenny, watching this experience, brings over other animals to place on the drum, and the children try each one in turn.

Frank, watching the children, sees that they are not focused on the sound of the instrument as much as they are on making objects move. He goes to the storage room and brings out a small, low trampoline and places it on the floor near the children. Elisa says, "Look, let's try them on the trampoline!" and the children proceed to repeat the experimentation, banging on the trampoline with a mallet.

Notice that Frank's original intention with the drum was to support the children's explorations of sound. As a careful observer, he pays attention to what questions the children are asking as they experiment, and shifts direction to focus on the movement of the objects, supporting the children as they take the activity in a different direction.

Mysterious Movement

There are a number of ways of moving objects that we will call mysterious. What this means is that experimenting with mysterious movement may not help children understand the reasons for the movement, but it can gain their interest and can focus them on the resulting movement instead. Two examples of mysterious movement have to do with surface tension and with magnets.

Interestingly, there are a number of published activities for young children that presume to be teaching the children about surface tension or about magnets. These activities are engaging for children, and as such are a provocation for children to look at movement. But children do not learn about magnetism by making objects move with magnets, nor do they learn about surface tension by making pepper move on the water surface with soap. We would argue that even many teachers who incorporate these activities, if questioned, would not have a deep understanding of magnetism or surface tension.

This raises an important question, because some in early childhood education advocate the use of "magic" or mystery in order to engage children. As a means of engagement or provocation, there is nothing wrong with this, but it is important to understand that the real focus is not magnetism or surface tension, but rather creating movement in interesting ways. Chaille and Britain (2003) discuss the nature of "magical" sources of change or movement as being ones that

> . . . have as their source some other unidentified, unknown, or even unknowable process. They are puzzling, beyond the children's understanding. Yet, as constructivists, we want children to experience themselves as sources of knowledge and not to see knowledge as coming from an external source. (p. 101)

So, as you think about movement explorations, consider the ability of the child to construct knowledge from the experience, while not discounting the engagement that is possible through provocations that might involve "mystery."

Erika

Moving objects with a magnet

Tamami, a 4-year-old, is lying under a table with a clear Plexiglas top. On the table are several objects—a small cardboard box, plastic animals, and metal utensils. Using a magnet attached to a stick, Tamami is attempting to move the objects on top of the table. "Hey! I can't move the box, but look, I can move the spoon!" Adam, who is standing at the table, runs and gets a basket of small balls that include balls made of metal, plastic, and rubber. He takes the other objects off the table, and puts some of the balls on the table. They roll around, and Tamami tries to "grab" them from underneath with her magnet. "Look, Adam, I stopped one!" She proceeds to move the metal ball around, bumping the other balls with it.

Tamami and Adam are fascinated by the fact that the magnet

can move some objects and not others, but *why* this occurs is beyond their understanding. Their teacher, Deb, realizes this, and does not question them about the reasons for this, or even focus on which objects they can move with the magnet. Instead, she suggests they try making a maze on the table top to move the objects through to see how it's different than on the Plexiglas.

Frances has been teaching first grade for many years, and has done experiments with the children on surface tension; in her eyes they have been very engaged and successful. After talking with some children about their understanding of surface tension, however, she realizes that they missed the point, and don't understand it at all. After reflection on this, she changes the activity.

> *The next year, she places small dishes of milk with drops of food coloring in them, and has the children use a dropper to put soap into the water. As the children begin to exclaim over how the food coloring moves away from the soap, she asks them questions about how the coloring is moving, and what happens when they drop it in a different place. She does not talk about surface tension, as she used to.*

Frances's willingness to rethink her curriculum is admirable, and shows the importance of talking to children about their understanding, and listening carefully to their responses.

Questions to Consider

1. Can you explain magnetism? If you can, how would you explain it to a 5-year-old child?
2. Look through some teacher resources that include activities, and try to identify ones that incorporate mystery. How could you adapt those activities to take advantage of the interest they generate without expecting children to understand the magic behind the activity?

Spinning

This form of movement is unique enough that we are considering it as a separate category, as it can generate a number of different approaches to the study of movement. One of the simplest examples of spinning movement is tops.

Dan's mother has recently returned from Japan, and she brought back a collection of different tops. She shows them to Ellie, Dan's first-grade teacher, who asks to use them with the children as a provocation for studying spinning movement. Ellie shares the box of tops with the children, and Dan demonstrates how they work. He then asks if others want to try to spin the tops, and six other children begin attempting to spin them. The children remark that Dan's top spins longer than anyone else's. Leslie says, "No, mine went longer than Dan's!" Ellie suggests that they keep track with stopwatches, and brings them out. Because they have enough tops for half the class, she pairs the children up to time each other as they spin the tops, recording their times.

Later, during math time, Ellie uses the data they collected on the top spinning times, looking at the different ways of representing how the class did. They look at the wide range of times, and notice that there are very few low and very few high times. Much to her surprise, Ellie is able to introduce the concept of central tendency—calculating the mean and talking about what that represents, realizing that this concept is complex for first graders to understand. She also calculates the median, and the children have a lively discussion about which one best represents how the class did.

Ellie shares this experience with her teaching team, and they have a good discussion about the importance of a meaningful context for introducing complex concepts to young children. They also discuss how even if all of the children did not fully understand the mean and median, they are constructing a strong base for their later learning.

Questions to Consider

Think about the importance of your expectations about children's capabilities at different ages.
1. How could Ellie have limited the children's learning if she had *not* introduced the concepts of central tendency in this situation?
2. What is the balance between having expectations that are too high and expectations that may be too low?
3. What would your expectations be for 3- and 4-year-old children in introducing tops to them? How would you incorporate mathematics into experiencing tops with them?

Another way to study spinning is through the creation of twirly spinners ("helicopters") that lend themselves to lots of different kinds of experimentation.

Nicki's second graders have been studying different ways to move through the air, and they have done a great deal with paper airplanes and kites. She decides to introduce the class to "helicopters" after seeing a twirly wooden toy at the toy store. She finds a description of how to make twirlers out of tag board—a simple way to cut and fold the tag board to make the same kind of toy (see Figure 6-5).

Figure 6-5
Tag-Board Twirler

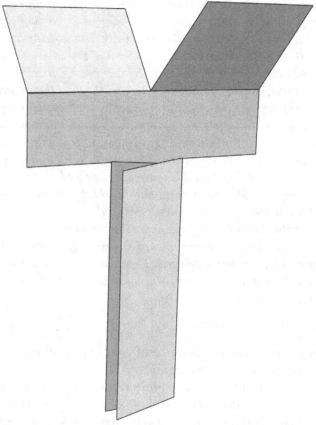

Source: Ken Davis

She begins by showing a video clip of a helicopter, and the children discuss how its movement is different from that of an airplane. Then she shows them the twirly wooden toy. They watch it twirl as it drops from her raised hand. She then provides the tag-board twirlers to cut out and create. On their work tables are also different sizes of paper clips.

Some of the children work alone and some pair up, and most of the resulting twirlers successfully fly. They wonder why some fly better than others, and find that how the flaps are folded seems to matter. Nicki points out the boxes of paper clips, and says to one group of children, "I wonder what would happen if you put a paper clip on the end?"

Some of the children begin to decorate their twirlers, and discover that the medium they use can affect how it flies. At the end of a couple of days *of experimenting, the children decide they want to fly their varied creations off the second-floor atrium in the library, so they can fly farther. Nicki takes movies of the event, as she has been documenting their different experiments all along.*

It's important to recognize the value of the time this project took, particularly in terms of the experimentation that it allows children to engage in, with tangible and immediate results. And it is also important that the teacher take the time to document this process, and make it explicit for the children, so that they will recognize the connections as they study science and mathematical inquiry.

The Movement of Time

Time is a concept that is difficult for young children to grasp. Unfortunately, many early childhood curriculum books describe ways of teaching time that result in superficial understanding of time, so children may "learn" to say what time it is by looking at a clock without understanding the concepts of time. We are challenged to think about ways of looking at time from the child's perspective—what can they see that represents time? The first-grade Common Core State Standard for Math emphasizes children telling and writing the time to the hour and half-hour, but children need many experiences with the application of measuring time before this standard will make sense.

There are ways that time is represented by movement. Think about things that move over time—what can children do to represent that movement, to measure it?

Nancy's first-grade class has been engaged in a study of light and shadows, and the children have spent time on the playground observing shadows— taking pictures and sketching them. One day, they do this both in the morning and later in the afternoon. After posting the pictures on the wall, Tommy remarks, "Look! The shadow of this tree has moved!" The children discuss this, and they decide to examine the movement of the shadows. The next morning, they go out onto the playground and place a piece of tape at the end of the tree's shadow. Every hour, several children go out onto the playground and mark the shadow, placing the time on each mark.

At the end of the day, the class goes outside, and sees the change in the shadow. Nancy leads the group in a discussion of why the shadow is different. "Well," says Tommy, "the sun is shining on the tree from a different direction. That's why the shadow is longer." The discussion continues, talking about how the sun is in different parts of the sky at different times. This opens up discussion of why the sun is in different parts of the sky, whether the sun is moving, how the earth is moving, and how time is one way of recording these changes.

The children begin to consult the many resource books Nancy has made available, and one of them finds a section on sundials as a way of measuring time. A project to create sundials follows.

Nancy has found a way for children to measure time in a variety of ways, connecting it to the movement of shadows as a concrete representation. The study of sundials contributes to the children's emerging understanding of time.

The study of growth can involve a focus on the big idea of transformation, as discussed in Chapter 5, but it can also incorporate the study of the measurement of movement, also supporting children's construction of concepts of time.

Marjorie's kindergarten class is engaged in a study of plants, and has planted fast-growing beans in the classroom. They have been measuring the growth of the plants on a daily basis, marking each day's progress. Marjorie would like to connect this to the measurement of time. She sets up a camera to take pictures of the plants every 30 minutes, explaining this to the children. After a week, she compiles the pictures into a time-lapse video, and shows it to the children. The video represents 7 days of growth, compressed into a 10-minute time period. The resulting discussion about speeding up time, and measuring it in different units, leads to other discussions—estimating the future growth over time, for example. The children decide to measure their height over time, just as some of their parents have done on a yearly basis at home. "Look, this line represents 1 month!" "She's growing faster than I am!"

Review Questions

1. What are the two elements of the big idea of movement discussed in this chapter? Elaborate on one of them.
2. Select two of the types of movement, analyze them, and develop activities for each of them relating to either math or science.
3. Find a science activity in a curriculum resource or textbook, or think about a movement activity you've already done with children. Think about how you could modify the activity to integrate mathematics into the experience.
4. Do the same thing using a mathematics activity. How could you modify the activity to integrate science into the experience?

Summary

In this chapter, we've explored the following elements of movement that lend themselves to the integration of mathematics and science: (1) the direction of movement, (2) the representation of movement, (3) movement of the surface, (4) different sources of movement, (5) mysterious movement, (6) spinning movement, and (7) the movement of time. There are probably other elements that could be generated, and you are encouraged to think about this issue yourself and generate other elements for exploration and experimentation. In the following part of the chapter, we will elaborate on two different areas of exploration, examining each for preschool-age children and for early elementary children.

Modules for Chapter 6: Movement

MODULE 6-1 FOCUS: DIRECTION OF MOVEMENT

Common Core State Standards for Math

Third Grade: Number and Operations-Fractions
Develop understanding of fractions as numbers.

Next Generation Science Standards

3-PS2-2. Make observations and/or measurements of an object's motion to provide evidence that a pattern can be used to predict future motion.

Integrating Math and Science: Sports

Setting: Third Grade

Molly knew that her third graders were huge basketball fans, so she set up a game for math that required the children to toss crumpled paper into plastic cups. The children were divided into small groups. Each group had a cup and made five paper balls. Each child stood a couple of feet from the table and tossed each ball toward the cup. Molly gave each group a piece of paper with five frames drawn on it on which to keep track of the balls they tossed. On each of the five squares the children would check or color in the square to indicate that a ball had landed in a cup.

1st Throw	2nd Throw	3rd Throw	4th Throw	5th Throw
X		X	X	

As the children tossed the balls they commented on how tight the balls were crumpled and if that made a difference in the accuracy of their tosses, how hard or lightly they needed to toss the balls, and if overhand or underhanded tosses worked better. When everyone finished they shared their tables, making fractions from the number of balls in the cups. Alan said, "I got 2 out of 5 balls in the cup." Molly asked Alan, "How did you show that in your Five Frame?" Alan said, "I drew a big X in the box, so I have two boxes with an X in them and three boxes without an X. I missed the cup with those balls." Molly asked the children, "How many balls would he have to get in a cup to fill up his Five Frame?"

The children enthusiastically replied that Alan would have to throw three more balls. Molly then had the children get back in their groups and think of ways to represent how many balls went into the cups and how many missed. They needed to write it as an equation or number sentence. After they had worked on this for a few minutes, Molly got them back together in a large group. "Let me show you how your number sentence could be written as a fraction. We could write a 2 and then a diagonal line like this, / , and then write the 5 for the total number of boxes. If you wrote your number sentences like a fraction, what would they look like?" After the groups all wrote at least one or two fractions, Molly had them talk about what their fractions meant.

Scenario Questions

1. What did Molly have to consider in order to set up a whole-class activity like this? What do you think some of her biggest issues might have been?
2. List some strategies Molly might have used to document or record the children's thinking during the activity. What strategy might the children use to record their throws?
3. What would the children need to know about behavior expectations before participating in an activity like this?

Content Questions

1. What other materials could be used to test hitting a target?
2. The standard for this activity works toward the children studying movement to make predictions. Work with a small group to list things in your life that require prediction of movement.
3. In this scenario there are at least three ways we work with fractions: area, length, and quantity. In this scenario the children are working with a set (quantity). What could the teacher do to emphasize working with area and length?
4. The children are creating fractions in this scenario and then thinking about how to represent them. How is this different from being presented with numbers on a worksheet and being asked to represent them?
5. The language of fractions—*numerator, denominator, decimal, percent, ratio,* and *proportion*—are words that are not used in general, day-to-day conversation. How would you define each word to someone who had never heard the word before?

Integrating Math and Science: Winter Pictures

Setting: Kindergarten

Common Core State Standards for Math

Kindergarten: Geometry

Analyze, compare, create, and compose shapes.

Analyze and compare two- and three-dimensional shapes, in different sizes and orientations, using informal language to describe their similarities, differences, parts (e.g., number of sides and vertices/"corners"), and other attributes (e.g., having sides of equal length).

Model shapes in the world by building shapes from components (e.g., sticks and clay balls) and drawing shapes.

Next Generation Science Standards

K-PS2-2. Analyze data to determine if a design solution works as intended to change the speed or direction of an object with a push or a pull.

Byran was implementing a seasonal study of trees throughout the school year. The first month of school the children had adopted a tree on the playground and had sketched and painted pictures of its leafy branches and rough bark. They documented the leaves changing colors several weeks later, and now everyone was commenting on how bare the branches looked. One day in the art center, Byran put out thinned-down black paint, large sheets of paper, and straws. He showed the children how to place a small puddle of paint close to the bottom of the paper and then blow gently to move the paint into curvy waves of lines across the paper. Some of the children became so intent on moving the paint they blew a little too hard and got light-headed; others carefully blew to try to re-create the branches of their playground tree. Elisa said, "I blew really lightly on the very end of this line, and my paint is very, very tiny." Noi exclaimed, after getting a little light-headed, "You blew lightly and my head is light!!" The children laughed at the different uses of the word "light." They also compared how different amounts of paint required different strengths of blowing. The children also became fascinated by the shapes the paint was creating. Some of them tried to purposefully create triangles and circles, and re-creating tree branches was largely forgotten, although a few children pointed out that if you looked through the branches outside you could actually see some of those shapes.

After the pictures dried, the children added details of things around the tree or drew birds and animals they thought might want to visit their trees.

Scenario Questions

1. It is apparent that these children have had experiences with paint before Byran put these materials out for them to experiment with. What do you think he had to do to prepare them for this activity? Why would it be inappropriate for this to be their first experience with paint?
2. What are some topics of discussion Byran might have with the children after listening to their comments? What other curriculum areas were touched on by the children?
3. How could Byran have prepared the children for the light-headedness they felt when blowing too hard?

Content Questions

1. How we make an object move depends on its properties. Make a list of the differences between making solids move as compared to liquids.
2. It might be confusing to children to think about wind and the act of blowing as being similar. How would you help children understand the difference between blowing with your mouth and the wind?

Children's Literature with a Focus on Directing Movement

These titles emphasize directed movement.

Ballard, C. (2008). *Exploring forces and movement.* New York: PowerKids Press.
   This is an introduction to many ways to make things move.
Dahl, M., & Shea, D. (2006). *Pull, lift and lower: A book about pulleys (Amazing science: Simple machines).* Minneapolis, MN: Picture Window Books.
Heelan, J. R., & Simmonds, N. (2000). *Rolling along: The story of Taylor and his wheelchair.* Atlanta, GA: Peachtree.
   This book was co-published as a Rehabilitation Institute of Chicago Learning Book. It integrates the need for directing movement with the image of the capable child.
Keller, L. (2012). *Bowling alley bandit.* New York: Henry Holt and Company.
   This is the first in a series using Arnie the Doughnut as the main character. Havoc takes place at a bowling alley when one of the characters cannot throw anything but a gutter ball.
Llewellyn, C., & Abel, S. (2004). *And everyone shouted, "pull!": A first look at forces and motion (First look: Science).* Picture Window Books.
   A farmer gets help from his animals to get his produce to market.
Stille, D. R., & Boyd, S. (2004). *Motion: Push and pull; Fast and slow. (Amazing science).* Minneapolis, MN: Picture Window Books.
   Introduces expanded ideas about motion.

Willems, M. (2009). *Watch me throw the ball!* New York: Hyperion Books. Mo Willems has become very well known for his book *Don't Let the Pigeon Drive the Bus*. This book is the first in a series starring Elephant and Piggie. Elephant has a serious talk with Piggie about throwing a ball.

Websites

Making Things Move
This website is a science unit sample for several different ways to act on objects to make them move. It is designed for grades K and up.
Quarked
This is an entertainingly designed website about subatomic science. The content knowledge is obviously not for use directly with young children, but can deepen your own understanding about physics. There are games that children who have had experience throwing balls at targets would enjoy.
Science Games for Kids: Forces in Action
This offers children a chance to experiment with weight and gradient. It lends itself to setting up actual experiments that children could then try on their own.

Further Exploration of the Big Idea for Teachers

1. Make a simple pendulum from a pencil, tape, string, and a large washer. Tape the pencil to the edge of a table. Attach the string to the pencil by tying it loosely around the pencil. Tie the other end around the washer. Lift the washer gently and let it swing back and forth. Count the swings. How many swings happen in a minute? Does holding the washer higher impact the number of swings? Try different lengths of string and different weights of washers. How would a chart help you predict the number of swings with different materials?

2. Create a list of all the games that require directed movement. What considerations do players have to keep in mind to successfully play these games? Choose one of the games on your list and make a concept map of all the physical science ideas that could be part of the game.

3. Use plastic rulers with a concave center down the middle to create mini-ramps. Experiment with different kinds of balls and marbles to roll them into a cup held by someone else. How far apart can you place the ruler and the cup and still get the ball into the cup? What do you have to think about in order to estimate where the ball will end up? How can you measure this distance? How does the height of the ramp impact the distance the marble rolls?

Further Exploration of the Big Idea for Children

1. There are commercial games that require children to direct movement. Inexpensive bowling games and target games can engage children in experimenting with changing distance and force to make things roll and fly.
2. Other toys that support directed movement are plastic jumping frogs and tiddly winks.
3. Let children roll toy car wheels through paint in boxes, creating parallel lines. As they tilt the box they can experiment with the placement of lines or mixing of colors.

MODULE 6-2 FOCUS: CHAIN REACTION

Common Core State Standards for Math

Second Grade: Measurement and Data
Measure and estimate lengths in standard units
Represent and interpret data

Next Generation Science Standards

K-2-ETS1-1. Ask questions, make observations, and gather information about a situation people want to change to define a simple problem that can be solved through the development of a new or improved object or tool.

K-2-ETS1-2. Develop a simple sketch, drawing, or physical model to illustrate how the shape of an object helps it function as needed to solve a given problem.

K-2-ETS1-3. Analyze data from tests of two objects designed to solve the same problem to compare the strengths and weaknesses of how each performs.

Integrating Math and Science: Rube Goldberg Machines
Setting: Second Grade

One day the second graders came to school and found several books in their classroom library that showed how one thing could make another thing happen. One of the books was about a little pig who doesn't want to get out of bed to turn off the lights, so he designs a complicated way to flip the switch from his bed. The pictures throughout the book show the details of the process, with wires, pulleys, wheels, and other assorted objects working together to turn out the light. Jody was particularly engaged with this story and asked her teacher if the class could make something like this in their project area. Barb, the teacher, pointed out that the pig had a problem to solve and that his invention helped him solve the problem. "What problem could our class solve with a chain-reaction machine?" asked Barb. This got several of the children very excited and there were many conversations over the next few days about various things they could do. Barb supported their interest by bringing in books about Rube Goldberg, a turn-of-the-century cartoonist who drew wildly complex ways to do the simplest things. Finally, they decided to build a machine that would roll a pencil into a box that held pencils that needed to be sharpened.

Scenario Questions

1. What are some of the things the teacher did to plan for this project? What do you think some of her goals might have been? What do you think her classroom looked like?
2. How did the teacher use engagement to plan this project?
3. How does the teacher see the role of children in her classroom?
4. What do you think she will need to do next in order to support the project that the children are planning on building?
5. Look at the three science standards for this scenario. What do you think the children will do in their work that will connect to each standard? For example, the first standard states that children will "Ask questions, make observations, and gather information about a situation people want to change to define a simple problem that can be solved through the development of a new or improved object or tool." In the scenario, the children have been challenged by the teacher to find a problem they can solve by designing a Rube Goldberg machine. What else could the teacher do to strengthen the connection to each standard?

Content Questions

1. How is a chain reaction in a situation like this different or similar to cause and effect?
2. How would you describe the relationship between weight and force? How could you test your description?

Integrating Math and Science: The Three Little Pigs in the Block Center

Setting: Preschool

Head Start Child Development and Early Learning Framework

Math

> Understands directionality, order, and position of objects, such as up, down, in front, behind
>
> Sorts, classifies, and serializes (puts in a pattern) objects using attributes, such as color, shape, or size

Science

> Participates in simple investigations to form hypotheses, gather observations, draw conclusions, and form generalizations.
>
> Uses senses and tools, including technology, to gather information, investigate materials, and observe processes and relationships.

Joseph's preschoolers had been interacting with a variety of books that were variations on "The Three Little Pigs." They had compared the different versions, preferring the ones where the wolf met some kind of punishment, but agreeing that the wolf and pigs might become friends too if they were nice to each other. Esme declared that she could blow as hard as a wolf and would prove it in the block center. Several children decided they too could build houses for wolf play. This led to days of small house constructions and then vigorous blowing to see if the block houses would fall down. Joseph observed the children blowing with their mouths with no luck in knocking the block houses down, and suggested there might be other ways to do it without simply blowing. He helped the children think about other ways they could move one thing that would then push the houses down. Esme decided that she was going to make a ramp with a large cylinder block at the top, which she could then push. It would roll down the ramp and hit the houses harder. The first few times she tried this the cylinder rolled off the end of the ramp at an angle, completely missing the house, but when she got the distance and angle correct, the house fell down. Two other children who had continued with their own experiments became interested in helping Esme with her problem. They tested different sizes and shapes of blocks over a period of several days and finally came up with a construction that could not be knocked down by the rolling cylinder.

Scenario Questions

1. The teacher in this scenario had gathered different versions of a popular children's story. What could have been some of the reasons he did this?
2. The teacher followed the children's interests and leads in this situation, but what could he have done if the children had not decided to build houses? How could he have encouraged this in a different way?
3. What other concepts might be part of *The Three Little Pigs*? For example, the children could also explore building with other materials—table-top blocks or cardboard blocks, for example.

Content Questions

1. Newton's three laws of motion are the laws of inertia, mass and acceleration, and action and reaction. How would you describe these laws?
2. Can you describe an example for each law? What do early childhood teachers need to understand about these laws in order to teach young children?
3. Discuss the nature and importance of *variables* in experimentation. What does it mean to hold a variable "constant," and how would that apply to the children's experimentation in the block corner?

Children's Literature with a Focus on One Thing Making Another Thing Happen

Geisert, A. (2005). *Lights out.* Boston, MA: HMH Books for Young Readers.
A small pig has to go to bed, but wants to turn out his lights without getting up. He creates an elaborate way to turn off the light. The book clearly illustrates how each part of the system works to create a chain reaction.
Numeroff, L. J. (2010). *If you give a mouse a cookie.* New York: HarperCollins.
Numeroff, L. J. (1998). *If you give a pig a pancake.* New York: HarperCollins.
Numeroff, L. J. (1991). *If you give a moose a muffin.* New York: HarperCollins.
This series of books illustrates an amusing cyclical chain of events.
Slade, S., & Schwartz, C. (2010). *What if there were no bees?: A book about the grassland ecosystem (Food chain reactions).* Minneapolis, MN: Picture Window Books.
Slade, S., & Schwartz, C. (2010). *What if there were no grey wolves?: A book about the temperate forest ecosystem (Food chain reactions).* Minneapolis, MN: Picture Window Books.
Slade, S., & Schwartz, C. (2010). *What if there were no sea otters?: A book about ocean ecosystem (Food chain reactions).* Minneapolis, MN: Picture Window Books.
The loss of one part of a food chain is explored in this series.
Suen, A., & Carrick, P. (2007). *Wired.* Charlesbridge.
This book is written on two levels, an easy-to-read level and a more in-depth level. It explains how electricity gets into our homes.

Websites

Rube Goldberg Machines
The official site for Rube Goldberg machines and related contests.
YouTube videos
There are many videos illustrating the power of chain reactions. Here are a few that are inspirational for teachers. Some could be shown to children:

Honda Car Commercial
All the parts of a Honda were used in this musical chain reaction.
OKGo: This Too Shall Pass
This music video incorporates the band and a wildly colorful chain reaction
   set to the song "This Too Shall Pass."
Target—Fresh Machine (Rube Goldberg)
Commercial using many of the products sold at Target.
Japanese Wooden Xylophone
Commercial using different tonal qualities of wooden xylophone-type instru-
   ments to play "Ode to Joy."
PBS Zoom
This gives children a chance to problem solve with movable parts in an
   electronic environment.
Japanese Rube Goldberg Machines
These are small chain-reaction machines that use everyday objects.

Further Exploration of the Big Idea for Teachers

1. Build a Rube Goldberg machine that will deliver a ball into a
   cup. Use the following basic materials: pipe insulating tubes cut
   in half lengthwise (this creates a gutter that is a good size for
   marbles), rulers that have indentations on top that create a
   gutter down the length of the ruler, dominoes, masking tape,
   modeling clay, and marbles. Other materials that are available
   can be added for height, weight, and stability. Use the challenge
   of having to use at least one long section of the tubing, one ruler,
   and enough dominoes to make a small chain. The end result
   should be the marble going into a cup. The marble has to stay in
   the cup, so if the cup is lying down there has to be a way to keep
   the marble inside.
2. Make a picture book illustrating a food chain or life cycle, to be
   used in a children's classroom.
3. Build a domino chain reaction. Create the challenge of making the dominoes split into different directions, and go uphill.
   Dominoes come in many different sizes and weights, so you may
   have to experiment with different brands to find the ones that fall
   as expected.

Further Exploration of the Big Idea for Children

1. Put dominos or a set of thin rectangular blocks in the block center. Show children how they can be set up to knock the next one
   over. Find pictures of dominoes set up and ready for a chain reaction and place those in the block center, too.

2. Collect cardboard tubing and masking tape. Ask children to create marble runs with as many different turns as possible. Give them materials that they can use to measure the distance of the marble as it goes out the end of the tubing.
3. Slightly older children can be challenged to use ramps, levers, and other small simple machines. Have them design their machines separately and then figure out how the machines can work together to make something happen.

7   Balance and Symmetry

Learning Outcomes

After working with the ideas in this chapter, you should be able to:

- Define and describe key elements of the big idea of balance.
- Analyze different explorations of balance, including symmetry, comparisons, the use of representations, and games that incorporate balance.
- Create applications for the integration of math and science in the study of balance.

Common Core State Standards for Mathematics

Kindergarten: Measurement and Data
Describe and compare measurable attributes.
Classify objects and count the number of objects in categories.

Kindergarten: Geometry
Identify and describe shapes.
Analyze, compare, create, and compose shapes.

First Grade: Measurement and Data
Measure lengths indirectly and by iterating length units.
Represent and interpret data.

First Grade: Geometry
Reason with shapes and their attributes.

Next Generation Science Standards

K-2. Engineering Design
K-2-ETS1-1. Ask questions, make observations, and gather information about a situation people want to change to define a simple problem that can be solved through the development of a new or improved object or tool.
K-2-ETS1-3. Analyze data from tests of two objects designed to solve the same problem to compare the strengths and weaknesses of how each performs.

Head Start Child Development and Early Learning Framework

Scientific Skills and Method
The skills to observe and collect information and use it to ask questions, predict, explain, and draw conclusions.

Ken Davis

Balancing blocks

Balance is a big idea that is pervasive in children's lives, underlying questions and explorations in many domains. From physical balance on the playground as a child walks carefully on a wooden divider, to comparisons involved in the distribution of materials, balance is an important source of inquiry across mathematics and science.

Jonah is creating pipe-cleaner figures that are part of his preschool's project on the circus. He attaches metal beads to each end of a pipe cleaner to serve as the figure's arms. On one arm, he attaches two metal beads, and on the other, three. The figure falls to the heavier side. Jonah studies it for a minute, then adds another bead to the other side to even it out. The figure balances. He says, "Now they are the same!"

Jonah is engaged in comparisons of materials, in this case the weight of the materials, in making his decisions about how many beads to attach. His work involves the physical act of balance, an example of his construction of physical knowledge, as well as active comparisons and estimations of equality, an example of the construction of mathematical knowledge.

157

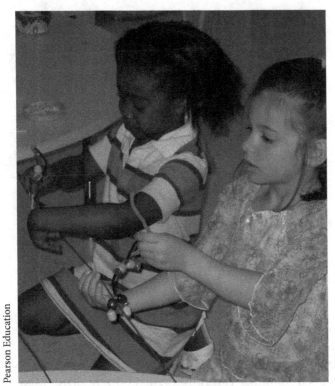

Pearson Education

Balancing the tightrope walker

ELEMENTS OF THE BIG IDEA OF BALANCE

The act of balancing implies the estimation and/or measurement of size, weight, number, and mass. In its simplest form, it involves the comparison of A and B, and requires the determination of equivalency. In order for balance to occur, A has to equal B along the relevant dimension, depending on the context. Balance as a big idea necessitates and supports three key elements: (1) making comparisons through estimation and measurement; (2) patterns; and (3) the establishment of equality, the basis for algebraic thinking, which involves arithmetic. In terms of science, balance is an integral part of the construction of physical knowledge, particularly relating to conservation.

Comparisons

Comparisons can be either approximate (through estimation) or determined through measurement. Jonah, the 4-year-old in the previous example, was able to estimate equivalence by direct comparison, and to test his idea through experimentation. Often direct comparisons do not work, and more precise measurement, or more experimentation, is necessary.

Barbara's second-grade class has received a bag of seeds, and wants to divide the bag in half to share with the other second-grade class. To encourage more precise measurement, she tells the children that each class needs exactly the same amount. The children decide to use the pan balance, which they have been exploring. They begin by estimating half of the bag and putting it into one of the pans; the other half goes into the other pan. It does not balance. One of the children suggests that they try again, but Emily says, "We can just move a little bit from one pan to the other until they are the same." Through trial and error, putting a little bit at a time into the higher pan from the lower pan, the children eventually get the two sides in balance.

This example incorporates both estimation and measurement, using weight as the way to establish equivalence of two quantities. In both preschool and elementary classrooms, there are numerous opportunities to make comparisons and to encourage both estimation and measurement.

Questions to Consider_____

1. What are some common situations in classrooms where estimation and measurement can be encouraged?
2. What resources would be helpful to have available for the purpose of encouraging estimation and measurement (think of the pan balance in the previous example)?

Patterns

Patterns can be viewed as a form of balance, in that they involve the reproduction of a visual image, a sound, or an object over and over. (We also address patterns as a big idea in Chapter 4.) Understanding patterns is important for both math and science. In math, patterns are a building block for much of arithmetic and geometry. In the Head Start Standards, *patterns* is one of the five elements to be focused on. In science, patterns are a sign of regularity—in sound, in light, and in nature. Regularity and irregularity, detection of differences in patterns, is essential for **classification** in many domains, and one of the foundations of experimentation and the scientific method.

Erin's first-grade class is studying the patterns of music, and her class has listened to different types of music—reggae, rock, and African marimba. Her teacher, Esperanza, asks them to form small groups to brainstorm different ways they might represent the patterns they hear.

Erin's group comes up with three ways—clapping, marks on paper, and objects, and other groups come up with these and others. As a whole group, the many ideas are collected on a piece of chart paper. The children then divide into groups to elaborate on each of them.

Erin is in the group using objects, and they decide that there are at least two types of beats—so they choose attribute blocks to use to represent the beats, with large circles as the loud beat and small circles as the small beat. They then set out to apply their system to the different forms of music, arriving at different arrays of objects.

The results are a variety of different kinds of patterns—the objects are displayed on a table, the marks on the board, and the clapping in a digital recording. This leads to a discussion of the regularities in the three forms of music. Esperanza then plays other forms of music that do not follow the same kind of regular patterns—a modern atonal classical piece and a Japanese koto recording. The children note their inability to establish a pattern, and talk about the differences.

The Establishment of Equality

Children are constructing both physical and mathematical knowledge through their interactions with the world. One of the bases for understanding the physical world is conservation—that things in the world, such as number, mass, and weight, stay the same unless something is added or taken away. This construct, described by Piaget (1977) as one of the building blocks of intellectual development, is grounded on the idea of equivalence. In order to understand conservation, a child must first be able to establish that two things are the same. Here's an example of conservation of mass:

Two kindergarten children, David and Maria, want to share an apple. Their teacher cuts it in half, and Maria wants hers cut into smaller pieces, so the teacher cuts one half into three other pieces (see Figure 7-1). David says, "That's not fair! She has more than me!" Maria, who understands the concept of conservation, says, "No, David, see? If I put my pieces together they are the same as yours." She shows him, putting her pieces together and putting her half

Figure 7-1
Comparing Halves of an Apple

Source: Ken Davis

side by side with his. David, unconvinced (because he has not yet constructed the concept of conservation of mass), continues to complain.

The establishment of equality is essential to the construction of understanding of conservation. Children do not learn conservation by being taught directly—rather, they construct it through numerous interactions with objects and materials, making comparisons of size, number, quantity, and mass. Through these experiences, children have opportunities to compare along many dimensions, and number becomes an important representational tool for them to use.

Think about the second graders using the pan balance. If they were dividing larger objects that can be counted instead of birdseed, then numbers could be used as a tool for establishing equivalency.

Olivia's first-grade teacher, Kate, brings in 14 small bird feeders to share with the other first-grade class, and asks the children to figure out how many each class should get. The children work first individually to figure this out, using pencil and paper. Olivia draws 14 circles on her paper, and then puts a mark by one and a different mark by the next one. When she is done, she counts the number of marks, determining that there are seven X's and seven O's:

$$X \ O \ X \ O \ X \ O \ X \ O \ X \ O \ X \ O \ X \ O$$

Will draws two rows of bird feeders. On one side, he draws one, then draws another on the other side. As he draws, he counts from 1 to 14.

1	2
3	4
5	6
7	8
9	10
11	12
13	14

He then counts the number of bird feeders in the first row, arriving at the number 7.

After the children are done working individually, Kate asks them if they want to share what they figured out. Some children have concluded that the answer is 7; others have different answers. She asks if one of them would like to share how they figured it out. Olivia and Will each share their strategy for arriving at the answer.

Kate, Olivia's and Will's teacher, is acknowledging that children have a variety of strategies for solving problems, and that the children may be at different points in their understanding of numbers. She encourages the children who have arrived at an incorrect answer to explain what they did, and in some cases, they recognize their mistakes as they explain it. She could have also introduced objects to represent the bird feeders, and some of the children could have used them to represent their thinking.

How is this the basis for **algebraic thinking**? Algebra is a tool for representing numbers with letters, and then using this tool to explore arithmetic. Giving children opportunities to represent objects in establishing equivalency is supporting this, helping arithmetic become a tool of thinking rather than a set of memorized techniques.

Questions to Consider

Olivia's teacher could have brought in the bird feeders, and asked the class to divide the number 14 by the number 2. Let's say the class had spent time memorizing simple division ("8 divided by 2 is 4, 10 divided by 2 is 5, etc."). How would this teaching strategy differ from what is described in the scenario? What do children learn in each of these experiences, besides the answer?

EXPLORATION OF BALANCE

There are many opportunities to explore balance. We will concentrate on three: (1) The study of symmetry; (2) comparisons and tools of measurement; (3) the use of representations, including numbers; and (4) using games that incorporate balance as physical knowledge.

The Study of Symmetry

Children are fascinated with symmetry, which can be seen as a representation of balance. Symmetry involves the replication of elements across the midline, and there are many avenues for exploring symmetry. The use of mirrors is one key way to explore symmetry, and there are many ways that children can study patterns and pictures using mirrors.

After looking at the Mirror Puzzle Book *(Walter, 1985) and having a discussion of what symmetry is, Liza, Rick's kindergarten teacher, has put out a number of mirrors on a table, and has suggested that children can use them to find things that are and are not symmetrical. She has also put out some printed digital pictures for the children to use, including pictures of faces, buildings and flowers, as well as different cardboard shapes, including triangles, squares, and circles.*

Ken Davis

Creating symmetry with a mirror

Rick begins by using the mirror on the pictures on the table, and then starts going around the room, holding the mirror up to other objects to see whether they look symmetrical. He asks the teacher if they can go out to the playground to use the mirrors, where they use the mirrors to look at leaves, rocks, and the design on the fence.

The children begin to make a chart that lists "things that are symmetrical" and "things that are NOT symmetrical."

Liza sees that the children are interested in symmetry, and seem less interested in mirrors. They go on a walk around the neighborhood looking for things that are symmetrical, and the children begin to bring things in from their homes. Rick brings in a collection of seashells, some that are symmetrical and some that are not. Karen's mother has a collection of butterflies in a box, and Karen notices that they are symmetrical in their patterns; she asks her mother to come in to share her collection with the class.

Liza generates more ideas about how to study symmetry. Because it is a snowy winter, she decides to use the book Snowflake Bentley (Martin, 2009) to launch a study of snowflakes, and discovers a number of websites relating to snowflakes and their designs and patterns. The children create their own snowflakes, using print blocks and folded paper. The print blocks provide particular challenges, as the children must think carefully about each side of the paper to reproduce the other side. They also begin to use rulers to check the symmetry of their patterns, determining the placement of the block from the middle of the paper on each side.

Questions to Consider

1. Think about how symmetry is represented in art, in music, in literacy. What are some examples of symmetry in these areas?
2. How could a teacher support the connections across the different curriculum domains—symmetry in nature, in literacy, in the arts? What could she say or do to support the children making these connections?

Comparisons and Tools of Measurement

Making comparisons is an important element of the study of balance. Think about the different variables that can be compared. Children can compare length, number, volume, weight, size or mass, time, distance, speed, shape, and angles. Tools of measurement, such as the rulers used in the making of snowflakes, or the pan balance in determining equal amounts of birdseed, are important ways to make comparisons and to establish balance. Although children of different ages may be more or less familiar with tools of measurement, it's helpful to have many available and to both support and encourage their use. Some tools to consider are rulers, meter sticks, tape measures, compasses, stop watches, pan balances, weight balances, levels, scales, measuring cups of various kinds, Unifix cubes, and string.

Depending on the children's age and experiences, they may be more or less interested in the different variables, and more or less capable of using the different tools in a meaningful way. For example, younger children can use string to make measurements of length. Children can learn that a non-standard tool, such as string, can be compared to other objects for measurement. This comparison between objects that can't be moved is called transitivity. They learn that if the string is as long as the wall, then the comparison with the edge of the table means that the table is as long as or shorter than the wall.

However, by introducing rulers, which can be used in the same way as a piece of string, the relationship between numbers and units is implied. When those numbers are then used to represent length, children are given more and more experiences that will support their construction of numbers. Similarly, a balance can effectively compare the weight of objects; when the balance also incorporates numbers to represent the different weights of the objects it is adding to the child's experiences with number in a natural and authentic way. It is important that children learn to make comparisons without numbers before and at the same time as they use numbers, however—otherwise, the numbers are learned without their underlying meaning. Children who don't understand number concepts, for example, can learn to measure using a ruler in a way that leads to errors—because the numbers are meaningless to them, and they only know the "rule" that the larger number is longer.

Angelina and Rurik are arguing about which one of them has the longer road in the building area of their preschool. Rurik's road is straight, and Angelina's has curves in it, but they both start and end at the same place. Rurik insists

Comparing the lengths of roads

that his is just as long as hers. He uses a tape measure to show her. "See, they are both 4 feet long!" Angelina says, just as insistently, that hers is longer, because it has curves in it. She takes a piece of string, and lays it out against her road, then stretches it out and measures it with the tape measure. "No, see, mine is 6 feet long." Because Rurik does not understand the conservation of length, he cannot accept her answer— he only looks at the starting and ending points of the road.

It's not unusual for young children to learn how to use a tool without understanding, and it's important to think about what the child does and does not know about the number concepts underlying the tool use.

Questions to Consider

1. Think about how children might use another tool (e.g., glass measuring cups) to make comparisons without understanding what they are measuring.
2. What kinds of experiences would Rurik need to construct an understanding of conservation of length?
3. Why do you think these understandings can't be taught directly? What happens when you try to teach such understandings directly?

The Use of Representations

When representations are used to represent balance, simple arithmetic and the underlying principles of algebra are introduced. For example, with a math balance that has hanging weights (Figure 7-2), children can see visual representations of addition and equations.

So, for example, the child can see that a weight hung on the 5 mark can be balanced by another weight on the 5 mark, *or* by two weights, one hung on the 2 mark and one on the 3 mark. What is important is that the numbers are representing weights, rather than being used alone, so that the child can connect the numbers to the objects being represented.

Figure 7-2
Math Balance

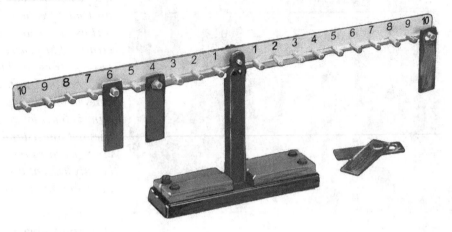

Source: Ken Davis

It's also important to recognize that there are developmental issues here. Younger children, like David and Maria comparing the halves of the apple, would not necessarily be able to conceptualize the numerical representation of the apple parts. Older children would, however. So, for example, if David and Maria were first graders, they could weigh each person's apple—David the half apple, and Maria's three pieces. The numerical representation of each half could be represented as follows:

David's apple: 5 ounces

Maria's apple: 2 ounces + 2 ounces + 1 ounce = 5 ounces

In this way, the representation of the equality of the two halves is made explicit using numbers and a simple equation.

Looking again at the distribution of bird feeders from the earlier scenario, the children can be encouraged to represent each set of bird feeders in a variety of ways—with drawings, tally marks, and numbers, for example. Kindergarten through second-grade children are varied in their understanding of number concepts, a fact that is often unrecognized in the mathematics taught to young children. When children are given opportunities to use a variety of representations, including but not restricted to number, they actually come to see the meaning of the numerical representation, and learn from peers the many possibilities. It is the *teacher* who provides this range of opportunities, which both respects each child's level of understanding and supports them as they come to deeper understanding of numbers.

The challenge of teachers of young children is to acknowledge the wide range of understandings of mathematics, as there are preschool-age children who may have an understanding of one-to-one correspondence, for example, and some second-grade children who do not.

Questions to Consider

Find a sample of an arithmetic problem in a textbook for first-grade children.

1. How does it provide for a variety of strategies for children to use in solving the problem?
2. If it doesn't, how could you as a teacher modify it so that this is possible?

Josie, the director of a preschool that has 3- to 5-year-old children in age-separated classrooms, engages her teachers in a school-wide project, inspired by some of the children's interests in the Summer Olympics, particularly the track and field competitions. Each class-room teacher decides to approach the project in slightly different ways, but they all agree that one of the shared goals is to focus on measurement.

Sue, the teacher of the 3-year-old classroom, begins the project by showing the children a video clip of a short sprint competition, and asks the children if they would like to create their own race. "We can't run that fast!" says Robert. "Yes we can," says Lisa, "I can run faster than you." The children decide to go out onto the playground and run races. After some excited running alongside each other, Robert says that they need to start at the same place. After determining the starting point, the children run as far as they can until they stop. "I won!" says Dan. "No you didn't, you just went farther than me, but I ran faster than you!" says Robert.

James, the teacher of the 5-year-old classroom, decides to show the children a video clip of the long jump to provoke their ideas and interest. His class decides to do the long jump, and the children immediately set up a starting point and a jumping point before they begin. The focus, then, is on measuring the length of the jump, and there are many different ideas about how to do this. Jess suggests that they mark the length using their feet, but Maren says, "Your feet are longer than my feet!" Debbie runs and gets a meter stick, and begins to use it to measure the length of the jump.

The teachers at the school meet to discuss the project, and compare notes on the different understandings of, and interests in, measurement across the age groups, as well as the differences between children. Sue, for example, notes that some of the children, like Robert, have an understanding of the "starting point," whereas others do not. James is surprised at how much prior understanding of measurement many of his children have.

Games That Incorporate Balance: Physical Knowledge

Some games that children play incorporate balance, and are useful supports for the development of physical knowledge that underlies logico-mathematical understanding (Kamii & Rummelsburg, 2008). Some commercial games, such as Don't Spill the Beans™ and Jenga™, can be used, or they can stimulate the construction of similar games by the teacher.

Marisa, a kindergarten teacher, has read Kamii and Rummelsburg's (2008) article and decides to try one of the balance games they describe. In this game, the children put a paper plate on top of an empty plastic bottle, and take turns adding Unifix cubes onto the plate, with the goal of keeping it from falling over. The children play this game in pairs, as they suggest in the article, and enthusiastically engage. Cory and Alice place Unifix cubes alternately on each side, beginning in the middle of the plate, until it falls over. They then start over, placing the cubes in a circular pattern as they alternate, and find that they can use more cubes with this strategy.

Marisa is encouraged by the spontaneous counting and comparisons that the children engage in during this game, and extends it by offering different sizes of paper plates and differently weighted attribute blocks (thin and thick circles and squares) to make the game more complex. The children talk about how two thin circles are the same as one thick one as they use them to balance.

Marisa sees the value of providing the children with these physical knowledge activities, based on Kamii and Rummelsburg's research, which showed an increase in the children's use of arithmetic despite the fact that the children did not directly study arithmetic in the classroom, but rather engaged in physical knowledge games. The links between children's engagement in experimentation in a balance game and the construction of logico-mathematical knowledge are important to support the incorporation of games of this sort into the early childhood curriculum.

Jenga™ is a game in which children remove, one at a time, blocks from a stack until the stack can no longer stand and falls over. Because this game is appropriate for children from kindergarten on (although some younger children can engage in it), Judith, who teaches 3- and 4-year-old children, decides to modify it to make it possible for her children to play.

Unit blocks used like a Jenga game

Judith builds a stack of unit blocks into a structure much like the Jenga™ game.

She poses the question to the children: Can you take out one block and keep the stack standing? The children quickly gravitate to this activity, and there is a good deal of stack falling, much to the children's delight. Judith notices that the goal of the game, from the children's perspective, is to figure out how to make the stack fall, rather than how to keep it balanced. She recognizes that this is an equally valuable experience for the children in constructing an understanding of balance.

As Judith reflects on this experience, she also realizes the difference in effect the scale of the activity has. Making a large structure fall is more dramatic than making a small structure fall. She also recognizes that this is how the children are exploring the materials, and decides to keep the activity as a choice to see how the experience changes over time.

Seth has been playing with the stacking blocks for several days, and he and Bobbi declare that they are going to see whether they can keep a stack from falling. They begin to pull a block out slowly, and when they see that the structure is going to fall, quickly push it back into the structure and select a different block. Other children begin to try the same game, and gradually the group gravitates to trying to make the structure balance as long as possible.

Judith's prediction was confirmed—the children did need to see how they could make the structure fall before they could figure out how to make it stay balanced.

Questions to Consider _____

1. What is the difference between exploration of materials and play with materials?
2. Can you think of other situations where children first need to explore materials before they can engage in experimentation with them?
3. How do children learn about balance by making the stacks fall over?

Review Questions

1. What are the three elements of the big idea of balance discussed in this chapter? Elaborate on one of them.
2. Select one of the explorations of balance (symmetry, comparisons, use of representations, games) and analyze it.
3. Design an activity, project, or exploration that integrates math and science in the study of balance.

Summary

In this chapter, we've discussed three elements of the study of balance: (1) making comparisons through estimation and measurement; (2) the study of patterns; and (3) the establishment of equality, the basis for algebraic thinking that involves arithmetic. We've also explored four approaches to studying balance as a big idea: (1) the study of symmetry; (2) comparisons and tools of measurement; (3) the use of representations, including numbers; and (4) games that incorporate balance with a focus on physical knowledge. Although there may be other interesting approaches to incorporating both math and science into the study of balance, looking at these may help to generate further ideas. In the following section, we will elaborate on two different ways of exploring balance with both younger and older children, showing how they are connected to the math and science standards.

Symmetry
- property of an obj.
    butterflies
    geometric shape

Some animals are
Plants are
Only symmetrical
if rotated at
certain degrees

symmetrical - a transformation that leaves that object unchanged

Rotate it - identical to
120° orginal

Rotate it - not identical
90°

Science - bilateral symmetry
human body L + R side

Modules for Chapter 7: Balance

MODULE 7-1 FOCUS: BALANCE

Common Core State Standards for Math

Kindergarten: Counting and Cardinality
Count to tell the number of objects.
Third Grade: Measurement and Data
Represent and interpret data.

Next Generation Science Standards

K-2-ETS1 Engineering Design

K-2-ETS1-1. Ask questions, make observations, and gather information about a situation people want to change to define a simple problem that can be solved through the development of a new or improved object or tool.

K-2-ETS1-2. Develop a simple sketch, drawing, or physical model to illustrate how the shape of an object helps it function as needed to solve a given problem.

K-2-ETS1-3. Analyze data from tests of two objects designed to solve the same problem to compare the strengths and weaknesses of how each performs.

Head Start Child Development and Early Learning Framework

Math

Recognizes and names common shapes, their parts, and attributes.

Combines and separates shapes to make other shapes.

Compares objects in size and shape.

Integrating Math and Science: Houses in the Block Center

Setting: Preschool

Michelle's preschoolers were building houses in the block center. There were four children, each building his or her representation of a house. Christian's house was a small enclosure built with unit blocks on their sides, Kendra's house had blocks stacked together with no space inside, and the other children had variations of these designs. "My house is going to have a roof!" said Christian. He was carefully trying to place a flat board on top of his enclosure. Kendra watched him and looked at her house. "My house doesn't need a roof, it already has one," she said. Christian's attempt to get his roof to fit wasn't going very well because it required balancing the edges on all the blocks and the board was just barely big enough. Kendra offered some advice, "You need to make your house smaller so the roof will fit." She counted the blocks Christian had used, "One, two, three . . . you have three blocks on this side, and this side, and this side, and this side." She surveyed the structure as she sat back on her heels, "You need to use two blocks on this side, and this side, and this side, and this side," she said, pointing to each side. Christian thought about it for a moment and then took the house apart to rebuild it with fewer blocks. "Christian! Why'd you do that?" exclaimed Kendra, "you could'a just taken a block away from this side, and this side, and this side, and this side!" Michelle had been listening to this exchange and offered an extension of Kendra's thinking, "So, each side has to be the same for the roof to balance?" "Yeah!" said Kendra.

Scenario Questions

1. What do you think might have prompted house building in the block center? What themes of play are common in block centers?
2. Can you think of ways Michelle could have provoked house building in the block center if it wasn't occurring?
3. What concept was Michelle trying to reinforce? What other questions or problems could she use to extend this even further?

Content Questions

1. What attributes of unit blocks reinforce the concept of balance? One-to-one correspondence?
2. What would children do, and what concepts would be involved, if you introduced blocks that were half-sizes of the unit blocks?
3. What are ways to represent what the children are doing mathematically?

Integrating Math and Science: Circus Tightrope Walkers

Setting: Third Grade

Many third graders had gone to the circus and had become fascinated with the tightrope walkers. The children were talking about how scary that would be, and how they had used a really long pole to help with balance. Their enthusiasm was played out on the playground, with several of them walking along the balance beam that was a few inches above the ground. After trying this, they appreciated the performers' feats even more. Toni, their teacher, had heard their comments and had seen them trying out the balance beam on the playground. A few days later she showed the class a video of Nic Wallenda's walk that was a time-lapse recording. "The time lapse makes it easy to see the pole going up and down on the ends. I bet I could walk the whole balance beam if I had that pole," said Mark. "Aw, that pole is too big for our balance beam," said Carla. This led to a discussion about what could be used as a balance beam pole. They decided to try a broom and a classroom pointer. Toni set up a chart so they could keep track of the size of the pole, the height of the child, and the time staying up on the beam.

Scenario Questions

1. What do you think the teacher's purpose was in showing the children the time-lapse video?
2. What vocabulary do you think might be included in this activity?
3. Time-lapse photography is used for many different purposes. How could time-lapse photography help children understand the concept of time?
4. What are some ways that numbers and measurement can be incorporated into this activity in addition to the chart that Toni introduces?

Content Questions

1. What factors have to be taken into consideration in this kind of balancing?
2. How does a physical exploration of the concept of balance help children understand the concept of equality?
3. Gravity is part of the concept of balance. What does "your center of gravity" mean?
4. How can algebraic equations be used in considering the ideas of balance?

Children's Literature with a Focus on Balance

These titles explore the physical concept of balance and equality.

McCully, E. A. (1997). *Mirette on the high wire.* New York: Puffin Books.
   This Caldecott-winning book is about overcoming fear. Mirette is a 19th-century French girl who meets a former tightrope walker who is now living at Mirette's mother's boarding house. Mirette learns to walk the tightrope to help her new friend conquer his fear.

LeSeig, T. (1961). *Ten apples up on top.* New York: Beginner Books.
   This classic follows a dog, lion, and tiger as they compete to see how many apples each can balance on his head.

Wood, A., & Wood, D. (1995). *Piggies.* New York: Sandpiper.
   This delightfully illustrated book is basically a finger-play to do with children. The focus on five fingers for each hand is an opportunity to talk about equal or same. The pigs are also doing some balancing acts.

Websites

Science for Kids

This is part of the official website for the American Chemical Society and offers a large variety of simple science activities that are appropriate for P–4. Search under "balance" and you will find activities that explore different perspectives of balance.

Exploratorium Science Snacks

The Exploratorium website contains many ideas and activities and much information about science, including a number of activities relating to balance.

Gamesgames.com

This website has fairly straightforward video games that involve some form of balance. In one game you slide sloths along poles by tipping the game field with the arrow keys. In another game you build towers by clicking on "drop" when a pendulum is in the right spot with a box. (Note: There are ads on this website.)

Further Explorations of the Big Idea for Teachers

1. Try to balance a pipe cleaner on some part of your body. What do you have to do to the pipe cleaner to get it to balance? What was the easiest way to balance it? What was the hardest way to balance it? What kind of conversation did this activity start? What words did people have to use?
2. Introduce beads or weights to the pipe-cleaner activity. What concepts do you find yourself thinking about as you try to balance the pipe cleaner with weights on each side?
3. Play Jenga™ or Pick-up Sticks™ with a small group. What do you have to consider before moving a piece?

Further Exploration of the Big Idea for Children

1. Place two different kinds of balances in an exploration center with a variety of materials. Try to vary the materials according to weight so that some things look similar but have very different weight.
2. Make mystery blocks. Use small shoeboxes weighted on one end or in the middle with cans, and some with nothing in them. What happens when the blocks don't act the way children predict?
3. Using plastic hangers, give children materials to hang from the hanger to make mobiles. Provide an assortment of different objects of different weights, wire, and string.

MODULE 7-2 FOCUS: SYMMETRY

Common Core State Standards for Math

Kindergarten: Geometry

Analyze, compare, create, and compare shapes

Math Practice 5

Use appropriate tools strategically

Next Generation Science Standards

K-PS2 Motion and Stability: Forces and interactions
Analyze data to determine if a design solution works as intended to change the speed or direction of an object with a push or a pull.

Head Start Child Development and Early Learning Framework

Math

Begins to make comparisons between several objects based on a single attribute.

Science

Begins to use sense and a variety of tools and simple measuring devices to gather information, investigate materials, and observe processes and relationships.
Develops increased ability to observe and discuss common properties, differences and comparisons among objects and materials.

Integrating Math and Science: Butterflies

Setting: Preschool

Mount Magazine in Arkansas is home to over 127 varieties of butterflies, which prompted a butterfly festival to be held each June. This was a great time in Jessica's preschool classroom to focus on the varieties and attributes of butterflies. Some of the activities the children had previously participated in involved painting pictures of butterflies, dressing up in butterfly wings, and reading The Very Hungry Caterpillar *(Carle, 1984). This year Jessica wanted to focus on the big idea of symmetry and butterflies. She put out mirrors that could be held in the middle of a picture of a butterfly. The children could then see that the butterfly wings looked the same with the mirror and without. Four-year-old Payton exclaimed, "Look! The wings are the same on both sides. The color is the same; the circle is the same. Everything is alike!"*

Scenario Questions

1. What ideas and knowledge do you think Jessica had reinforced about butterflies in the past? What children had learned about butterflies before Jessica changed her focus?
2. What can Jessica do to capture the children's comments and ideas about butterfly wings?
3. How do you think she has her classroom set up to meet children's need for exploration?
4. What can she do to reinforce scientific vocabulary?

Content Questions

1. Why is the study of the butterfly important? What do you know about butterflies?
2. How are butterflies similar to or different from other insects?
3. Many teachers use butterflies to study the life cycle of insects. What do children learn from this that can be applied to plants and other animals?
4. How does children's developmental age impact their ability to truly understand what is happening during the chrysalis stage?
5. How are butterflies supported in the environment? What are some of the butterflies that are common in your area? What kinds of place-based science topics could you study?

Integrating Math and Science: Hearts

Setting: First Grade

Tara's first graders were busy decorating their boxes for Valentine's Day. They had started by tracing stencils of hearts and were working really hard to get their scissors around the curves on the heart. "Hey, I can make my heart real easy," said Wendy. "This is the way my big sister did hers at home." She took a rectangular piece of paper, folded it rather haphazardly, and then began cutting on an outside edge. It soon became apparent that this was creating two shapes and not one heart. "Huh, what happened? I folded my paper, but it didn't make a heart," said Wendy. Maggie picked up the pieces and said, "Yeah, and one of the sides is a lot bigger than the other side." Tara asked the children, "Remember when we talked about the line of symmetry in math? What makes the sides symmetrical?" Maggie said, "You have to cut from the fold, see—like this! See, my heart has a side this big and the other side is the same size!" Wendy declared, "Well, I've seen pictures of REAL hearts and they don't look like this anyway."

Scenario Questions

1. How do you think the teacher set this activity up? What could have made a stronger connection to the idea of symmetry?
2. What did the teacher do to help the students with the vocabulary? What else could be done to increase the student's use of the concept of symmetry?
3. What are some of the issues involved in activities connected to holidays?
4. What would you do to respond to Wendy's last comment?

Content Questions

1. Symmetry is a way to describe geometrical shapes. The correspondence of shapes around a line or a point is a way of looking at symmetry. Why would it be important to explore both regular shapes and irregular shapes for symmetry?
2. Why is symmetry an important part of the concept of balance?
3. How could symmetry be used in science to help children make observations?
4. What is the connection between form, function, and symmetry?

Children's Literature with a Focus on Symmetry

Leedy, L. (2013). *Seeing symmetry*. New York: Holiday House.
 Leedy's book covers many different ways of finding symmetry and thinking about how to create symmetry.
Martin, J. B. (2009). *Snowflake Bentley*. New York: HMH Books for Young Readers.
 There are many examples of symmetrical objects in nature. Snowflakes offer an especially motivating way of thinking about symmetrical shapes. This biographical picture book also gives children background information about science and the passion scientists have for their subjects.
Murphy, S., & Floca, B. (2000). *Let's fly a kite*. New York: HarperCollins.
 Two children not only learn about the concept of symmetry, they also have to cooperate with each other.
Schrier, A. V. (2006). *Reading essentials discovering and exploring science: Symmetry in nature*. Logan, IA: Perfection Learning.
 Photography is used to create a new way of looking at nature.

Websites

Symmetry Game—Innovations Learning
This game will test your understanding of symmetry and will also help you
understand why children need to have physical knowledge reinforced
in order to understand many concepts. This website would also work for
older children.

Great Math Games
Great Math Games touches on several different aspects of symmetry that will
be useful for planning lessons. It also has many interactive games that
would be fun and informative for children.

Math Is Fun
This is a free-form tool that creates symmetrical designs.

Links Learning
This website presents content knowledge in a straightforward style. It would
work well for children who have already had physical knowledge experiences with folding lines of symmetry.

PBS Kids Go Cyberchase
At this interactive website, children can play with different forms of symmetry
and cartoon characters.

Mrs. Judd's Snowflake Station
This is an app for iPads that supports children in creating symmetrical designs.

Further Exploration of the Big Idea for Teachers

1. Make paper airplanes. How many different kinds of symmetry
   have to be used to make planes that fly? How does balance work
   in this process?
2. Research the process of folding paper to create art. Some forms
   of folded paper art are fairly common, such as origami, but there
   are many other ways artists use balance and symmetry in their
   structures. Andy Goldsworthy is an example of an artist who has
   taken symmetry and balance to new places in nature.
3. Make mobiles. Experiment with shapes and weight to create
   symmetrical mobiles and asymmetrical mobiles that require careful weight distribution.

Further Exploration of the Big Idea for Children

1. Make class books about the symmetry in nature. Give children
   stiff cardboard with heavy-duty clips at the top for individual note-
   pads. The children can sketch the symmetrical shapes in the classroom and outdoors.

Another way to capture images for a book or poster would be to give the children inexpensive cameras and have them take photos of the symmetry around them.

2. Give children one half of a picture of a face. They can glue it to a sheet of paper and draw the other half, paying close attention to symmetry and balance of features.

3. Put out different colors of paint and paper. Have children explore symmetry by placing a small amount of paint on the paper and then folding it in half. The opened paper will have a design of symmetry on it that can become a character in a story. Make sure the paint is thick enough to spread without running. Show the children that very small amounts work better than more.

8 Relationships

Learning Outcomes

After working with the ideas in this chapter, you should be able to:

- Define key ideas about relationships in math and science.
- Understand the role of cause and effect, part/whole, classification, and interdependence in math and science.
- Create applications for integrating a focus on relationships in math and science.

Standards Addressed in This Chapter

Common Core State Standards for Mathematics

Kindergarten: Counting and Cardinality
Know number names and the count sequence
Count to tell the number of objects
Compare numbers

Second Grade: Operations and Algebraic Thinking
A Work with equal groups of objects to gain foundations for multiplication

Next Generation Science Standards

K-PS2-2 Analyze data to determine if a design solution works as intended to change the speed of direction of an object with a push or a pull.
3-PS2-1 Plan and conduct an investigation to provide evidence of the effects of balanced and unbalanced forces on the motion of an object.

Head Start Child Development and Early Learning Framework

Science
Shows increased awareness and beginning understanding of changes in materials and cause-effect relationships

INTRODUCTION TO THE BIG IDEA OF RELATIONSHIPS

Constructing relationships is at the heart of logico-mathematical knowledge, and also underlies much of science in terms of the relationships of variables. In this chapter we emphasize the big idea of relationships, where this is the focus of children's explorations and experimentation. As in previous chapters, we center the discussion on a few elements of relationships that lend themselves best to integration of math and science in ways that engage children.

Let's start by looking at an example involving the first element we will examine, the exploration of **causal relationships**—those in which one thing leads to another.

Randy is the teacher of a first-grade class that has been reading about Rube Goldberg's inventions, looking at books and pictures, as well as viewing excerpts from videos (such as "The Way Things Go") that give sophisticated examples of chain reactions. The children become fascinated with this idea, and decide that they would like to construct their own chain reactions. They decide to do it in the form of a marble rollway, similar to the game of Mousetrap ™. Randy decides to first give them some experiences with marble rollways, and brings in pipe insulation, tape, and marbles. The class engages in free construction with the materials. After a follow-up whole-group discussion, Randy decides to divide them into small groups of three or four children, and each group is assigned the task of coming up with an element of the chain, incorporating some challenges that the children have generated. For example, one of the challenges is to set up a chain that involves a marble going through the air; another challenge is that a marble must knock something over. The challenges are written on cards, and each group picks two cards to use, with the understanding that groups can swap cards if they want.

The groups work over several days, designing their components, acquiring the materials needed, and then experimenting with the materials to construct the final

Figure 8-1
Make a Marble Ring a Bell

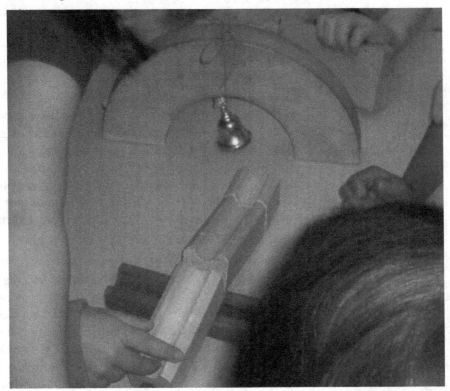

Source: Ken Davis

version. Randy requires each group to describe its component on a large card,
using symbols (Figure 8-1). Each group then shares the component with the
class, after which the group decides how to link all the components together into
one large rollway by creating a storyboard of the final rollway, using the com-
ponent cards created by each group. Once this is determined, more small-group
work on the links between components occurs. The final rollway is set up in the
multipurpose room, and other classes are invited to an unveiling.

This large-scale project creates an engaging context in which the
children work, and math and science can be seen throughout the process, in different ways depending on each group's particular challenges
and solutions to problems. For example, one group has the challenge
of using a lever in the component, and experiments with the length of
the lever to use to propel the marble. Another group struggles with the
problem of getting the marble to go fast enough down an incline to
propel it across a gap, experimenting with the height of the incline to
arrive at the optimal speed. All of the groups have to learn to measure

and record their experiments in order to arrive at the final version of their components. By facing the challenge of creating a chain reaction, the children focus not on a simple causation—A leads to B—but have to articulate the more complex transitive relationship of A leads to B leads to C, which makes each link more visible. Math and science are integrated at the very heart of this big idea.

Questions to Consider_____

1. What are some examples of "chain reactions" that occur naturally?
2. Can you think of examples of chain reactions in children's literature?
3. Why do you think that focusing on a chain reaction puts more emphasis on cause and effect?
4. In a previous chapter, Rube Goldberg contraptions were a provocation for children's engagement in the big idea of movement. Think about how the same project could incorporate multiple "big ideas," and how you as the teacher can facilitate the focus, or can decide to follow the children's interests and engagement in the project.

ELEMENTS OF THE BIG IDEA OF RELATIONSHIPS

We will address four elements of the big idea of relationships: (1) cause and effect, or the relationship between events (as seen in the rollways example); (2) part/whole relationships, particularly focusing on zooming in and out; (3) classification; and (4) interdependence and perspective-taking.

Cause and Effect

As we saw in the rollway example, examining chain reactions makes causal relationships more explicit and visible. There are also ways of focusing on simple cause-and-effect relationships. One way is through the study of gears, and another is through oppositional causal relationships, such as levers and pulleys.

Amy's kindergartners have been playing with some commercial gear toys (some examples are Gears! Gears! Gears!™ and Georello Tech Gear Set™), and seem interested in how the toys are working. She decides to explore how gears work with the children. She begins by asking them to draw gears, and to show how the gears move on their drawings. Rory carefully handles the gears as he makes his drawings, and decides to trace them onto his paper. Amy asks him to explain how one gear moves another, and he says, "See, when you turn this one, then this one turns." His gestures indicate that when he turns one in a clockwise direction, the other one moves in a clockwise direction too. Josie, who is sitting next to him, says, "No, silly, they turn the other way!" Rory and Josie have a lively discussion about how the gears move, with Rory initially defending his idea, and eventually being convinced otherwise.

Amy then suggests that the children make their own gears, and provides them with some self-hardening clay that they have used in another project. Some of the children make pointed teeth and some make squared ones, with lots of discussion about what will work and what won't. They also decide to make different sizes of gears, and study the gear toys for ideas. After the gears have hardened, the children try the gears on the table top, using all of the gears together.

Amy is observing the children throughout this process, and notices that they seem to understand the idea of the gear teeth, and how they need to fit together. She's interested to see what new understandings will come about as they experiment with different sizes of gears, particularly in terms of how fast the gears move depending on the gear that is being moved—does a small gear move another gear faster or slower than a large gear? She asks the children for their ideas during the morning meeting, and different ideas are shared. The resulting work on this project is unexpected:

Rory notices that when he moves the large gear with the small gear, it does not make a full rotation in sync with the small gear (Figure 8-2). He then switches the two gears, and sees that the larger gear does not have to make a full rotation to turn the small gear around. He counts the number of teeth that need to move on the large gear, and then counts the number of teeth on the small gear. He shares what he is doing at the morning meeting, and more of the children start counting and examining the relationship between the number of teeth turning and the size of the gear being turned.

Although Amy had not intended to introduce number as an element of the exploration of gears, she capitalizes on the children's spontaneous use of number in this context. She suggests that they make some more gears with different numbers of teeth, and provides a piece of chart paper to record the relationships they are finding. In this way, the exploration of gears has effectively integrated math and science in a meaningful and child-directed way.

Figure 8-2
A Small Gear Turning a Larger Gear

Source: Ken Davis

Questions to Consider _____

1. How could Amy have provoked the number relationship if the topic had not come about naturally?
2. What does it tell you about the children and about Amy's classroom that Rory thinks to use number in his explorations?

Levers are interesting ways to move an object, because when you push *down* on a lever, the object on the other end goes *up*. Similarly, when you pull down on a pulley, the object you are moving goes up. When you experience something that is unexpected, it is more noticeable, and the experience can lead to more explicit thinking about the relationship than if it is an expected or congruent relationship.

Lucinda's second-grade classroom has been reading a story that includes the use of a catapult to attack a castle. The children become interested in how a catapult works, and decide, with Lucinda's encouragement, to embark on a project to make catapults. As a class, they decide that they will try to catapult a ping-pong ball across the room, after a lively discussion about safety issues. To make the catapult, Lucinda and the children gather together materials, with the help of some parents. (Lucinda has put in the class newsletter a story of the

Figure 8-3
A Lever and a Catapult

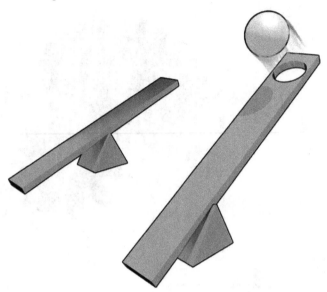

Source: Ken Davis

project, using the children's descriptions, so that the parents will understand that this is a science activity and not focused on weapons.)

Because a catapult incorporates a lever, they begin by experimenting with levers, creating a holder for the ball at one end of a piece of wood, and a fulcrum for the lever (Figure 8-3).

They experiment with different lengths of the lever, and with different heights of the fulcrum, exploring the relationships. They decide to make several catapults so that they can test out the most effective combination of lever length and fulcrum size. With ping-pong balls flying around the classroom, Lucinda records what she is hearing the children talking about. "Look! The higher the fulcrum, the farther the ball goes!" "I think when the lever is too long, it can't go as fast."

While looking at books about levers and how they work, Lucinda notices that many of them talk about *force* as a concept. She decides that this concept is beyond her children's understanding, and does not focus on force as a variable. However, she does use the word as she talks to the children about what they are doing, knowing that introducing vocabulary will help the children as they begin to construct their understandings.

Questions to Consider_____

1. Think about how Lucinda is documenting the children's experimentation. How can she use what the children are saying as they

experiment to assess their understanding? How can she use it to communicate to parents and others about what they are doing?

2. Look at science activities that incorporate levers, and see what they say about "force." Do you think Lucinda made a good decision to not explicitly introduce the concept of force? Can *you* explain what force means in physics?

Part/Whole Relationships

One of the ways to explore part/whole relationships is to introduce children to the idea of zooming in and out. This is something that fascinates children (and adults!), and there are many good examples of video clips to provoke an interest in zooming. One occurs at the end of the movie *Men in Black* (1997), in which the street scene zooms out to the earth, which zooms out to show the earth as a marble in a game being played by an alien. Another, particularly appropriate for older children (K–3), is the video "The Powers of Ten" (do an Internet search for "Powers of Ten") that begins with a couple lying on a beach and zooms out into the universe, then zooms in to inside their bodies and to the level of atoms.

Wendy is showing the book Zoom *(Banyai, 1998; you can also search for a video version of this book) to her third-grade class, intending it as a provocation for their exploration of part/whole relationships. This is a wordless book, in which each page is a zoom-out on one part of the previous page. So, the picture of a rooster on the first page is followed by a picture of a room on the second page in which there is a framed picture with a rooster in it on the wall, and on it goes; each page is a zoom-out of the previous page.*

After talking about the book with the class, she takes a digital photograph of the book sitting in their library in the classroom, and poses the question to the children: How could we zoom out from here? Excited, Jake says, "We zoom out to the school," and Mark says, "And then we zoom out to the neighborhood of the school."

At this point, Wendy has a number of possible directions she can take with the children. She decides to use this as an entryway into mapping, which can incorporate a good deal of the mathematics that she wants to explore with the children.

She begins by having the children map the classroom, intending to move on to mapping the school. For both projects, the children find they have to make measurements of the different parts of the room, and she introduces the idea of representing the area of a space. The map, including dimensions of each part of the room and areas of spaces, is put together on a large piece of chart paper. The children ask if there is a way to do this on the computer. Stefanie says, "My Dad uses a computer to do his work!" Her father is an architect, and has shown Stefanie how he designs spaces using a computer program. Wendy asks him to come show the class what he does, and he suggests a simpler computer program that would work for their purposes. Some of the children take on the computer design part of the project, while others continue to work on chart paper.

When they have completed this project, the children decide to do the same with the school. As they brainstorm how to create a map of the school, and begin exploring the school to decide how to approach this problem, one of the children sees a map of each floor that shows where the emergency exits are located. Wendy makes copies of these maps for the children to use.

The children's interest in this project is not waning, so Wendy decides to support taking it to the next step of zooming out. She introduces the children to Google Earth, which some of them have already seen.

The children locate their school, and discuss the idea of the "bird's-eye" perspective of a map. Projecting the neighborhood of the school onto a large piece of paper, the children trace the buildings onto large pieces of paper that can be put together to make the neighborhood. But Google Earth does not identify the buildings, so the children decide to go out into the neighborhood to identify the buildings they have seen on their "map" of the neighborhood.

Mapping poses many opportunities for the incorporation of mathematics—think about scale, for example, which brings fractions to life for the children. The children begin to think deeply about the idea of zooming out, particularly as they move to Google Earth. Wendy has also introduced computer technology as a tool for both mapping and zooming out to a bird's-eye perspective.

Another way to focus on part/whole relationships involves the study of scale, something addressed in maps but also explored in other ways.

Jorge's first-grade class has been playing soccer on the playground, and in the classroom they have been working with clay. Jorge starts to make a clay figure representing himself playing the game on the playground. The children at the table with him notice what he is doing, and start talking about making a whole team of soccer players, reproducing the game on the table. Their teacher, Jamie, overhears their discussion, and suggests they undertake it as a project.

While continuing to work on the clay figures, they also take pictures of the soccer field with children playing on it, and have a discussion about how big the field will have to be. Jamie suggests that they measure the field, borrowing an electronic tape measure from the custodian. They draw out the field on the whiteboard, and then add the players, represented by stick figures.

Jorge puts a piece of chart paper on the table, saying "This is the soccer field." Then he places his clay figure on the paper. A discussion ensues. "The field isn't big enough!" "It won't hold all the players that way!" The children decide that the field needs to be larger, and Jamie suggests that they measure the clay figures. She introduces the concept of scale, showing the children how maps use different scales depending on the map. The children struggle to figure out how big the soccer field needs to be, using the measurements they have for the clay figures and the relationship between their heights and the actual soccer field.

Jamie has been looking for a way to introduce children to meaningful uses of fractions, and is pleased that this came up spontaneously. When they begin to study fractions, she incorporates word problems using the soccer game they have created.

The study of scale doesn't have to incorporate numbers. Younger children can look at scale in terms of smaller and larger, and using technology can support this exploration, as in the following scenario:

Sierra's class of 4-year-olds is engaged in a study of faces. Her teacher, Jim, has taken digital photographs of each child. He prints out three versions of each—small, medium, and large—and cuts them out. He places them on a table, all mixed up, and is interested to see what the children might do with them. Some of the children gravitate to the table, including Sierra, who starts trying to find the three versions of her picture. Other children do the same, and then they excitedly match the different sizes. Sierra holds one up, and says, "Hi, I'm little Sierra, where is little Linda?" The two girls' pictures "talk" to each other. Then Sierra says, in a lower voice, "and I'm big Sierra!" Linda responds, also in a lower voice, "Hi, big Sierra, I'm big Linda!"

Jim is interested to see their spontaneous sorting of the three versions by size, and the matching that they do. He sees this as an opportunity to support the construction of one-to-one correspondence.

Jim reads the children the story of Goldilocks and the Three Bears, a story they are all familiar with. After the story, Linda says, "Hey, let's make houses for our pictures!" The children begin to draw different sizes of houses on paper to correspond with the size of each picture, then place the pictures on the corresponding "house."

Without incorporating numbers directly, Jim has provided numerous experiences for the children that will support the development of important number concepts, including seriation and one-to-one correspondence.

Questions to Consider

1. What do you think would happen if Jim introduced more than three different sizes of the pictures of the children? How would this further support their ideas of seriation?
2. What are some other materials that would lend themselves to supporting the construction of seriation? One-to-one correspondence?
3. How could number be incorporated into this activity in a meaningful way?

Classification

Children's construction of the understanding of classification involves relationships, particularly when we look at concepts of **class inclusion** and **hierarchical inclusion**. Very young children are able to identify characteristics of objects, and learn to separate groups of objects by shared characteristics. Understanding that an object can have two characteristics, one that includes another characteristic, is more difficult and requires experiences with materials and objects that focus on both the shared and unshared characteristics. For example, a knife and a spoon are different utensils, so both belong to the classification "utensils," but they each also belong to the group of "knives" or "spoons." So, a knife is both a knife *and* a utensil, and the classification "utensil" includes "knives." Members of a class are in relationship with each other with regard to the shared classification.

Betsy's group of 5-year-olds has decided to set up a grocery store in the dramatic play area. Betsy brings out a large bin filled with plastic and rubber objects, including many food items, but also including plastic animals and people, and poses the problem to the children of how they should sort through the objects to find what they need for the grocery story. Megan says, "I know, let's make two piles—those things that will go in the grocery store, and those things that don't." Steven says, "Yes, but we also need to have separate piles for the fruits and vegetables." The children decide to sort the objects into three piles, one for things that don't go in the grocery store, one for fruits and vegetables, and one for other things that go in the grocery store. A few of the children are engaged in this activity for quite some time. When they are done, Betsy asks the children,

"How many things go into the grocery store? How many things don't go into the grocery store?" The children count the objects in each pile, reporting the results of their counts. Betsy says again, "So, is there a way to figure out how many don't go in the grocery store?" Steven says, "Yes, we can count them!" He proceeds to put the objects together, and then counts them. Megan says, "Wait, you don't have to count them again, you can just add the two numbers."

Betsy realizes that the step to seeing the fruits and vegetables as also part of the "things for the grocery store" group is difficult for most of the children, Steven included, while some, like Megan, already understand the concept of class inclusion. Giving them experiences such as this, however, will support this construction of class inclusion for all of the children.

Questions to Consider

1. Why doesn't Betsy just tell the children how they can figure out this problem? Wouldn't that be easier than having Steven count all of the objects?
2. How does this experience support Megan's thinking?

Charlie's group of 3- and 4-year-olds likes to play with a set of attribute blocks. The blocks are all together in a bin, and have attributes of color, size, and thickness. Charlie realizes that these children do not have an understanding of class inclusion, but he wants to give them experiences that will support their thinking about classification. He finds a set of small trays, and puts the trays in the bin with the attribute blocks.

As the children play with the blocks, they take out the trays, and begin to put the blocks into each tray. Charlie notices that they are spontaneously classifying the objects, usually by one attribute—by color or by size, but not both. This confirms his thoughts about their understanding and the importance of giving them these opportunities.

Questions to Consider

1. Why doesn't Charlie ask the children to classify them into multiple groups?
2. How is this experience supporting the children's construction of class inclusion?
3. How is Charlie using his observations as information for assessment?

These experiences with classification are important for both math and science. Class inclusion underlies the understanding of number, as each number represents the group of numbers preceding it.

Classification is also essential for understanding much of the natural world. For example, think about the classifications of living things, and the multiple classifications that need to be understood. We need to be careful about teaching rules for classification as always being true because there will always be exceptions. It is better to focus children's attention on what makes certain rules true—that way, they are always thinking about differences and similarities.

Older children can engage in more complex multiple classifications, and are better able to engage in hierarchical inclusion, which is the concept that one object can be a member of many classes. For example, a lion is simultaneously a lion, a mammal, *and* a living thing. Visual representations, such as **Venn diagrams**, are both comprehensible and useful for older children's classification experiences.

Karen's second-grade classroom has decided to take on the challenge of organizing the classroom library, and she sees this as an opportunity to address issues of classification and representation of classification. They begin by brainstorming the different categories of books. As they do this, some of the categories are included in other categories. For example, there are books about animals, and some of them are fiction/story books, whereas others are nonfiction resource books. The children decide that both categories are important to have represented in their library. The list on the board looks like this:

Books about animals

Nonfiction

Fiction

The children begin to identify the books about animals, and put them into two piles. They then begin to identify the books about famous people, and find that some of these are fiction or nonfiction.

Karen draws two diagrams on the board:

Animals	**Famous people**	**Transportation**
Fiction/nonfiction	*Fiction/nonfiction*	*Fiction/nonfiction*

Fiction	**Nonfiction**
	Animals
	Famous people
	Transportation

The children vote on which way they should classify the books, and decide on the second one. Kerry says, "Whether a book is fiction or not fiction is a bigger thing than what the book is about."

Kerry is expressing the idea of hierarchical inclusion—why something represents a higher level of classification. The use of diagrams supported the children in seeing this relationship.

Perspective-Taking and Interdependence

Although taking a "bird's-eye perspective" could be seen as perspective-taking, and certainly introduces the idea, seeing it as the perspective of the bird brings in a slightly different emphasis, one that relates to the idea that there are multiple perspectives that are different. Perspective-taking has implications in both the social domain and the cognitive domain, and these two are intertwined. In the social domain, it implies the development of empathy, understanding the feelings of another person. It also can imply understanding the impact of one's actions on the world. For example, the act of putting waste in a stream, from the perspective of a factory, may be an efficient way to dispose of waste. From the perspective of the fish in the stream, this act has different implications and meanings. So, making perspective-taking explicit supports children's understanding of interdependence in the social and natural world, an important goal and value in our schools. In the cognitive domain, perspective-taking makes any given problem more complex, as it can be looked at in different ways. For example, the efficiency of waste disposal is complicated by thinking of the effects of the particular solution. Instead of looking at "A leads to B," we must look at "A leads to B, which then has an impact on A as well as on C" (Figure 8-4).

Anne reads the story of the blind men and the elephant to her second-grade class. She then takes the children out to the playground with their clipboards and drawing pencils, and positions them in a circle around a large play structure. She asks them to draw some part of what they see. When they have finished their sketches, they lay them out on a table in the classroom, and talk about the different things each of them focused on and drew. She then asks them to imagine that one of the pictures is the only one they have ever seen of the structure, and that based on that, and that alone, they have to describe what the entire structure looks like. The children write in their writing journals, and read the descriptions to each other in small groups.

In a whole-group discussion, they discuss what they learned by doing this. Dot says, "These people all thought they were right just from knowing one

Figure 8-4
Causal Relationships and Interdependence

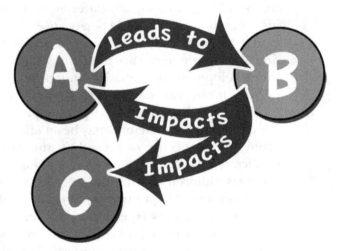

Source: Ken Davis

Zooming in with digital cameras

thing." "Yeah, it's sort of like when you only hear one side of a story!" Doug adds. Anne says to the group, Well, it's pretty amazing how limited you are if you only see one part of something."

Because she understands its importance, Anne has effectively integrated perspective-taking across different curriculum domains.

In a similar fashion, Kris's class of 4-year-olds has been learning how to use digital cameras, and she decides to focus on perspective-taking:

Kris takes a group of five children out to the playground after showing them how to zoom with the digital camera. She asks them to take some pictures that zoom in on one part of something on the playground. When they get inside, she has each child pick two pictures from the ones they took, and prints them out.

The next day at morning circle, she asks the children to project their pictures, and the group tries to guess what each is a picture of.

Both Kris and Anne have used different means to focus the children on physical perspective-taking, which is important for understanding many concepts in both mathematics and science.

Review Questions

1. What are some of the key ideas to use in integrating math and science around the big idea of relationships?
2. Discuss and analyze the role of cause and effect, part/whole, classification, and interdependence in math and science education.
3. Design an activity, project, or exploration that integrates math and science in the study of relationships.

Summary

In this chapter, we have described four elements of the big idea of relationships that can serve to integrate math and science: (1) cause and effect, or relationships between events; (2) part/whole relationships; (3) classification; and (4) perspective-taking and interdependence.

Cause and effect can represent simple to complex relationships. Part/whole relationships can be thought of as one thing or multiple things at the same time. Classification is the logical-mathematical thought process of applying rules for comparing and contrasting. Perspective-taking is looking at the complexity of interactions.

Through these—and other—elements of the big idea of relationships we can effectively integrate math and science in the early childhood classroom. In the modules to follow, we will examine some specific ways to do that.

Modules for Chapter 8: Relationships

MODULE 8-1 FOCUS: PART/WHOLE

Common Core State Standards for Math

Kindergarten:Geometry

Analyze, compare, create, and compose shapes.

Third Grade: Number and Operations—Fractions

Develop understanding of fractions as numbers.

Next Generation Science Standard

3-LS4-2 Use evidence to construct an explanation for how the variations in characteristics among individuals of the same species may provide advantages in surviving, finding mates, and reproducing.

Head Start Child Development and Early Learning Framework

Domain 3: Mathematics
Geometry and Spatial Sense: Begins to recognize, describe, compare, and name common shapes, their parts and attributes.

Integrating Math and Science: Quilts

Setting: Toddler Preschool Classroom

Alexis, a part-time student in the local university's early childhood teacher education program, also worked at a child-care facility in her neighborhood. Her math methods class at the university was focusing on teaching children about fractions, which wasn't her favorite topic, but she was learning some new things she hadn't thought about before. And her science methods class had been talking about why observation was so important. This was why, on this particular day, she had a pile of colorful quilts that had been made by people in her family.

Alexis spread two of the quilts on the floor of the toddler classroom, quilts that had really bright geometrical shapes used in the quilting patterns. She then put soft shapes from a toy collection on top of the quilts. As the 18-month-olds got up from their afternoon nap, they noticed the quilts and shapes and immediately wanted to explore this new terrain. As the children crawled and walked on the quilts, Alexis pointed out shapes in the quilts that matched the soft-sculpture toys. "Look, Mai! This triangle is red, just like these in the blanket." Alexis handed Mai the soft red triangle. Mai looked at the toy and promptly put one corner in her mouth. "Ha ha," laughed Alexis, "you put the corner of that triangle in your mouth!" Mai held the triangle out to Alexis with no obvious intent to give it back. "Look over here, Mai, this square has two red triangles in it." Mai plopped down and laid the soft-sculpture toy on top of the square. "Yea! You found the triangles in the square!"

This game went on for a minute or two and then Mai toddled off to a new toy, but Alexis noticed that another child was sitting on the square and was pointing to another square of red triangles.

Before Alexis had taken her math methods class, she would have never thought about doing an activity like this with toddlers, but they had talked in class a lot about how children needed many different experiences with language and shapes in order to later understand math concepts that involve fractions and geometry. Finding shapes within shapes was a great way to help the children notice patterns and parts of bigger shapes. Alexis planned on leaving the quilts out for the children to play with for a few days; she wanted to see if their interest led her to other ways of supporting their language and learning about shapes.

Scenario Questions

1. What other considerations about choosing materials do you think Alexis thought about? How does this relate to the importance of using materials that children have had experience with?
2. Why would it be important for Alexis to say "corner" and "triangle"?
3. What kind of language development did Alexis expect with this activity?
4. How could parts and wholes be emphasized at snack time?

Content Questions

1. What do children need to understand about parts and wholes before they can manipulate fractions using numbers?
2. What other kinds of materials would lend themselves to exploring parts and wholes?

3. The relationship between a part and its whole is something we can think about, but is not necessarily a concrete concept. How does the developmental task of conservation impact a child's ability to understand fractions?

4. What are the differences between regular shapes and irregular shapes? Why is it important to include both in our teaching?

5. Squares are special kinds of rectangles. Researchers (e.g., Cross, Woods, & Schweingruber, 2009) have found that using double-naming works well to teach children about squares ("Yes, that's a square-rectangle"). What other ways can you use double-naming when exploring shapes with young children?

Integrating Math and Science: Making Books

Setting: Third-Grade Classroom

There were many examples of children's illustrations in Jacob's third-grade classroom. The children enjoyed drawing and painting pictures to add to the stories they wrote. This prompted Jacob to bring in more illustrations into his math lessons and at the same time encourage children's science vocabulary.

"Today we are going to learn the special names of groups of animals. Do you know what we call several cows?" The children thought that was an easy one. "Herd!" many of them called out. "Well, I bet there are some you don't know—here's a list." Jacob distributed copied lists of different animals that were familiar to the children, but had little-used group names. "What I want you to do," Jacob told the children, "is to choose an animal and then illustrate what a fraction of the group might be doing in their natural habitat. How many animals are in your group will help you decide what number, or denominator, goes on the bottom of your fraction, and then how many are doing different behaviors in their habitat will tell you what number, or numerator, goes on top in your fraction." The children were very engaged in creating their groups and thinking of things different parts of the groups could be doing. This led to researching the animals so the illustrations would be correct. Jacob added the requirement that fraction symbols be written at the top of the pictures. As the illustrations were finished, Jacob could see that some of the children understood the concept of fractions, but some needed more experience with the three-dimensional fraction models used during math activity time.

Scenario Questions

1. Why did Jacob use animals the children were familiar with?
2. What do you think Jacob noticed when he looked at the children's pictures? What would tell him that some children didn't understand the concept of fractions?
3. Do you think this was the first time the children had used fraction symbols? Why or why not?

Content Questions

1. The Common Core State Standard for Math dealing with fractions at this level is multi-layered. Can you give a concrete example of each part of the standard?
2. How does a fractional counting sequence differ from simply having fractional pieces? Why is it important to use the correct language to describe a fractional counting sequence?
3. How we define the whole is very important. We can talk about parts of one whole or we can talk about fractional parts of sets. Can you think of an example for each?

Other Areas for Integrating Fractions and Part/Whole Relationships

Social Studies: Equal shares during snack time or at class parties can be talked about. You may hear children say, "I got the bigger half." This is an opportunity to clarify that if it is truly "half," both pieces will be the same size.

Art: Looking closely at classic pieces of art can foster a rich discussion of all the things that can be seen in a larger picture. Shapes, colors, lines, and familiar objects can all be discovered in paintings that are easily found on the Internet.

Music: With younger children, simply enjoying the rhythm of familiar tunes reinforces part/whole relationships. Asking

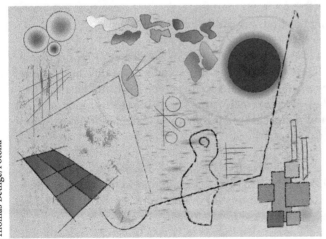

Thomas Bethge/Fotolia

Shapes within shapes

preschoolers to find the beat in a song that has more than one tempo helps them think about the differences within a melody. With older children, looking at the written form of music helps them see that music is made up of smaller parts that create a recognizable whole.

Children's Literature with Focus on Part/Whole Relationships

These titles emphasize part/whole, fractions, perspective, and classification.

Munsch, R., & Martchenko, M. (1983). *David's father.* Toronto, Canada: Annick Press.

> This story about a giant for a father includes several items that have to be over-large for the giant.

Hoban, T. (1986). *Shapes, shapes, shapes.* New York: Greenwillow Books.

> Tana Hoban's photography opens up new worlds in all of her books. *Shapes, Shapes, Shapes* is particularly good at presenting smaller shapes within larger shapes.

Hoban, T. (1997). *Look book.* New York: Greenwillow Books.

> In another Tana Hoban book, we are first presented with a small cut-out in the page that we can look through to see a piece of the next page, revealing puzzling shapes and colors. Only by turning the page do we recognize a familiar object in our world.

Jocelyn, M. (2004). *Hannah's collections.* Toronto, Canada: Tundra Books.

> Hannah has to take a collection to school to share, but she has so many it's difficult to decide which one to take. She solves her problem in a very creative way.

Websites

Virtual Manipulatives

Many activities involving fractions are available on this website.

Mathwire

This website has collected hundreds of classroom activities to support teaching math. It is searchable using key themes, standards, and topics. A large number of worksheets on this website are not necessarily the best way to teach a topic, but there are also many worksheets that can support the child's organization of materials for classification activities and part/whole problems.

Illuminations

This highly organized teaching resource from the National Council for the Teaching of Mathematics (NCTM) is a searchable website that contains detailed lesson plans for a wide range of math topics. This website also has online activities for children. Put your grade levels in the search box and then click "online activities."

Cool Math for Children

This website has multiple games for a variety of math topics. There are two games for fractions; one is simply recognizing mixed fractions and the other requires one-step addition to create "one."

Further Exploration of the Big Idea for Teachers

1. Think about how you use fractions in your daily life. Do you cook? Do you build things that require fairly exact measurements? What kinds of tools do you use to do these things? Create lists with a small group of all the tools people use that at some point involve fractions. Discuss with your classmates things children could do to use these same, real tools.

2. Review the definitions of physical and logico-mathematical knowledge. Look at the materials in a math or science catalog that are intended for teaching about fractions. Which materials would involve both types of knowledge? Which would focus on only one? Choose one of the materials and discuss in your group why you chose that material or object and how you think you would use it in a classroom.

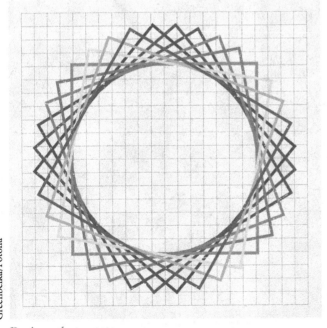

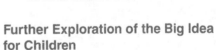

Greenbelka/Fotolia

Designs that rotate

Further Exploration of the Big Idea for Children

1. Have the children create designs by rotating polygons and tracing each rotation. Give the children markers or crayons and encourage them to find different shapes in their rotated designs and color the new shapes. Have them look for smaller shapes that match larger ones.

2. Have children make their own picture finders. The children can use frames cut from heavy paper to place on detailed illustrations to find smaller pictures within larger pictures. Old calendar illustrations are very useful for this activity if they have detailed photographs or paintings.

MODULE 8-2 FOCUS: CHAIN REACTIONS

Common Core State Standards for Math

Kindergarten: Measurement and Data

Describe and compare measurable attributes.

Classify objects and count the number of objects in each
category.

First Grade: Measurement and Data

Represent and interpret data.

Next Generation Science Standards

K-PS2-1. Plan and conduct an investigation to compare the
effects of different strengths or different directions of pushes
and pulls on the motion of an object.

K-PS2-2. Analyze data to determine if a design solution works as
intended to change the speed or direction of an object with a
push or a pull.

2-PS1-2. Analyze data obtained from testing different materials
to determine which materials have the properties that are best
suited for an intended purpose.

Integrating Math and Science: All Fall Down

Setting: Kindergarten

*The kindergartners decided that their block structure needed a fence, so
they began using dominoes to create a circle around the structure. They
had to use different kinds of dominoes because no one set had enough.
The task became a little tricky when dominoes fell over, causing the whole
line to fall. Krish said, "Hey, I know what to do, let's leave a space here
and here so if they fall over, they all won't go." "That's a good idea," said
Kim, "but I kind of like it when they fall over!" The children immediately decided that making the dominoes fall was more fun than building
the fence, so the task became seeing how far they could make the line of
dominoes go. Kim said, "I think the white dominoes fall harder than the
black." Krish said, "Let's see how many of each color we have, and then
we can just use the same colors together." Once they had grouped the dominoes into four color groups, their teacher suggested that they keep track by
writing the amount for each color on a poster so they would know if they
lost any.*

Scenario Questions

1. What could the teacher do next to strengthen the connection between the activity and the math standard? What questions could be asked?
2. What materials could be introduced to strengthen the connection to the science standard for properties of materials?
3. The activity in this scenario came out of free play and teacher observation. What could teachers do to make sure a problem like this presented itself?

Content Questions

1. What do we mean by "property" and "attribute"?
2. *Taxonomy* is a term used often in scientific writing. How are taxonomy and classification the same or different? How do scientists use the term *taxonomy*?
3. How can causality be represented by symbols and expressed in mathematical terms?

Integrating Math and Science: Boats

Setting: Second Grade

Ashley's second graders had just read Who Sank the Boat *by Pamela Allen. In this story a series of animals gets into a boat and the boat sinks when the smallest creature gets in. "I don't think it's fair to blame the mouse," said Mia, "just 'cause he was last wasn't the reason the boat sank." "Yeah," said Michael, "those other animals all made the boat go lower in the water, so it was their fault too." Ashley asked, "Do you think the design of the boat had anything to do with it?" "Sure," said Joey, "they needed a bigger boat!"*

Ashley showed the children an exploration she had set up in their science center. They would experiment with different designs of boats made from 5-inch by 5-inch pieces of aluminum foil to see how many pennies each boat could hold. They would shape the boat, place it in a few inches of water in an old aquarium, and then carefully lay pennies inside the boat. They would count the number of pennies it took to sink each boat design. A chart tablet by the science center was used to record a drawing of each boat and how many pennies it held. Ashley added labels so the children could classify the boats by shape.

At the end of the week Ashley gathered the children together again for a science discussion. "Our boat was long and narrow, like a canoe," said Marcy, "and it held 27 pennies before it sank." "Ours was flat on the bottom, and it held 34 pennies," said Michael, "so it was a better design." Over the next 2 weeks several children pursued the question of boat design, even trying out different materials for the boat, such as clay.

Ashley observed that some children thought clay would always float and that was why it made a good boat. She started a new exploration activity with different types of materials the children could test. A new chart was started so children could classify the materials by how well they floated.

Scenario Questions

1. The classroom in this scenario had a science activity center. What would be the pros and cons of using a center versus exploring the boats as a whole-class activity?
2. The children did their record keeping as a whole group. How could this be set up so they could keep their own observations? What are the advantages of having a public display of the results?
3. The second graders read the book on their own, but the teacher could have read it to the whole class. If she had read it to the whole class, what questions might she have used before she began?

Content Questions

1. How does water displacement work in making things float?
2. Sink and float activities are very common in early childhood classrooms. The way we set up an activity will lead children to construct certain ideas about why things sink or float. How would you explain why a steel ball will sink, but a steel boat will float, or a ball of clay versus clay shaped like a cup?
3. Properties of materials are not always obvious by looking. Density is one property that can't be necessarily seen. How does the density of materials impact sinking and floating?

Children's Literature with a Focus on Cause and Effect

Allen, P. (1996). *Who sank the boat?* London: Puffin.
  A cow, a donkey, a sheep, a pig, and a tiny mouse decide to go for a row on the bay, with disastrous results.

Brett, J. (2009). *The mitten.* New York: Putnam Juvenile.
  A little boy loses his mitten in the snowy woods. A series of animals each tries to make it their home.

Charlip, R. (2010). *Fortunately.* Logan, IA: Perfection Learning.

> One situation leads to another in a chain reaction of misadventures.

Cuyler, M., & Catrow, D. (1996). *That's good! That's bad!* New York: Henry Holt and Company.

> A little boy's adventure with a balloon creates a chain reaction of startling proportions.

Suen, A., & Carrick, P. (2007). *Wired.* Watertown, MA: Charlesbridge Publishing.

> The chain reaction of how a lamp is lit in a house creates a fascinating journey of electricity from the source to our homes.

Tolstoy, A., & Goto, S. (2003). *The enormous turnip.* Mooloolaba, Queensland: Sandpiper Books.

> A traditional tale of a Russian farmer who encourages his turnip to grow, which it does. It then takes a series of helpers to pull it up.

Websites

Playfully Inventing and Exploring with Digital and Other Stuff
This website provides a general description of a variety of chain-reaction activities.

Ethemes for Teachers
This website, available through the University of Missouri, has a great collection of Internet resources about a variety of topics. The collection for Rube Goldberg provides information and lesson plans.

Rube Goldberg Gallery
Rube Goldberg was a well-known cartoonist in the first half of the 20th century. His detailed cartoons depicted highly engineered solutions for everyday problems. His name has become an adjective referring to overly engineered solutions. There are many examples on the Internet of how children have made their own Goldberg machines.

Eco Kids
This is a hands-on activity website that covers several science topics, such as wildlife and climate change.
One food-chain activity is appropriate for readers or non-readers with help. It animates two natural food chains with information about what the consequences are when the chain is broken.

PBS Zoom
This website has an interactive Goldberg machine. Children can manipulate the parts of the machine to deliver a hamburger.

Fantastic Contraption
Children can create increasingly intricate machines by adding wheels and connectors.

Further Exploration of the Big Idea for Teachers

1. Brainstorm with a small group all of the different ways you classify things in your life. Groceries, laundry, papers, and clothing may be just a few things. Pick one and compare with others what kinds of sorting schemes they use. How can we make classification and sorting activities more authentic for children?

2. Have each person bring in something that can serve as a component of a Rube Goldberg–type machine (a pinwheel, a tube, a pulley, etc.). In small groups, determine how the components can go together to create a chain reaction, and then have the large group put all the components together into one machine.

3. Study a chain-reaction machine that you find on a website, and then analyze all the different ways of creating movement that are demonstrated in the machine.

4. Read the article "Science Concepts Young Children Learn Through Water Play" by Carol M. Gross (2012). Choose a different science concept and make your own table that explores the definition, exploration, and dialogue you could plan, as well as math concepts that could be added.

Further Exploration of the Big Idea for Children

1. Live insects or spiders can be kept for short periods of time in the classroom. An insect cage or jar with holes in the lid can allow for viewing by the children with magnifying glasses. Provide many different pictures of the insects for the children to compare with the live insects. For instance, ladybugs are common in many parts of the country, and many pictures can be found in books and on the Internet. Internet websites with factual information about ladybugs could be shared. Set up a classification chart so children can record how the ladybugs are alike and how they are different.

2. Give the children a problem to solve that requires multiple steps in moving something from one place to another.

9 Developing Your Own Curriculum: Big Ideas and Planning

Learning Outcomes

After working with the ideas in this chapter, you should be able to:

- Describe different approaches to determining the big idea
- Explain a variety of strategies for thinking about curriculum planning
- Describe different approaches to curriculum planning
- Understand how to use other areas of the curriculum to strengthen math and science integration

As we have stated from the beginning of this book, we are not providing you with a curriculum guide or specific plan for how and what to do to integrate mathematics and science. Instead, we are hoping to generate a way of thinking about integrating the curriculum around big ideas, to do so in a way consistent with constructivism, and to do so while addressing standards in both disciplines. We have elaborated on some big ideas in order to illustrate how this might work—at various grade levels, and with different possible activities, units, or projects.

In this final chapter, we encourage you to think about how to develop your own curriculum within the same format. First, we discuss different approaches to deciding on the big idea to focus on, and then we suggest some approaches to planning your curriculum over time.

DETERMINING THE BIG IDEA

There are several approaches you can take to determining your big idea:

- Coming up with new big ideas to explore
- Re-thinking an activity, project, or unit
- Starting with a standard or standards
- Starting with children's interests
- Starting with an event (e.g., flooding in your town, a circus in town)
- Starting with an interest of yours

Coming up with New Big Ideas

In this book, we have used the following big ideas as illustrative: *patterns, transformation, balance and symmetry, movement,* and *relationships.* There are other big ideas that might be of interest and relevant for your classroom. In Chaille (2008), there are chapters on the big ideas of *light, zooming in and out, playing with sound, upside down and inside out,* and *chain reactions,* and subsequently we have worked with the big idea of *spaces and enclosures* with teachers. In Chaille (2008), the process of identifying a big idea is described as thinking of it as a topic that includes many different types of projects and activities, and then further examining this topic to clarify the underlying concepts that children will be exploring and learning.

The Next Generation Science Standards use Cross-Cutting Concepts, and these are also big ideas that can serve as inspiration for integrating the curriculum.

Re-thinking an Activity, Project, or Unit

We like to think of this as a "big idea makeover," meaning that you think through and unpack something you already do that you feel is engaging and successful, and frame it in terms of the underlying big idea, integrating math and science in meaningful ways in the process, as in the following scenario:

Marcie had always taught a weather unit in her first-grade classroom. In the past she had focused on charting the weather for each day and then collecting those charts for the month. She and the other first-grade teachers had also invited a local TV weather person to come and talk to the children about severe weather. This year Marcie wanted to integrate her weather unit and strengthen the connections between math and science through the big idea of relationships and patterns. This meant going beyond simply talking about the daily weather in their location. She started with a whiteboard projection of a map of the United States that showed lightning strikes across the country in colored graphics. She asked the children to think about why there was more lightning in the Midwest than in the Northwest. The children were excited to share what they had experienced about storms. She wrote down all their theories on chart paper. They then found questions among the theories that reflected the most popular ideas, such as, "what is lightning?" "what makes lightning?" "why is there lightning before thunder?" and "why is it so bright?" She looked at the Common Core State Standards for Math (CCSSM) and the Next Generation Standards (NGSS) and saw that she could reinforce numbers and operations with the big numbers that this topic would generate, and sound vibration working in waves had a strong connection as well. This opened up many areas of inquiry she had never before thought of including in her weather unit.

In this example we see that using big ideas helped the teacher see the opportunities for an in-depth study that got at the heart of experience and learning for the children.

Starting with Children's Interests

It's important when a group of children become interested in something to honor that, when possible, by incorporating children's interests into the classroom work. As a teacher, you can see and hear when children are developing a particular interest that might warrant deeper exploration. This might be triggered, for example, by one child bringing into the classroom an item from home, something that is received with enthusiasm by others. For example, a child might bring in a bird's nest that was found in the backyard, or a stamp collection found when cleaning out an attic, and you notice the children's continuing discussion and interest in this item. You also might notice that a group of students are taking books out on one subject—perhaps boats, or sharks—and seem to be reading and talking about a particular topic. You can then take this interest and think through whether and how you might pursue it in a way that would connect to a big idea and be a vehicle for math and science integration.

Families can also provide a starting point. Children quite often come to school eager to share things their families have done over the weekend or a trip being planned. Family members can be sources of inspiration when they are asked to share their expertise at school. Quite often teachers have to encourage family members to share by providing suggestions about aspects of their jobs or hobbies children will find interesting. Once children see someone's family member sharing at school, they quite often think about what their own family members could share, and it becomes much easier to get family participation.

One third grader's dad was a roofer. The dad brought his tools and some materials to the class one day and explained what the tools were used for and why some roofing materials were better than others. The children had many ideas about why it was important to keep rain out of your house. This started a project in the classroom to investigate the properties of water. Materials were tested to see what absorbed water and what repelled water. Children discussed materials used for roofing in different parts of the world and why those materials would work in one place, but not another. The teacher did not know the dad's sharing would be so engaging, but she was prepared to connect it to the curriculum and integrate the ideas.

Starting with an Event

During a weather event, such as flooding, or other natural disasters such as earthquakes, children are often not only interested in the event but also need to know more about why it is happening. This is particularly true of local events, but something covered extensively in the media that happens far away—such as a tsunami in Indonesia—can be the basis for deeper exploration of math and science. Your task is to pay attention to what children want to know and are interested in related to this event, and then to develop your curriculum to capture this interest and the children's need to understand. Other interesting events might include something like the circus coming to town and setting up in a visible place, or an athletic event that is getting lots of media attention.

Starting with Where You Are

Consider your local context, and capitalize on the features, resources, and destinations available to you. This could include bodies of water, museums, parks, fountains, and farms. Also consider local businesses that could be the source of projects and activities, as in the following examples:

- A working bakery can be an important resource for work on transformation.
- A farmer's market can be the source of inspiration for the study of growth.
- An exhibit at an art museum could be the focus of a study on light.
- A sports arena could be a provocation about spaces and enclosures.
- A visitor's center at a wildlife refuge could support the study of relationships.

Become familiar with all the resources in your community, and cultivate relationships. One of them could become the basis for a deep exploration that is grounded in the children's community.

Start with an Interest of *Yours*

This starting point is less commonly discussed, but it is important to honor your own interests and think of them as possibilities for exploration with the children in your classroom. If you are passionate about something, and think through carefully whether, how, and why you could explore it with young children, then your own passion will play a role in inspiring the engagement of the children. And, you as a teacher will be modeling your own love for learning.

Let's say you become interested in caves after a family trip. You could think through the big idea that exploring caves could relate to—perhaps light, or perhaps spaces and enclosures—and think this through as you would any other potential integrating exploration.

The next step would be to learn more about the science and math involved in your interest. It's a good idea to use a notebook at this stage to collect science and math content that you can refer to. Many websites can help you with this; starting points include the websites of the National Science Teachers Association and the National Council for Teachers of Mathematics.

Starting with the Standards

Another approach is to take one of the standards in either mathematics or science, and use that as the basis for developing integrating experiences for young children.

For example, in math children are expected to tell time. We know that understanding the passage of time and the representation of that understanding is not just a matter of drawing the hands on a clock or labeling a picture of a digital clock. Teachers understand that it is important to integrate the standard of telling time into many different aspects of the day:

- They keep schedules prominently displayed and refer to them often.
- They have the children create visual representations of the day, or week, or year. They connect the daily number line or calendar to events.
- They use science concepts to explore the shadows thrown by objects at different times of the day.
- They use literature that focuses on different aspects of telling time and refer to the characters in the stories in math problems.
- They have the children do projects that focus on the changes they have gone through as they grew.

In other words, they are constantly looking for ways to help children think about time in ways that bridge math and science.

THE PLANNING PROCESS: STRATEGIES FOR THINKING ABOUT PLANNING

Although the intent of this section is not to give you an explicit blueprint for how to plan—many teachers have systems and strategies honed from years of experience, or are given a particular approach to use in their school—we hope the following guidelines will help you think through your year:

Strategy 1: Be planful and intentional and *be flexible and responsive:* As described in Chapter 1, the concept of *progettazione* from the schools in Reggio Emilia requires the delicate balance between careful planning, with as much detail and specifics as possible, and the flexibility and nimbleness to change those plans based on what children do and how they respond.

Strategy 2: Plan for both the long term and the short term: Consider your whole year first, and occasionally re-examine your year plan. Determine the outcomes that you desire for your children, and work backward from there ("backward design"). After you have a skeleton of the year, you can then zoom in to whatever unit of time makes sense for you—probably monthly, and then weekly. The long-term plan should be in broad strokes, without too many specifics. Then zoom in to the first month, or the month ahead, and get as specific as possible. Think of this as a process of zooming in and out.

Strategy 3: Be as specific as possible in your short-term plans: Incorporate the following elements in any way that makes sense to you, or in any format that you are either required or encouraged to use in your school:

- Intention for the activity, project, or unit: What are your goals?
- Materials needed: Be very specific, include sizes and sources.
- Introduction: How will this be introduced to the children? What will you say? How will you provoke their interest?
- Predictions: What do you expect the children to do? Try to envision what will happen.
- Anticipated learning: Based on your predictions of what they will do, what do you think children will learn?

- Plan for documentation and assessment: How will you keep track of what happens and of what individual children are learning?

Strategy 4: Revisit and revise your plans often: As you engage in this planning process, you will be continually revising your plans. For example, as you think about what children will do, how they will engage in this experience, you might realize there are possibilities that are not desired, and you can then modify the materials, setup, or introduction to head off these possibilities. You may also need to modify plans based on what happens along the way—experiences, projects, units, or activities may take more or less time than is planned; events can happen that alter what transpires; or this particular group of children might have different needs and interests than you anticipated. Again, as stated earlier, this is part of the process of combining flexibility with thorough planning. It does not mean that you throw out your plans; you just reconsider them and revise them continually.

THE PLANNING PROCESS: WHAT DOES IT LOOK LIKE?

Although every context is a little different, most teachers are in a situation where there are guidelines and expectations for a particular grade level or age group. This is usually true in the public school elementary system, and it is also true in many preschool contexts, including Head Start. This is where you should start when there are explicit guidelines available. In other cases, the expectations (or intentions) are constructed by the teachers in a collaborative process as they come together to decide what the focus of the curriculum might be over the year ahead.

Planning for Integration and Inquiry

We can think of travel as a metaphor for planning. If you are going on a spring break trip to the beach, you think about what you are going to need once you get there. You consider the fact that driving may take longer, but you will be able to take more with you, and if you fly you will have to consider more carefully what to pack. You are thinking about being out on the beach, so bathing suits and suntan lotion are important, but then you think about what the weather might do in early spring so you think about also taking a sweatshirt for colder, windier beaches. You find yourself standing in front of your closet considering what you own that will work and what you might have to purchase for the trip; you are *assessing* your options. You are comparing what you believe you will need to what you already own, but you are also thinking about what might happen.

Teachers go through the same process when considering how to set up an environment that is focused on integrating math and science. They must think about where they want to end up and what they already have that will help them get there. Imagination is tapped when thinking about how each space in the classroom is going to be used, and what the possible needs of the children may be. Teachers are also thinking about how they want the curriculum to unfold. Even in classrooms where curriculum guides are in place teachers can use authentic learning as their guide. There are a variety of ways to organize the curriculum for integration of math and science.

The Project Approach

We introduced the Project Approach in Chapter 1. It offers a powerful way to plan for math and science integration.

The Project Approach is organized into three phases (Katz & Chard, 2000). Phase 1 is the beginning of the process of finding out what children know about a specific topic, and what their questions are about the topic. During this part of the project there is a lot of conversation, many questions are recorded, journals and other records are kept of children's ideas, and resources are collected.

Phase 2 is the development of the project. Children actively pursue the answers to their questions. They interview specialists, and they use materials, books, technology, and other media. Children's individual interests are all supported in this part of the project as they investigate the aspects of the topic that interest them the most. As they find answers and construct meaning, they draw, write, create movies and comics, build, and act out their new knowledge.

Phase 3 is the conclusion of the project. In this phase all the new information constructed by the children is shared with a wider audience in some way. Children plan for this part of the project just as much as they did during their participation. They proudly become the docents for their classroom museums or guides to their art galleries. They share at the school morning meeting or set up a presentation for parents during a parent night.

Planning with the End in Sight

Teachers plan for assessment at the beginning of the project. They know that there will be unexpected things to document, but a purposeful teacher plans ahead of time in order to capture everything needed to share with parents, teachers, school administrators, and the children.

Neil knew that his second graders would be expected to know facts about plants for one of the tests his school system used. He began his planning by looking at the materials that were left in his classroom by a former teacher, but there were mainly a lot of worksheets showing parts of plants, the life cycle of the plant, and the needs of plants. He thought about the empty shelf below the window in his room and realized that if the children grew their own plants he would be able to assess their knowledge about all of the discrete or specific bits of information the children would have to know for the tests. He gathered a list of plants that would be easy and fast to grow in the classroom and presented several choices to the children. As the project unfolded, he carefully kept records of what the children understood about plant growth. He made sure that various parts of the project included records that the children kept themselves, showing their awareness of vocabulary.

The Five E Learning Cycle

In early childhood education we often hear the phrase "hands-on learning." It is acknowledged that children need physical experiences in order for learning to take place. However, learning goes beyond simply manipulating objects. Nuthall (1999), for example, found that students need three to four experiences with a concept. The five E learning cycle (Brown & Abell, 2007) recognizes this need by organizing a plan around the learner's need to interact through different levels of thinking.

The five E's are:

Engage: At this point we want to present an interesting problem, encourage predictions, or suggest an activity that will get children's curiosity involved.

Explore: The children begin the activity that will support their exploration to begin answering the problem.

Explain: The children can explain their ideas about what is happening during exploration. This is not meant as the moment for the *teacher* to explain.

Extend: The ideas from the children's explanation are taken to a new level of application to other problems or the real world.

Evaluation: The teacher captures the children's understanding through multiple means in order to plan the next engagement.

The curriculum guide for Brenda's school system stated that first graders needed to be able to compare artificial sources of light to natural sources; second graders needed to also be able to understand the concept of opaque and transparent; and third graders needed to include the concepts of reflect, refract, and absorb. To Brenda that meant her kindergartners needed lots of experiences thinking about light. Brenda was also thinking about how the kindergartners needed many opportunities to learn counting and classifying strategies. She decided that she would spend 2 weeks using light as her science focus, with the possibility of more specific activities based on the children's interests and understandings. She used the five E lesson plan as her guide:

Engage: *Brenda would read the book* Moonbear's Shadow *by Frank Asch and ask the children to think about their shadows, when they saw them and what might be causing them.*

Explore: *Three science stations would be set up around the room. Each science station would have books about light, dark, shadows, and colors.*

One would be a large utility box with a curtain on the front. The box would be a good setting for creating shadows using objects and flashlights.

The second station would be a light box with transparent, opaque, and translucent materials available for free play. A three-column chart would enable the children to keep a record of which materials let light shine through, which let a little light through, and which wouldn't let light through at all.

The third station would be the overhead projector with opaque and transparent shapes for exploration of the properties of the shadows thrown.

Each station would have a chart where children's comments and questions could be written down.

Explain: *At the end of the week Brenda planned on reading the book* Light: Shadows, Mirrors and Rainbows *by Natalie Rosinsky. Her questions would include helping the children connect some of the explanations from the book back to their comments and questions on the charts. They would use counting and classification strategies to keep* *track of how many materials were tested and how many were translu- cent and/or opaque.*

Extend: *A new science station using mirrors would be added the second week so the children could further their exploration of some of the ideas brought up in Natalie Rosinsky's book.*

Evaluation: *Brenda planned on using the children's comments from the charts and from the group times when they read the books to create a journal page where each child could write or draw a picture that showed their answer to "What I know about light." She also prepared a rubric that had the major concepts from her objectives so that she could record each child's level of understanding.*

This planning was different from when Brenda first began teach- ing. In her first couple of years of teaching Brenda would focus on put- ting materials out for children to explore, but there was little structure for supporting their thinking. With the five E lesson plan, Brenda was able to meet her district expectations, but even more than that, she was able to set appropriately high expectations for the children's problem- solving and logical thought processes.

For younger children, the five E process could be less structured, and lends itself to supporting the negotiated, back-and-forth curric- ulum development of a constructivist classroom, as in the following scenario:

Jonah, the teacher of classroom of 4-year-olds, had observed the children notic- ing some interesting shadows on the wall. Capitalizing on this, and wanting to pursue the big idea of "light" with the children, he decided to provoke fur- ther interest in light by providing a basket of flashlights and different kinds of opaque, translucent, and colored transparent paper to the children for initial exploration (Engage). As the children played with these materials, they noticed the different ways the light shone through the different kinds of paper. He then introduced several shadow puppets, and the children had the idea of making their own puppets with different materials (Explore). Jonah collected a set of children's books, both fiction and nonfiction, about shadows and light for the children to use (Explain). He observed that the children were then using their own bodies to create shadows after reading One Snowy Day *by Jack Keats, and set up a canvas shadow screen with a large projecting light (Extend), and the children created shadow stories, projecting themselves on the screen. Jonah recorded some of the children's comments and discussions about how to enact different actions, as well as digital photographs of their shadow play (Evaluation).*

USING OTHER AREAS OF THE CURRICULUM TO STRENGTHEN MATH AND SCIENCE

In Chapter 1 we talked about multidisciplinary, interdisciplinary, and transdisciplinary curriculum integration. Constructivist teachers of young children are always looking for ways to make the curriculum areas work better together rather than only in separate blocks of time, but the realities of the school day quite often force teachers to focus on specific curriculum subjects individually. However, this doesn't mean that we have to give up on integrating the curriculum.

Connecting Language Arts, Math, and Science

The Common Core State Standards for English Language Arts focus on using nonfiction books along with fiction. This is a perfect place to bring in what are called **text sets**. A text set is usually a small group of books that represent both a fiction and nonfiction view of a topic. The use of both genres of books is a powerful tool for helping children construct knowledge. For example, *Diary of a Worm* by Doreen Cronin and Harry Bliss could be paired with *Wiggling Worms at Work* by Wendy Pfeffer. Children could be asked to sort the facts from fiction in *Diary of a Worm* or to take the factual information in *Wiggling Worms at Work* and add something to the narrative of *Diary of a Worm.* Either way, children will be thinking about what they now know about worms and how that compares to information in a literary device such as a diary. There are a number of websites with text set information, including The Reading and Writing Project, Worlds of Words (Arizona State), and Text Project.

Connecting Children's Literature, Math, and Science

Any curriculum area can be integrated using children's literature, but this strategy is particularly powerful in math and science. The key is to use specific strategies that can be applied to any book. For example, we can use literary structures and the Common Core State Standards for Math to focus on problem finding (Wilburn, Keat, & Napoli, 2011). For example, *Officer Buckle and Gloria* by Peggy Rathmann is a story about Officer Buckle, who is the safety officer for the local school system. He visits schools to give safety talks, which are very boring to the children until the day he shows up with Gloria, a German shepherd. It turns out that Gloria has special illustrative powers for Officer Buckle's talks that really make the children sit up and pay attention. The literary elements for this story connect to math and science in the following ways:

- Plot: How are the actions in the story connected? How does one thing make another thing happen? (Relationships)
- Characters: Gloria could come to the classroom and help us illustrate math and science problems. How could she show us the water cycle? How could she show us how many ways we could count children in our classroom? (Movement)
- Objects: The special letter in the story is written on a star-shaped paper. How many ways could we draw a star? How many stars could we draw in a minute? (Burns, 2007) (Patterns)
- Setting: How many guidelines do we have for our class? What guidelines do we need for science activities in our classroom? (Relationships)
- Illustrations: How could we estimate how many children are in the auditorium listening to Officer Buckle? How could we estimate how many would see him on television? (Transformation)
- Time Frame: How many different ways could we keep track of our daily schedule? What changes can we see happening over the course of a day? A week? A month? A year? (Wilburn et al., 2011) (Transformation; Patterns)

Cognitively Guided Instruction

Another strategy comes from Cognitively Guided Instruction (CGI). CGI is a research-based professional development program that uses children's thinking to teach math. It is not a curriculum, but is based in the practices of effective teachers who listen to children's thinking about math. In the CGI approach, there is no one math strategy. Children are encouraged to find multiple ways to solve problems that make sense to them (Carpenter, Fennema, Franke, Levi, & Empson, 1999).

According to CGI, there are many different problem types (Table 9-1). Teachers need to use the different types of problems so that children's thinking is flexible and multiple ways of thinking are supported.

Teachers can use children's literature to develop different math problems using the different CGI problem types. For example, if we are

Table 9-1 CGI Problem Types

Joining Problems

Join: Result Unknown	Join: Change Unknown	Join: Start Unknown
(JRU)	(JCU)	(JSU)
Amy had 5 cookies. David gave her 4 more cookies. How many cookies does Amy have now?	Amy had 5 cookies. David gave her some more. Then Amy had 9 cookies. How many cookies did David give her?	Amy had some cookies, David gave her 4 more and then she had 9 cookies. How many cookies did Amy have before David gave her some?
$5 + 4 = \underline{}$	$5 + \underline{} = 9$	$\underline{} + 4 = 9$

Joining Separating Problems

Separate: Result Unknown	Separate: Change Unknown	Separate: Start Unknown
(SRU)	(SCU)	(SSU)
Amy had 9 cookies. She gave 4 of them to David. How many does she have now?	Amy had 9 cookies. She gave some to David. Now she has 4 cookies. How many did she give David?	Amy had some cookies. She gave 4 cookies to David. Now she has 5 cookies left. How many cookies did Amy have before she gave some to David?
$9 - 4 = \underline{}$	$9 - \underline{} = 4$	$\underline{} - 4 = 5$

Joining Part-Part-Whole Problems

Part-Part-Whole: Whole Unknown	Part-Part-Whole: Part Unknown	
(PPW:WU)	(PPW:PU)	
Amy has 4 vanilla cookies and 5 chocolate cookies. How many cookies does she have altogether?	Amy has 9 cookies. 4 are vanilla and the rest are chocolate. How many chocolate cookies does she have?	
$4 + 5 = \underline{}$	$9 - 4 = \underline{}$ or $4 + \underline{} = 9$	

Joining Compare Problems

Compare Difference Unknown	Compare Quantity Unknown	Compare Referent Unknown
Amy has 9 cookies. David has 4 cookies. How many more cookies does Amy have than David?	Amy has 5 cookies. David has 4 more cookies than Amy. How many cookies does David have?	Amy has 9 cookies. She has 4 more than David. How many cookies does David have?
$9 - 4 = \underline{}$ or $4 + \underline{} = 9$	$5 + 4 = \underline{}$	$9 - 4 = \underline{}$ or $\underline{} + 4 = 9$

Joining Multiplication and Division Problems

Multiplication	Measurement Division	Partitive Division
Amy had 2 piles of cookies. There are 4 cookies in each pile. How many cookies does Amy have?	Amy had 8 cookies. She them to some other children. She gave each child 2 cookies. How many children got cookies?	Amy had 8 cookies. She wants to give them to 4 children. If she gives each child the same number of cookies, how many cookies will each child get?
$2 \times 4 = \underline{}$	$8 \div 2 = \underline{}$	$8 \div 4 = \underline{}$

Carpenter et al. (1999).

using *Diary of a Worm* (Cronin & Bliss, 2003) we could use the following CGI problem types:

> Join, Result Unknown: Worm found a newspaper on the ground and then a little later he found 2 more newspapers. How many newspapers did he find all together?

> Separate, Change Unknown: Worm had 8 oranges. He gave some to his sister and now he has 3 oranges. How many did he give his sister?

> Part-Part-Whole, Whole Unknown: Worm has 2 history books and 3 science books. How many books does he have?

As you can see, problem types can be used with any context. Science and math literature can then be used to reinforce other concepts and support children's thinking about connections.

Starting with a Standard

Another strategy that could be applied to children's literature is to focus on one of the Common Core State Standards for Math. For example, in the book *Hannah's Collections* (Jocelyn, 2004), Hannah wants to take her many collections of things to school to share, but can't take them all. She comes up with a plan for taking samples of her collections. In connection with this story, we could focus on the Common Core State Standards for Math covering number and operations for third grade. Many different problem types could be designed around thinking about Hannah's collections. Children in the class could share their own collections or classroom collections could be considered. For instance, children could problem solve how to count the books in the classroom, how to keep track of the number of books, how to organize and classify particular sets of books, and how to apply multiplication to the counting.

Connecting the Arts, Math, and Science

The arts include visual art, dance, movement, music, and drama. For purposes of thinking about integration, we look at these art-related areas as different ways to represent thinking. Children who are second-language learners and other children who are developing vocabulary need highly visual support in the curriculum. So when young children are learning about the water cycle, for example, they need to move through the cycle using the whole body. They need to sing about the process and make up new ways to move. They need to be able to paint pictures of the parts of the water cycle they understand so they can show others their understanding. Each new representation then deepens their own construction of how the world works. These representations also give us as teachers an idea of how children are thinking.

When people visit Reggio Emilia schools, they are impressed by the children's artistic representations of learning (Hertzog, 2001). Some may think there is an art or dance class that is focusing on these topics; however, art is not seen as a separate curriculum area in Reggio Emilia preschools. It is an integral part of the classroom, as one of the many languages of children that represents their thinking. The teachers focus on the child's thinking and providing access to and support for a variety of media. If art instruction is necessary, it is given as needed and/or when materials are introduced.

In American classrooms, a constructivist teacher will plan on teaching children strategies that can be used when the child needs them. For example, at the beginning of the year the teacher might do guided instruction about the care and use of paint. The children will be taught how to control the amount of paint on the brush, how to clean the brush, and how to store their paintings, but they will not necessarily be given a specific assignment or object to paint. Then, when they want to illustrate their ideas about what a stormy sky looked like or their observations of the plant they are growing, they can use the paint with minimal teacher supervision.

There are a number of useful websites for integrating math and science with the arts. These include Smithsonian Education, which has resources, website links, and lesson ideas for teachers, and the National Science Teachers Association (NSTA) blog focusing on many topics of planning for math and science integration in early childhood classrooms. Most museums have helpful websites with numerous website links to explore, with many directed at classroom teachers and many directed at children.

Connecting Social Studies, Math, and Science

Our focus on social studies with young children is quite often a focus on the need for civic responsibility. When we talk about social studies we are using information from many different fields: geography, political science, economics, psychology, civics, history, anthropology, and religious studies. In early childhood it is more common to begin with the child, family, and community. Math and science can easily be reinforced by connecting topics common to big ideas and social studies with children's everyday life experiences, as in this scenario:

Hunza had her first graders choose symbols that represented the ways they traveled to school each morning. Six of the children walked to school, eight rode the school bus, five were brought to school by family members in cars, and seven were brought to school by child-care centers. She had the children create a bar graph with their chosen symbols. There was a lot of discussion about the information contained in the bar graph, and this generated more comments and questions. One comment that Hunza decided to explore because of classroom discussion, was the number of wheels represented by the different vehicles. This led to interesting math problems, such as, "If there are 3 buses and 4 cars how many wheels are there?" Hunza used the big idea of balance to direct the children's thinking toward another math problem: "If there are 2 buses with a total of 16 wheels, how many cars would we need to have the same number of wheels?" This then led to an exploration of the relative sizes of the tires on the different vehicles and a discussion about how tires are measured and what they are made from. Hunza knew that social studies standards for her school system were being addressed and that math and science concepts were being used and reinforced. The children were actually thinking beyond the standards with her support.

Questions to Consider

1. Different school structures encourage different types of planning. Teachers generally find that planning together can strengthen their teaching. What do you think some of the advantages and disadvantages of group planning might be?
2. How do we make sure children have a place in the planning? What classroom structures encourage or discourage children's input and planning?
3. If you had $500 to spend on materials for a new classroom, what would be your first consideration? What would be the most important thing to spend money on? Where could you save money?

Review Questions

1. What are two different approaches to determining the big idea?
2. Name and define three strategies of curriculum planning.
3. Describe one approach to curriculum planning by creating a project for integrating math and science that uses other areas of the curriculum.

Summary

In this text we have attempted to provide a framework for authentically integrating mathematics and science in the early childhood curriculum. Constructivism provides a framework for doing this—putting the emphasis on how children think about the world in integrated ways. When you use as the starting point the big ideas that engage children, and that permit the meaningful integration of math and science, the process is one that resonates with your learners. You are able to effectively support them in constructing their understandings of the world with experiences that allow them to make connections. In so doing, children will carry forward a deep understanding of the basic ideas that support them conceptually in building even deeper understandings. And, as important, you will be fostering their inherent motivation and interest in the world around them.

Websites

National Science Teachers Association
National Council of Teachers of Mathematics
Both websites of these national organizations have many resources for teachers relating to content knowledge and curriculum planning, and blogs for teachers relating to curriculum planning and implementation.

National Aeronautics and Space Administration (NASA)
Many resources on both content knowledge and the 5E approach to curriculum development.

The Project Approach
An excellent website that includes a section on developing and implementing projects, with examples.

An Everyday Story
A website that discusses how to approach planning inspired by the work of Reggio Emilia.

5E learning cycle
There are several websites that further explain this process.

Math Made Fun
A website with many resources and links relating to Cognitively Guided Instruction.

Read Write Think – International Reading Association
Includes classroom resources on incorporating children's literature into science studies. A good example is the children's book *Diary of a Worm* as a provocation.

Smithsonian Education
This website has resources, websites, and lesson ideas for teachers and children relating to science and other disciplines.

References

Beane, J. A. (1997). *Curriculum integration: Designing the core of democratic education.* New York, NY: Teachers College Press.

Berk, L. E., & Winsler, A. (1995). *Scaffolding children's learning: Vygotsky and early childhood education* (Vol. 7). Washington, DC: National Association for the Education of Young Children.

Bodrova, E., & Leong, D. J. (1996). *Tools of the mind: The Vygotskian approach to early childhood education.* Englewood Cliffs, NJ: Merrill.

Brooks, J. G., & Brooks, M. G. (2000). *In search of understanding: The case for constructivist classrooms.* Washington, DC: Association for Supervision and Curriculum Development.

Brown, P., & Abell, S. L. (2007). Perspectives: Examining the learning cycle. *Science and Children, 45*(4), 58–59.

Burns, M. (2007). *About teaching mathematics: A K–8 resource* (3rd ed.). Sausalito, CA: Math Solutions Publications.

Cadwell, L. B. (1997). *Bringing Reggio Emilia home: An innovative approach to early childhood education.* New York, NY: Teachers College Press.

Cadwell, L. B. (2003). *Bringing learning to life: A Reggio approach to early childhood education.* New York, NY: Teachers College Press.

Carpenter, T., Fennema, E., Franke, M., Levi, L., & Empson, S. (1999). *Children's mathematics.* Portsmouth, NH: Heinemann.

Casey, B., Kersh, J. E., & Young, J. M. (2004). Storytelling sagas: An effective medium for teaching early childhood mathematics. *Early Childhood Research Quarterly,* 167–172. doi: 10.1016/j.ecresq.2004.01.011

Chaille, C. (2008). *Constructivism across the early childhood curriculum: Big ideas as inspiration.* New York, NY: Allyn & Bacon.

Chaille, C. & Britain, L. (2003). The young child as scientist: A constructivist approach to early childhood science education. New York, NY: Allyn & Bacon.

Clements, D. H. (1999). Subitizing: What is it? Why teach it? *Teaching Children Mathematics, 5,* 400–405.

Cross, C. T., Woods, T. A., & Schweingruber, H. (2009). *Mathematics learning in early childhood: Paths toward excellence and equity.* Washington, DC: National Academies Press.

Dewey, J. (1900). *The school and society.* Chicago, IL: University of Chicago Press.

Edwards, C., Gandini, L., & Forman, G. (Eds.). (1993). *The hundred languages of children: The Reggio Emilia approach to early childhood education.* Norwood, NJ: Ablex Publishing Corporation.

Edwards, C., Gandini, L., & Forman, G. (Eds.). (1998). *The hundred languages of children: The Reggio Emilia approach to early childhood education* (2nd ed.). Norwood, NJ: Ablex.

Frost, J. L., Wortham, S. C., & Riefel, S. C. (2011). *Play and child development.* Upper Saddle River, NJ: Pearson.

Ginsburg, H., Jacobs, S. F., & Lopez, L. S. (1998). *The teacher's guide to flexible interviewing in the classroom: Learning what children know about math.* Needham Heights, MA: Allyn and Bacon.

Glanfield, F., Bush, W. S., & Stenmark, J. K. (2003). *Mathematics assessment: A practical handbook for grades K–2.* Reston, VA: National Council of Teachers of Mathematics.

Gross, C. M. (2012). Science concepts young children learn through water play. *Dimensions of Early Childhood, 40*(2), 3–11.

Harris, P., Smith, B. M., & Harris, J. (2011). *The myths of standardized tests: Why they don't tell you what you think they do.* Lanham, MD: Rowman & Littlefield.

Hertzog, N. B. (2001). Reflection and impressions from Reggio Emilia: "It's not about art!" *Early Childhood Research and Practice, 3,* 1.

Ilg, F. L., & Ames, L. B. (1965). *The Gesell Institute's child behavior: From birth to ten.* New York, NY: Harper Collins.

Johnston, P. (2004). *Choice words: How our language affects children's learning.* New York, NY: Stenhouse.

Kamii, C. (1985). *Young children reinvent arithmetic: Implications of Piaget's theory.* New York, NY: Teachers College Press.

Kamii, C., & Rummelsburg, J. (2008). Arithmetic for first graders lacking number concepts. *Teaching Children Mathematics, 14*(7), 389–394.

Katz, L., & Chard, S. (2000). *Engaging children's minds: The project approach.* New York, NY: Ablex.

Kieff, J. E., & Casbergue, R. M. (2000). *Playful learning and teaching: Integrating play into preschool and primary programs.* Upper Saddle River, NJ: Pearson.

Kohn, A. (2000). *The case against standardized testing: Raising the scores, ruining the schools.* Portsmouth, NH: Heinemann.

Kostos, K., & Shin, E. (2010). Using math journals to enhance second graders' communication of mathematical thinking. *Early Childhood Education Journal.* doi: 10.1007/s10643-010-0390-4

Kroesbergen, E. H., Van Luit, J. E. H., Van Lieshout, E. C. D. M., Van Loosbroek, E., & Van de Rijt, B. A. M. (2009). Individual differences in early numeracy: The role of executive functions and subitizing. *Journal of Psychoeducational Assessment, 27*(3), 226–236.

Leonhardt, A. (2005). Using rubrics as an assessment tool in your classroom. *General Music Theory Today, 19*(1), 10–16.

Leung, F. K. S., Graf, K., & Lopez-Real, F. J. (2006). *Mathematics education in different cultural traditions—a comparative study.* New York, NY: Springer.

Lilburn, P., & Ciurak, A. (2010). *Investigations, tasks, and rubrics to teach and assess math, grades 1–6.* Sausalito, CA: Math Solutions Publications.

National Governors Association Center for Best Practices and the Council of Chief State School Officers. (2010). Common Core State Standards Initiative: Preparing America's students for college and career. Retrieved from http://www.corestandards.org/read-the-standards/

Nuthall, G. (1999). The way students learn: Acquiring knowledge from an integrated science and social studies unit. *The Elementary School Journal,* 303–341.

Papic, M., & Mulligan, J. T. (2007). The growth of early mathematical patterning: An intervention study. In J. Watson & K. Beswick (Eds.), *Mathematics: Essential research, essential practice* (pp. 591–600).

Piaget, J. (1977). *The development of thought: Equilibration of cognitive structures.* New York, NY: The Viking Press. (Originally published 1975)

Seefeldt, C. (2005). *How to work with standards in the early childhood classroom.* New York, NY: Teachers College Press.

Stevens, D. D., Levi, A. J., & Walvoord, B. E. (2012). *Introduction to rubrics: An assessment tool to save grading time, convey effective feedback, and promote student learning.* Sterling, VA: Stylus Publishing.

Vars, G. F. (1996). The effects of interdisciplinary curriculum and instruction. In P. S. Hlebowitsh & W. G. Wraga (Eds.), *Annual review of research for school leaders* (pp. 147–164). Jefferson City, MO: Scholastic.

Viruru, R. (2006). Postcolonial technologies of power: Standardized testing and representing diverse young children. *International Journal of Educational Policy, Research & Practice, 7*(1), 49–70. Retrieved from Education Research Complete database.

Wang, A. (2009). Optimizing early mathematics experiences for children from low-income families: A study on opportunity to learn mathematics. *Early Childhood Education Journal, 37*(4), 295–302.

Wiggins, G., & McTighe, J. (2005). *Understanding by design.* Upper Saddle River, NJ: Pearson.

Wilburn, J., Keat, J., & Napoli, M. (2011). *Cowboys count, monkeys measure and princesses problem solve: Building early math skills through storybooks.* Baltimore, MD: Paul H. Brookes Publishing Company.

Wurm, J. P. (2005). *Working in the Reggio way: A beginner's guide for American teachers.* St. Paul, MN: Redleaf Press.

Yoshina, J. M., & Harada, V. H. (2007). Involving students in learning through rubrics. *Library Media Collection, 25*(5), 10–14.

Glossary

algebraic thinking A representation of arithmetic in which letters representing numbers are used according to the rules of arithmetic.

Asperger syndrome High-functioning behavior found on the autism spectrum. Children diagnosed with Asperger syndrome generally exhibit normal language development, but can struggle with social development.

attribute A variable characteristic of an object or material.

auditory Relating to the sense of hearing.

backward design An approach to curriculum planning that begins with the goals and standards.

big idea An overarching abstract or generic idea that incorporates multiple concepts and connects multiple activities and projects across disciplines.

causal relationships When the variation of one element in a relationship affects the other one.

child-centered curriculum An approach to curriculum that is driven by children's interests and questions.

class inclusion The understanding that some classes or sets of objects are also sub-sets of a larger class.

classification Sorting objects or materials into categories according to one or more attributes.

Cognitively Guided Instruction A professional development program that uses children's thinking to teach math, encouraging multiple strategies and problems.

composition What something is made up of.

conservation Understanding that two things that are equivalent remain the same despite changes in order or appearance, based on logic and/or compensation.

constructivism A theory of learning that says that children have theories or ideas about the world, and that they are constantly applying these theories in an attempt to understand and construct new knowledge.

content The information that is being discussed or taught.

context The setting that something occurs in and the effect of the relationships in that setting. What is happening takes on a new meaning depending on the context.

decomposition Taking something apart, either literally or taking apart an idea.

differentiation The information that is being taught is changed to meet the needs of the individual. The concept does not change, but the way it is presented takes into account the individual.

documentation Samples of children's work used to purposively show learning.

Down syndrome Presence of all or part of chromosome 21, which results in physical attributes and mild to moderate intellectual challenges.

equivalency Determining that two things are the same, either through measurement or estimation.

estimate An idea, based on given information, about something that isn't known for sure.

estimation A close guess of a value, made without measurement.

experimentation Trying out different ways of testing ideas.

force The push or pull upon an object resulting from the object's interaction with another object.

formative Information collected about learning and then used to plan for instruction.

growing patterns Recognizing the next step in a sequence to predict an outcome.

hierarchical inclusion In classification, the larger set includes the sub-set (e.g., daisies are also flowers); in number, the idea that each number includes all previous numbers (e.g., the number 20 includes the number 19).

inquiry-based learning An approach to curriculum that centers around children's authentic inquiries.

interdependence Mutual dependence, or mutual reliance, between things; the interconnections between and among elements, such that each is dependent on the other.

interdisciplinary approach An approach to curriculum that focuses on skills that apply across disciplines (e.g., math, literacy).

John Dewey Educational philosopher who advocated for curriculum integration and the application of school to life experiences.

logico-mathematical knowledge A type of knowledge (from Piaget's theory) relating to the abstracted relationships that are constructed by children through interactions with objects and materials; for example, size (big, little) is an abstract relationship depending on the objects being compared and exists in the mind.

model A model represents our thinking about a topic, issue, a way of doing something. It might be something described or it could be something created with physical materials.

multidisciplinary approach An approach to curriculum in which different subject areas are organized around the same theme or topic.

natural materials Manipulatives that help children make connections with their world. These could be different items depending on the child's experiences in the natural world.

phenomena Things or experiences we see and notice.

physical knowledge A type of knowledge (from Piaget's theory) relating to the empirical physical world; constructed by children through interactions with objects and materials; for example: round things roll down an incline.

project approach An approach to curriculum that connects experiences through projects that incorporate multiple activities and disciplines around a topic.

properties The terms *property* and *attribute* are sometimes used in the same situation. *Property* can be a more specific descriptive term, especially if used in science and math.

Reggio Emilia A city/region in Northern Italy; often used to refer to a dynamic, intentional approach to developing curriculum through interaction and negotiation between and among children and teachers.

repeating patterns Patterns with a unit that repeats.

rubric Criteria and standards used to make evaluation decisions.

scientific method Systematic experimentation that involves empirical, measurable observations to test a theory.

sequencing Placing objects in a series based on when they occurred.

seriation Placing objects in a series based on size or other property.

spatial structure patterns Mental organization of visual data.

subitizing Recognizing a quantity without one-to-one counting.

summative Information collected to record achievement of goals.

symmetry The quality of being made up of exactly similar parts facing each other on two sides of an axis or midline.

teacher-directed curriculum An approach to curriculum that is directed or initiated by the teacher.

text sets A set of books including fiction and nonfiction books focused on a topic.

theory A general principle or set of principles that explains facts or events of the natural world; an idea that is the starting point for argument or investigation.

transdisciplinary approach An approach to curriculum that sees experiential learning as incorporating and integrating across disciplines.

transitivity Comparing two or more quantities when direct physical comparison is not possible by using an intermediary object; for example, if A is smaller than B, and B is smaller than C, then A is smaller than C.

variables Attributes of objects or materials that can be acted upon or changed; for example, the speed of an object going down an incline, the angle of the incline, or the force used to push the object.

Venn diagram A diagram that uses circles to represents sets and their sometimes overlapping or embedded relationships.

Name Index

Abel, S., 147
Abell, S. L., 217
Allen, P., 205
Almon, J., 9
Ames, L. B., 21

Bagnato, S., 48
Ballard, C., 147
Banyai, I., 187
Beane, J. A., 11
Bell, D., 22
Berk, L. E., 4, 22
Bjorkman, S., 120
Bliss, H., 220, 223
Bodrova, E., 4, 22
Boyd, S., 147
Brett, J., 97, 205
Britain, L., 137
Brooks, J. G., 72
Brooks, M. G., 72
Brown, P., 217
Buehner, C., 97
Buehner, M., 97
Burns, M., 73, 221
Burns, R. C., 11

Cadwell, L. B., 16
Campbell, R., 92
Campbell, S. C., 92
Carle, E., 175
Carpenter, T. P., 111, 221
Carrick, P., 153, 206
Carter, M., 69
Casbergue, R. M., 4
Casey, B., 84
Catrow, D., 206
Chaille, C., 16, 72, 101, 137, 209
Chard, S., 12, 216
Charlip, R., 206

Ciurak, A., 40
Clements, A., 120
Clements, D. H., 22, 82
Cronin, D., 220, 223
Curtis, D., 69
Cuyler, M., 206

Dahl, M., 147
Dahlberg, G., 9
Davis, K., 40, 65, 124, 128–130, 140
dePaola, T., 115
DeViney, J., 69
Dewey, J., 11
Drake, S. M., 11
Driscoll, M., 92
Duncan, S., 69

Edwards, C., 5, 12, 16, 34
Ehlert, L., 92
Empson, S. B., 111, 221
Evanshen, P., 69

Falk, J., 69
Fennema, E., 111, 221
Floca, B., 177
Forman, G., 5, 12, 34
Franke, M L., 111, 221
Fromental, J., 120
Frost, J. L., 4, 22

Gandini, L., 5, 12, 34
Ganeri, A., 92
Gardner, H., 9
Geisert, A., 153
Gilden, R., 22
Ginsburg, H., 43
Goldberg, R., 206
Goldstone, B., 120

Goldsworthy, A., 116, 177
Goto, S., 206
Graf, K., 25
Gross, G. M., 207

Halle, T., 48
Hamilton, M., 92
Harada, V. H., 40
Harris, J., 10, 48
Harris, P., 10, 48
Harris, S., 69
Hart, L., 115
Heelan, J. R., 147
Hertzog, N. B., 224
Hoban, T., 200
Hsiang Yeh, H., 48
Huber, D., 49

Ilg, F. L., 21

Jacobs, S. F., 43
Jocelyn, M., 97, 115, 200, 223
Johnston, P., 31
Jolivet, J., 120

Kamii, C., 125, 168
Katz, L., 12, 216
Keat, J., 220
Keats, J., 219
Keller, L., 147
Keller, T. E., 47
Kersh, J. E., 84
Kieff, J. E., 4
Kohn, A., 48
Kostos, K., 42

Leedy, L., 177
Leong, D. J., 4, 22

Leonhardt, A., 40
LeSeig, T., 173
Leung, F. K. S., 25
Levi, L., 111, 221
Lewin-Benham, A., 9
Lilburn, P., 40
Llewellyn, C., 147
Lopez, L. S., 43
Lopez-Real, F. J., 25

Martchenko, M., 200
Martin, J. B., 163, 177
Martinez-Beck, I., 48
McCully, E. A., 173
McTighe, J., 10
Miller, E., 9
Moss, P., 9
Mulligan, J. T., 80
Munsch, R., 200
Murphy, S., 120, 177
Muttock, S., 22
Myller, R., 120

Napoli, M., 220
Numeroff, L. J., 153
Nuthall, G., 217

Otoshi, K., 97

Pallotta, J., 97
Papic, M., 80
Pfeffer, W., 220
Piaget, J., 4, 125, 160

Quinn, H., 47

Rathmann, P., 220
Reed, M., 120
Riefel, S. C., 4, 22
Robertson, W. C., 111
Rody, M., 69
Rosenberry, L., 69
Rosinsky, N. M., 115
Rummelsburg, J., 168

Sarama, J., 22
Schrier, A. V., 177
Schwartz, C., 153
Schweingruber, H. A., 22, 47, 198
Seefeldt, C., 47
Shea, D., 147
Shin, E., 42
Shlva, K., 22
Sidman, J., 92
Simmonds, N., 147
Siraj-Blatchford, I., 22
Slade, S., 153

Smith, B. M., 10, 48
Stille, D. R., 147
Suen, A., 153, 206
Swinburne, S. R., 92

Tolstoy, A., 206
Tout, K., 48

Vars, G. F., 11
Viruru, R., 48

Wang, A., 25
Wiggins, G., 10
Wilburne, J., 220, 221
Willems, M., 148
Wilson, R., 69
Winsler, A., 4, 22
Wood, A., 97, 173
Wood, D., 97, 173
Woods, T. A., 22, 198
Wortham, S. C., 4, 22
Wurm, J. P., 16, 34

Yolen, J., 115
Yoshina, J. M., 40
Young, J. M., 84

Zaslow, M., 48

Subject Index

AAAS Science Links for Teachers, 92
"AB" pattern, 79
Absorbency of paper towels, 106
Academic environment, 55–57
Accessibility of materials, 60–61
Accommodation, 23
Acorn Naturalists, 69
Algebraic thinking, 162
Alibris, 91
All Fall Down, 203
An Everyday Story, 226
Analytic rubrics, 39
Ancient Egyptian math system, 25
Animals in the classroom, 67–68
Ants, 87
Aquarium, 29
Arnie the Doughnut, 147
Artifacts, 48
Arts, 224–225
ASCD. See Association for Supervision and Curriculum Development (ASCD)
Assessment, 18–49
  authentic, 33
  culture and context, 24–26
  cyclical nature of, 27
  documentation. See Documentation
  EdTPA, 48
  formal/informal, 39
  formative, 19, 20
  guiding teaching decisions, 27–29
  interviewing, 43–46
  principles of, 26–29
  principles of development, 21–26

questions to ask, 44
responding to children's needs, 22–24
standardized testing, 48
standards, 46–48
teacher language, 31–33
trajectories of development, 21
understanding child's thought process, 44
validity, 27
vocabulary development, 29–33
websites, 49
whole child, 29
Association for Supervision and Curriculum Development (ASCD), 11
Astronomy, 92
Attribute, 103
Authentic assessment, 33

Backward design, 10, 214
Balance and symmetry, 6, 61, 71, 156–179
  comparisons, 158–159, 164–165
  conservation, 160, 161
  establishment of equality, 160–161
  estimation, 158
  games, 168–169
  module (balance), 171–174
  module (symmetry), 175–179
  patterns, 159–160
  physical knowledge, 168–169
  representations, 165–168
  symmetry, 162–163
  tools of measurement, 164–165
  transitivity, 164
  underlying standards, 157

Balance of natural and commercial materials, 58–60
Balancing blocks, 157
Behaviorism, 4
Big idea makeover, 210
Big ideas
  balance. See Balance and symmetry
  characteristics, 7
  children's interests, 210–211
  coming up with new ideas, 209–210
  concepts, and, 6
  defined, 6
  events, 211–212
  local context, 212
  movement. See Movement
  overview, 71
  patterns. See Patterns
  re-thinking an activity, project, unit, 210
  Reggio Emilia, 16
  relationships. See Relationships
  standards, 213
  teacher's interests, 212–213
  transformation. See Transformation
  unplanned integration, 5
Boats, 204–205
Boomwhackers, 95
Boston Children's Museum, 73
Bozeman Biology, 98
Budget limitations, 61
Building materials, 38
Bulletin board, 63
Bulletin board trim, 57–58
Butterfly, 102–103, 175–176

Calendar illustrations, 202
Calendar time, 55–56
Cardboard incline with
    "tunnel," 130
Carrots, 3
Catapult, 186
Cause and effect, 183–187
CGI. *See* Cognitively guided
    instruction (CGI)
Chain reaction, 150–155,
    203–207
Child-centered curriculum, 10
Children
    center of curriculum
        approach, 7
    diversity, 8
    natural mathematicians and
        scientists, 26
    "one hundred languages," 34
    theory-builders, 3
    "wired" to learn, 4
Children's literature, 220–221
Children's museums, 73
Chrysalis, 103
Circle time, 62–63
Circus tightrope walkers, 172–173
Class inclusion, 190, 191
Class-made books, 34
Classification, 80, 159, 190–193
Classroom Architect, 69
Classroom environment, 58–68.
        See also Environment for
        learning
Classroom pet, 118–119
Clay, 37–38
Clipboard, 105
Close observation, 36, 112–116
Clustered dots (panels), 80
Cognitively guided instruction
    (CGI), 221–223
Collections, 96, 97
Color mixing, 106
Colors, 98
Common core math standards, 9,
    27, 46, 47
    algebraic thinking, 110–111
    balance, 157, 171
    chain reaction, 150, 203

close observation, 112, 113
counting and cardinality, 181
direction of movement,
    144, 146
estimation, 117
fractions, 196
geometry, 157, 175, 196
measurement and data, 123,
    157, 203
movement, 123
nature, 89
operations and algebraic
    thinking, 181
organizing information, 94–95
part/whole relationships, 196
patterns, 77, 85
relationships, 181
symmetry, 157, 175
transformation, 101
Common Core Standards—
    Mathematics, 17
Comparisons, 158–159,
    164–165
Compass, 164
Composition, 102
Concepts, 6
Conceptual subitizing, 82
Connections, 86–87
Conservation, 160, 161
Conservation of mass, 160
Constructivism, 4, 11, 226
Constructivist curriculum
    framework, 15
Constructivist educator, 72
Constructivist teachers,
    220, 224
Content knowledge, 72–73
Content standards, 9, 47. *See also*
    Standards
Cookie cutters, 37
Cool Math for Children, 201
Counting bears, 58
Cross-cutting concepts, 210
Curriculum integration
    cognitively guided instruction
        (CGI), 221–223
    connecting arts, math and
        science, 224–225

connecting children's
    literature, math and
    science, 220–221
connecting language arts, math
    and science, 220
connecting social studies, math
    and science, 225–226
constructivist curriculum
    framework, 15
    historical overview, 11–12
    models of, 12
    project approach, 12–14
    standards, 224
    taking the child's perspective, 5
Curriculum planning, 214–219
    five E learning cycle, 217–219
    integration and inquiry,
        215–216
    long-term plan, 214
    plan with end in sight, 217
    project approach, 216
    revising the plan, 215
    short-term plan, 214
    strategies, 214–215

Daily rubric for child input, 40
Day and night, 90–91
Decomposition, 102
Designs that rotate, 201
Dice, 82
Differentiation, 66–67
Digital cameras, 61, 105, 194
Direction of movement, 126–129,
    144–149
Discovery Education, 98
Display areas, 63–64
Diversity, 8
Documentation, 33–43
    building materials, 38
    clay, 37–38
    defined, 33
    journaling, 41–43
    methods of, 33–34
    observational drawing, 35–37
    representations, 34–35
    rubrics, 39–40
    three-dimensional materials,
        37–38

Documentation panels, 34
Documenting growth, 109
Dominoes, 154
Don't Spill the Beans, 168
Dough toys, 37
Down syndrome, 23

Eco Kids, 206
EdTPA, 48, 49
Educational goals, 8
Environment for learning, 50–69
  academic environment, 55–57
  accessibility of materials, 60–61
  animals in the classroom, 67–68
  balance of natural and
    commercial materials,
    58–60
  children's individual needs, 66
  circle time, 62–63
  classroom environment, 58–68
  communicating with families
    and others, 68
  differentiation, 66–67
  display areas, 63–64
  learning centers, 64–65
  physical environment, 57–58
  routines, 55
  sharing of ideas, 62–63
  technology, 61–62
  vignettes (Blue Room/Green
    Room), 52–55
  websites, 69
Equality, 160–161
Equivalence, 103–104, 158
Establishment of equality,
  160–161
Estimation, 105–107, 111,
  117–121, 158
Ethemes for Teachers, 206
Events, 211–212
Experimentation, 107–108
Exploratorium
  (San Francisco), 73
Exploratorium Science
  Snacks, 174
Exploring the Science
  of Light, 98
Eye contact, 62

Fantastic Contraption, 206
Fibonacci numbers, 92
Fire engine, 13
First Hand Learning, 115
Five E learning cycle, 217–219
5E learning cycle, 227
Foil boats, 126, 135
Folded paper art, 178
Forced rotation system, 64
Formal assessment, 39
Formative assessment, 19, 20
Fractions, 189, 199
*Framework for K–12 Science
  Education*, A, 46
Frogs, 66, 67

Gamesgames.com, 174
Gears, 183–185
General knowledge development,
  28
Globe, 64
Google Earth, 188
Graffiti wall, 68
Great Math Games, 178
Group discussion, 62–63
Growing patterns, 80–82
Growth, 108–110, 142

Hands-on learning, 217
Hangers, 174
Harvard Graduate School of
  Education, Center for
  Astrophysics (CfA), 92
Head Start child development
  and early learning
  framework
  balance, 157, 171
  chain reaction, 151
  estimation, 117
  geometry and spatial
    sense, 123
  movement, 123
  organizing information, 94–95
  part/whole relationships, 196
  relationships, 181
  symmetry, 157, 175
Hearts, 176–177
"Helicopters," 139

Hierarchical inclusion, 190, 193
Holistic rubrics, 39
Honda Car Commercial (YouTube
  video), 153
Houses in the block center,
  171–172
Hypothesizing, 41

Ice, 117–118
Icicles, 117
Illuminations: Resources for
  Teaching Math, 98, 200–201
Incline experiments, 124, 125
Informal assessment, 39
Inquired-based learning, 7
Insects, 31, 32, 87, 207
Interdependence, 193
Interdisciplinary approach, 12
Interlocking cubes, 84
Interviewing for assessment,
  43–46

Japanese Rube Goldberg Machines
  (YouTube video), 154
Japanese Wooden Xylophone
  (YouTube video), 154
Jelly beans, 105
Jenga, 168, 169, 174
Joining compare problems, 222
Joining multiplication and
  division problems, 222
Joining part-part-whole
  problems, 222
Joining problems, 222
Joining separating problems, 222
Journaling, 41–43

Kiln, 36

Language arts, 220
Learning centers, 64–65
Leaves, 89
Lesson plans, 98
Levels, 164
Levers, 183, 185, 186
Life cycles, 92
Light tables, 62
Links Learning, 178

Local businesses, 212
Local context, 212
Logical-mathematical
    thinking, 102
Logico-mathematical
    knowledge, 125
Long-term plan, 214

Magnetism, 136, 137
Magnifying glass, 105
Making books, 198
Making Things Happen, 148
Mandala, 77
Map, 64
Mapping, 188
Math and science learning
    centers, 64–65
Math balance, 166
Math Is Fun, 178
Math Made Fun, 227
Math Wire, 98
Mathwire, 120, 200
Mazes, 127–129
Measuring cups, 164
Measuring sticks, 105
Men in Black (film), 187
Meter stick, 164
Mice, 119
Mini-ramp, 148
Mirrors, 162–163
Model, 61
Modeling, 27
Modeling clay, 36–37
Modeling dough, 36
Modification, 23
Moon, 85, 86
Movement, 122–155
    direction of, 126–129,
        144–149
    incline experiments,
        124, 125
    module (chain reaction),
        150–155
    module (direction of
        movement), 144–149
    moving surface, 133–134
    mysterious, 136–138
    representation of, 129–132

sources of, 134–136
spinning, 138–141
time, 141–142
underlying standards, 123
Movement of surfaces,
    133–134
Mrs. Judd's Snowflake
    Station, 178
Multidisciplinary approach, 12
Multiplication charts, 98
Mysterious movement,
    136–138
Mystery blocks, 174

NAEYC. *See* National Association
    for the Education of Young
    Children (NAEYC)
National Aeronautics and
    Space Administration
    (NASA), 226
National Association for the
    Education of Young
    Children (NAEYC), 9, 27
National Council of Teachers of
    Mathematics (NCTM), 9,
    27, 73, 226
National Geographic, 115, 116
National Geographic Kids, 92
National Library of Virtual
    Manipulatives, 121
National science education
    standards (NSES), 27, 47
National Science Teachers
    Association (NSTA), 9, 46,
    73, 224, 226
Natural disasters, 211
Natural materials, 60
Nature Explore, 69
NCTM. *See* National Council of
    Teachers of Mathematics
    (NCTM)
Negotiated dance, 8
Next generation science
    standards (NGSS), 46
    balance, 157, 171
    Bozeman Biology (website), 98
    chain reaction, 150, 203
    close observation, 112, 113

cross-cutting concepts, 210
direction of movement,
    144, 146
estimation, 117
movement, 123
nature, 89
organizing information,
    94–95
part/whole relationships, 196
patterns, 77, 85
relationships, 181
symmetry, 157, 175
transformation, 101
NGSS. *See* Next generation
    science standards (NGSS)
Normal development in
    education, 20
Notebook, 41–43
NSES. *See* National science
    education standards (NSES)
NSTA. *See* National Science
    Teachers Association
    (NSTA)
NSTA Early Childhood Education
    Position Statement, 17

Observation, 104–105
Observational drawing, 35–37
OKGo: This Too Shall Pass
    (YouTube video), 153
Okta's Rescue, 98
Old calendar illustrations, 202
One-to-one correspondence,
    189, 190
One-unit pattern, 79
Open-ended questions, 44
Oppositional causal
    relationships, 183
Optical illusions, 98
Organizing information,
    87, 94–99
Origami, 178
Out-of-print books, 91

Pan balance, 161, 164
Paper airplanes, 178
Part/whole relationships,
    187–190, 196–202

Patterns, 76–98
  balance and symmetry, 159–160
  classification, 80
  connections, 86–87
  growing, 80–82
  interlocking cubes, 84
  module (nature), 89–93
  module (organizing
    information), 94–99
  one-unit, 79
  organizing information, 87,
    94–99
  prediction, 84–86
  repeating, 78–79
  seriation and sequencing, 83
  spatial structure, 79–80
  subitizing, 82–83
  underlying standards, 77
Patterns of growth, 109
PBS Kids Go Cyberchase, 178
PBS Zoom, 206
PBS Zoom (YouTube video), 154
Peer interaction, 63
Pendulum, 148
Perspective-taking, 193–195
Phenomena, 85
Physical environment, 57–58
Physical knowledge, 168–169
Piagetian theory, 4
Pick-up Sticks, 174
Picture finders, 202
Pipe-cleaner activity, 174
Place value, 45
Plant growth, 109
Plastic bears, 60
Plastic boxes, 105
Plastic knives, 105
Play, 108
Playfully Inventing and Exploring
  with Digital and Other
  Stuff, 206
Polygon, 116
Posters, 63
Powell's City of Books, 91
Powers of Ten, The (video), 187
Prediction, 84–86
Problem-based learning, 12
Progettazione, 16, 214

Project approach, 12–14, 216
Properties, 102
Pulley, 183

Quarked, 148
Quilts, 196–197

Read Write Think–International
  Reading Association, 227
Reading and Writing Project, 220
Reggio Children, 17
Reggio Emilia, 5, 15–16
  artistic representations of
    learning, 224
  big ideas, 16
  documentation, 33
  drawings, 34
  environment, 57
  materials, 60
  progettazione, 16
  website, 69
Relationship building, 102–103
Relationship-building
  knowledge, 102
Relationships, 180–207
  cause and effect, 183–187
  classification, 190–193
  interdependence, 193
  module (chain reactions),
    203–207
  module (part/whole), 196–202
  part/whole, 187–190
  perspective-taking, 193–195
  underlying standards, 181
Repeating patterns, 78–79
Representational building, 37
Representations, 34–35,
  165–168
Rocks, 60, 112–113
Roll of register tape, 57
Rotting pumpkin, 112
Rounding numbers, 107
Routines, 55
Rube Goldberg Gallery, 206
Rube Goldberg machines, 150,
  153, 154
Rubric, 28, 39–40
Ruler, 164

Scale
  map, 188, 189
  tool of measurement, 61, 105,
    164
Scholastic Tools: Class Setup
  Tool, 69
Schools Out: Lessons from a
  Forest Kindergarten, 69
Science and math journals, 41–43
"Science Concepts Young
  Children Learn Through
  Water Play" (Gross), 207
Science for Kids, 174
Science Games for Kids: Forces
  in Action, 148
Science IDEAS, 115
Science knowledge and skills,
  chain reaction, 151
Science museums, 73
Science notebook, 41
Science With Me, 116
Scientific method, 124, 125
Scribbling, 35
Sequencing, 83
Seriation, 83, 190
Shadows, 98, 142
Shapes, 22
Shapes within shapes, 199
Short-term plan, 214
Smartboard, 61
Smithsonian Education, 224, 227
Social studies, 225–226
Solar system, 26
Spatial structure patterns,
  79–80
Spiders, 207
Spinning movement, 138–141
Spoons, 105
Sports, 144–145
Stage theories, 21
Standard room design elements, 66
Standardized testing, 48
Standards
  assessment, 46–48
  big ideas, 213
  cautionary note, 47
  common core. *See* Common
    core math standards

Standards (*Continued*)
curriculum integration, 224
NGSS. *See* Next generation
science standards (NGSS)
NSES, 27, 47
overarching goals, 9
positive benefits, 47
teachers, and, 47
Star-gazing, 92
Stars, 115
Stop watch, 164
String, 164
Subatomic science, 148
Subitizing, 82–83
Summative evaluation, 19
Sundial, 142
Surface tension, 136
Symmetry, 162–163. *See also*
Balance and symmetry
Symmetry Game—Innovations
Learning, 178

Tag-board triangle, 101
Tag-board twirler, 140
Tape measure, 164
*Target–Fresh Machine (Rube
Goldberg)* (YouTube
video), 154
Teacher
acts with intention, 11
content knowledge, 72
interests, 212–213
language use and language
learning, 30
overarching vision, 10
scribe, as, 41
standards, 47
Teacher-centered curriculum, 10
Teacher language, 31–33
Teacher-made tests, 39

Teacher performance
assessment, 48
Teaching Channel, 49, 98
Technology, 61–62, 131
Telling time, 213
10 frame, 82
Text Project, 220
Text set, 220
The Private Eye, 115
The Project Approach, 226
Theories, 3
Theory-building, 3, 4, 125
Thermometer, 61
Three-dimensional materials,
37–38
Three little pigs in the block
center, 151–152
Time, 141–142, 213
Tools, 60
Tools of measurement, 164–165
Tops, 138
Trajectories of development, 21
Transdisciplinary approach, 12
Transformation, 7, 71, 100–121
equivalence, 103–104
estimation, 105–107, 111,
117–121
experimentation, 107–108
growth, 108–110
module (close observation),
112–116
module (estimation),
117–121
observation, 104–105
relationship building,
102–103
underlying standards, 101
Transitivity, 164
Trays, 105
Triangle, 22, 80, 81

Turtle, 67
Tweezers, 105
Twirly spinner
("helicopters"), 139

Unifix cubes, 164
Unplanned integration, 5
U.S. Geological Survey, 120
Utah Education Network,
Science Education
Resources, 92, 98

Validity, 27
Variables, 125
Venn diagram, 192
Vibration, 135
Virtual manipulatives,
121, 200
Vocabulary development, 29–33
Vygotskian theory, 4

Wall calendar, 55–56
Weather events, 211
Weight balance, 164
What is the Reggio Emilia
Approach? An Everyday
Story, 69
Whole child, 29
Wind, 31
Winter pictures, 146
Word wall, 42
Worlds of Words, 220

YouTube, 49, 103, 153–154

Zero, 97
Zooming in and out,
187, 194, 214